MECCA AND MAIN STREET

MECCA

❧ AND ❧

MAIN STREET

Muslim Life in America After 9/11

GENEIVE ABDO

OXFORD

UNIVERSITY PRESS

OXFORD
UNIVERSITY PRESS

Oxford University Press, Inc., publishes works that
further Oxford University's objective of excellence
in research, scholarship, and education.

Oxford   New York
Auckland   Cape Town   Dar es Salaam   Hong Kong   Karachi
Kuala Lumpur   Madrid   Melbourne   Mexico City   Nairobi
New Delhi   Shanghai   Taipei   Toronto

With offices in
Argentina   Austria   Brazil   Chile   Czech Republic   France   Greece
Guatemala   Hungary   Italy   Japan   Poland   Portugal   Singapore
South Korea   Switzerland   Thailand   Turkey   Ukraine   Vietnam

Copyright © 2006 by Geneive Abdo

Published by Oxford University Press, Inc.
198 Madison Avenue, New York, NY 10016
www.oup.com

First issued as an Oxford University Press paperback, 2007
978-0-19-533237-7

Oxford is a registered trademark of Oxford University Press

The Library of Congress has cataloged the hardcover edition as follows:
Abdo, Geneive, 1960–
Mecca and Main Street : Muslim life in America after 9/11 / Geneive Abdo.
p. cm.   Includes bibliographical references and index.
ISBN-13: 978-0-19-531171-6
ISBN-10: 0-19-531171-X
1. Muslims—United States—Social conditions.
2. Muslims—United States—Attitudes.
3. Islam—United States.
4. United States—Ethnic relations.
5. United States—Race relations.
6. Social integration—United States.
I. Title.
E184.M88A22 2006
305.6'970973—dc22
2006015485

1 3 5 7 9 8 6 4 2
Printed in the United States of America
on acid-free paper

Contents

༓

Acknowledgments

ﻣﻦ

I am forever grateful to the main characters in this book. They shared intimate details of their lives with me during a period of unease at home and abroad. Many taught me not only what it is to be a Muslim in America, but how their faith can help ease the difficulties of living in the contemporary world.

From the beginning, Yusra Gomaa was my guide through the Islamic community, my researcher, and a model for the young generation of Muslim Americans. Her intelligence, determination, and belief in the central theme of this book were a great inspiration. Her life story appears later in these pages.

In Chicago, many friends and acquaintances helped along the way. My conversations over a few years with Dr. Umar Faruq Abdallah, Dr. Scott Alexander, and Dr. Abdul Malik Mujahid taught me to take note of the many nuances of Muslim life that are documented throughout the book. In Detroit, Saeed Khan and Patrick Cates were the first activists I met who opened my eyes to the diversity of mosques. Through them, I met Dr. Ihsan Bagby, whose admirable field research on this subject greatly enhanced my own work.

There are also the life-long helpers, the people who have provided stimulation and inspiration since I began writing about contemporary Islam more than a decade ago. I am grateful to Dr. John Esposito for his unwavering support. Cynthia Read, my editor at Oxford University Press, has maintained faith in my work, even when my ideas have contradicted conventional wisdom. She is a rare and gifted editor in American publishing. Jonathan Lyons, who edited and read every page, was an invaluable critic.

I am grateful to my agent, Laura Langlie, who lowered my stress level and helped beyond the call of duty. The novelist Christina Baker-Kline improved my narratives and storytelling.

This book was funded in part through a grant from the Earhart Foundation. I owe the foundation many thanks for its continuous support.

MECCA AND MAIN STREET

Prologue: Beginnings

ৡৡ

I first thought about writing this book, often with mixed emotions, during the days following September 11, 2001. My ambivalence turned to conviction one chilly afternoon in 2003 as I strolled through a San Francisco neighborhood with Maad Abu Ghazalah. Maad was running for a seat in the U.S. Congress, and I had asked if I could campaign door-to-door with him. I wanted to see how one of America's most liberal cities might respond to a Muslim and an Arab seeking public office. I had never been to San Francisco until that day, but I believed the stereotype of a city with open-minded, tolerant citizens. Certainly this enlightened thinking would apply to Maad, especially because there are no immediate physical clues that he is an Arab. With his light skin, green eyes, and sandy brown hair, he could be Italian or Greek or French.

The neighborhood overlooked San Francisco Bay, giving homeowners a spectacular view of the clear, deep blue water. When we walked up the hill to the first set of houses and rang the doorbells, no one seemed to be at home. But after a few minutes, we found our first couple willing to open their door for a chat.

"Hello, my name is Maad Abu Ghazalah and I am running for Congress in your district," Maad told the couple, extending his hand past the front-door screen to offer them his campaign literature.

There were a few moments of silence. Then the man blurted out, as if Maad were nowhere in sight, "With this name, I would say this guy doesn't have a chance. M-a-a-ad Abu Ghazalah. Not a chance."

While I tried to keep my jaw from dropping, Maad did not flinch. He was apparently used to this kind of reaction. "I was born in Palestine. I live in San Francisco and graduated from Notre Dame. I am running for Congress because I'm concerned about our foreign policy," he replied, deadpan.

The woman tried to take the edge off her husband's remark. "We need to know where you stand," she told Maad, "because many people will just see your name and think, 'I don't want to go down that road.'"

Where Maad stood was beside the point. He was against the Iraq war. He favored bringing the troops home—views the couple said they shared. But that was obviously not enough for them.

As we continued walking along the street, I wondered why Maad put himself through such unnecessary humiliation. I couldn't understand it. Here was a successful lawyer who certainly did not need to subject himself to bigotry and ignorance. We walked a bit more, but had little success persuading voters that Maad was their man for Congress. Only one person reacted favorably.

The cool breeze and the human chill from the San Franciscans, whom I thought would be free thinkers, made me want to end the campaigning. Maad agreed, somewhat reluctantly, after we had visited nearly every house along the street. I was curious to know how he felt, but we had just met that morning and I didn't feel comfortable asking him personal questions. I posed my question delicately: "So Maad, do you think you will continue campaigning? Do you think you are doing the right thing?"

He grinned a bit. "I have one vote and one hundred thousand to go," he said, referring to the one positive response. "I am not running to win. I am running so the next generation of Muslims might have a chance."

Later that day, on the plane out of San Francisco, I realized that the contemporary Muslim American experience should be documented. Life had changed dramatically for the country's six million Muslims. But because America was focused on Muslims living nearly everywhere else but at home—in Afghanistan, Iraq, Iran, Syria, and Pakistan—the story of their changing lives had been left untold.

For more than a century Muslims had lived in America in peace, blending into the ethnically diverse landscape. But suddenly, they were no longer in the shadows as an all but invisible minority. From now on, their every word would be noted, their every action seized upon by a nation gripped with fear and inflamed by political manipulation. The event that launched America's "War on Terrorism"—a war that many Muslims at home and abroad understand as directed at Islam itself—created for them a new American reality. Like the couple who greeted Maad Abu Ghazalah, much of America had embraced a black-and-white view: Muslims are terrorists; Islam is a religion of violence; Muslims are backward; Muslims are vengeful toward the West.

Mecca and Main Street: Muslim Life in America after 9/11 details the search by a diverse group of Muslims to find a way to live with dignity in this country. While many Muslims shared a growing desire to become more involved and educated about their faith long before September 11, in the wake of the attacks on Washington and New York, they felt an urgent need to embrace their beliefs and establish an Islamic identity as a unified community. A glance at the American horizon confirms this. A decade ago, it was unusual to spot a minaret. But now they can be seen in most major cities and many smaller ones, as well. Women in headscarves are an increasingly common sight in the nation's shopping malls, offices, schools and even health clubs. Employers are now asked to allow Muslim workers to take time off for daily prayers.

After living and working in the Islamic world for almost a decade as an author and journalist, I became interested in the Muslim American community when I returned to the United States shortly before September 11. I realized that some of the trends I had observed and documented in the Islamic world were also apparent here, especially among younger Muslims. After the attacks, it seemed vital for Americans to understand the Muslims living in their midst. Yet, much of the information available in the media has failed to inform or educate the public. My growing frustration led me to write this book.

The narratives I present are possible only because many generous Muslims were willing to tell me their stories. They welcomed me into their schools, mosques, Islamic centers, weddings, radio stations, and homes, even though I am an outsider to their community. Sometimes, telling me their stories was a form of catharsis; I was there with an open mind, well versed in their religion and culture, and willing to listen. Other times, they spoke out of desperation to get the word out. They live in the heart of America, but they are often defined solely by Americans' perceptions of Muslims abroad, whether they are insurgents in Iraq or Saudi oil tycoons in Riyadh. I have tried to tell their stories through their eyes, but with my voice.

In my travels, from New York to California, Texas, Ohio, Illinois, and Michigan, I discovered that September 11 has dramatically altered the way Muslims live in this country. These changes largely defy decades of history in a nation of immigrants, and they challenge the American ideal of diverse cultures linked by a shared attachment to common goals and dreams. Unlike other ethnic and religious groups who seek to become fully Americanized, many Muslim Americans, particularly the expanding younger generation of practicing Muslims, are involved in what their imams are calling a rejectionist movement. While gaining economic prosperity as members of the American workforce, they are trying to create their own world where they can find comfort in their faith and their communities. They are combining a desire to embrace Islam with negotiating the rigors of daily life in modern America.

Many Muslim Americans, the second generation in particular, are placing their Islamic identity first. (Throughout this book, I refer to second-generation Muslims as those whose immigrant parents were the first generation in their family to live in the United States.) Young Muslims born or raised in the United States are often more observant of Islamic practice than their parents. Many young women are wearing headscarves, even if their mothers didn't cover. And, unlike their parents, they believe their spiritual journey is also an intellectual one. This younger generation is not interested in blindly following the teachings of an imam simply because he is a religious figure; they carefully study the Koran and the Sunnah, the two sources of Islamic jurisprudence, to find rationality in religious practice. If an imam tells them, for example, that playing music is against Islamic teaching, they are likely to ask the imam to justify his opinion with a citation from the religious texts. These young Muslims are searching for purity in the faith while tailoring religious practice to their lives in America.

Their experience differs from that of their parents. The older generation began arriving from Islamic countries in great numbers almost a half century ago, after America's restrictive immigration laws were eased in the 1960s. But mentally these Muslims never left the Old Country behind. When they joined mosques in America, they wanted to observe the faith as they had back home, with aging imams citing Koranic verses that had little relevance to daily life in America.

One summer afternoon in 2004 at a gathering of young Muslims in Chicago, Sheikh Hamza Yusuf, an imam who is leading this new generation, accurately contrasted the past Muslim American experience with what the future should hold. His thinking had undergone many changes since he studied Islamic science and theology in the Middle East where he willingly accepted traditional interpretations of Islamic doctrine despite their lack of relevance to modern life. Once back in the United States, Sheikh Hamza realized that these readings of the faith were counterproductive in contemporary America. He shifted his ideas and refined the advice he gave his followers. "We have a crisis in faith. I sit in a *khutba* [Friday sermon] that violates the faith. . . . And I know we have to support the mosque, but if you go to a mosque and it is impossible to be there, you need to find another one. . . . I cringe when I think about the things I said ten years ago."

The men and women profiled in the following pages are all practicing Muslims, mosque-goers, most born in America as the children of recent immigrants. I chose these particular people not because they claim to represent all Muslim Americans but because they are the activists, journalists, imams, and human rights advocates who are shaping both the broader Muslim community's standing in America and Americans' views of the Islamic world. Islam is spreading rapidly around the globe, and the United States is no different; it is the fastest growing religion and, by some estimates, has already outpaced Judaism as the country's second faith.

The impulse within the young generation toward a well-defined Islamic identity is inspired by two developments. Devout Muslim Americans, much like their co-religionists across the Islamic world from Pakistan to Egypt, are experiencing a spiritual awakening. Many of the trends indicating an increase in piety among second-generation Muslim Americans are also visible in Egypt, Morocco, and Jordan and among young Muslims in Western Europe, as well. Over the last thirty years, an Islamic resurgence has spread throughout much of the world.

Then there is September 11, and the fallout from this tragic day in American history. After the attacks, a generation of believers who were already becoming more spiritual than their parents rose up to defend their faith. They felt under siege, with FBI agents raiding their mosques and homes, suspicious neighbors assuming every Muslim is suspect, and television news programs portraying Muslims as the new enemy of the West. Part of their defense was to adopt Islamic symbols—the *hijab*, the headscarf for women, and the *kufi*, the cap for men—in greater numbers. Many Muslims told me they felt impelled to learn more about their religion in order to explain the *true* Islam to America. Their future in this country depended upon it. They also felt a need for comfort that was unavailable in mainstream American society. They turned to their mosques, Islamic centers, Muslim Students' Associations on university campuses, and Islamic schools to ease the pain of increasing bigotry, stereotyping, and hate crimes. The role of the mosque was changing, and it changed even more after September 11. As in much of the Islamic world, in the 1970s and 1980s the mosque in America had been strictly a house of worship. But as Muslim Americans became more interested in developing their Islamic identity, the mosque became the center of social activity for those who prayed there.

After a brief period immediately following the attacks when Americans expressed an outpouring of support and tolerance for Muslims and Islam, surveys taken since September 11 show that public opinion has grown increasingly negative toward them. Data compiled by the respected Pew Forum on Religion and Public Life in the summer of 2004 demonstrated that almost half of Americans believe that Islam is more likely than other religions to promote violence, up from one quarter of Americans two years earlier. Pew also found 37 percent of those surveyed had an unfavorable view of Islam in 2004, an increase over the same period in 2003.

These feelings are acted out in ways small and large. Statistics compiled by the largest Islamic organization in the country, the Council on American-Islamic Relations, show an increase in anti-Muslim vandalism and other hate crimes over the last four years. During the years I spent researching this book, I had countless experiences with Americans who held negative opinions about Muslims, but who knew virtually nothing about Islam and had never met a Muslim. Some people talked about Muslims as if they were an alien species. Few Americans know the central tenets of Islam, its emphasis on social justice, or its acceptance of the Jewish and Christian prophets who came before the Prophet Muhammad. Few Americans know that world-class Muslim scientists, philosophers, and other scholars produced significant works during the Middle Ages, when Christian Europe was shrouded in darkness, disease, and ignorance. And how many Americans stop to consider the continuing impact of centuries of Western colonial occupation and domination on Muslim societies?

Most of the time, Americans' negative views focus on Islamic militancy. I am often asked: "If Islam does not promote violence, then why don't Muslims in this country condemn the September 11 attacks? Why don't they condemn the beheadings in Iraq? Why don't they disavow the militants acting in the name of Islam?" The truth is that nearly every Islamic organization in America condemned the events of 9/11 and other forms of violence, but the media rarely captures their voices and they go virtually unheard. Other times they are dismissed as disingenuous. And even as Islamic organizations have become more visible in the years since September 11, they have learned that visibility brings vulnerability. In effect, they lose if they remain silent, and are still targeted if they try to defend their true faith.

Much of the hostility toward Muslims reflects the lack of knowledge about Islam that has persisted since the first Muslims arrived in America more than three hundred years ago. As early as 1893, Muhammad Alexander Russell Webb, a former newspaperman and one of the earliest white converts to Islam, bewailed his fellow Americans' ignorance of the faith and the Prophet Muhammad. Sadly, little has changed since then. Instead of making an effort to understand Islam and the factors and history that have shaped its many modern forms and expressions, America's politicians and the media remain obsessed with any and all signs of extremism. The overriding question has been, "Are there militants on American soil?" Over the three years that I traveled to Islamic communities across America, I found no evidence of militancy. Are there strident voices critical of U.S. foreign policies? Without doubt. But these voices, at least for now, have not made the leap, as some European Muslims have done, toward violent radicalism.

Muslim Americans' successful creation of a strong Islamic identity is a departure from history. America had three historical encounters with Islam, none of which led to the creation of a true Islamic identity. The first Muslims to arrive in any number, beginning in the 1700s, were slaves from West Africa, and they never really had a chance. In the Deep South, where most black Muslims were sold, their enslavement, their forced conversions to Christianity, and other obstacles to practicing the faith made it impossible for them to create any real Islamic community.

The gradual collapse of the Ottoman Empire set off the next wave of immigrants, dating from around 1870 to the start of World War I. Many were Christians from Syria and Lebanon, like my own Maronite ancestors who eventually settled in San Antonio, Texas. There was also a significant number of Muslims, but they were more focused on preserving the religious and ethnic traditions of their homelands than on unifying into one Muslim American community. It was common for each ethnic group to have its own mosque, and various ethnic groups tended to settle in isolated pockets around the country, particularly in the Midwest, and remained cut off from each other.

The first attempt to carve out a national identity came from the African American community, when Noble Drew Ali founded the Moorish Science Temple in Newark, New Jersey, in 1913. Ali preached that African

Americans were a "Moorish" people and historically Muslim in culture and heritage. Two decades later, Wallace D. Fard, a silk peddler, claimed God sent him from the Muslim holy city of Mecca to save black America. His movement spawned the contemporary Nation of Islam, officially established in 1934 by the Honorable Elijah Muhammad. Like Nobel Drew Ali's Moorish Science Temple, the Nation of Islam was rich in Islamic symbols and terminology but offered little actual theology. The practice of the faith borrowed heavily from the services commonly conducted at black churches. Members sat on benches, sang, and listened to sermons on religious and social themes that did not address any aspect of Islam. What's more, Elijah Muhammad embraced ideas that openly violated basic Islamic principles. He declared that white people were the descendants of the Devil, and that he was a messenger of God, an idea heretical to Muslims who believe that the Prophet Muhammad was God's last messenger.

But, by putting Islam forward as an answer to racial oppression, the Nation of Islam effectively appealed to blacks who were searching for social justice and a new identity that would elevate them from imposed degradation. In the absence of a well-developed Islamic community with experiences in the Muslim world, there was virtually no one with religious authority to challenge such distortions of the faith. Eventually the challenge came from within the Nation itself.

Malcolm X, once the charismatic voice of the Nation of Islam, began publicly to challenge the movement's ideas after he returned in 1964 from a life-transforming pilgrimage to Mecca. Already, he had begun to question privately some aspects of the group's teachings. Similarly, and nearly at the same time, Elijah Muhammad's son Wallace Deen Muhammad, who was well versed in the Islamic holy texts, questioned his father's racist doctrine. In 1975, upon the death of his father, Wallace Deen began to discredit many of the separatist ideas upon which the Nation was built. He formed an alternative to the Nation, an organization eventually called the American Society of Muslims, but the results of Wallace Deen Muhammad's efforts were uneven.

Meanwhile, the liberalization of America's immigration laws in 1965 eased restrictions against immigrants from the Muslim world. Almost immediately, the face of Islam in America began to change. Now the immigrant community was growing alongside black Islam; in fact, immigrant Muslims soon outnumbered converts among African Americans. At the time, a global Islamic revival was taking root, sparked by the 1979 Islamic revolution in Iran and the Islamic triumph over Soviet rule in Afghanistan. These events influenced Muslims from Pakistan to Egypt, and many of the immigrants who arrived in America from these countries beginning in the 1970s wanted to practice their faith diligently. They began building mosques and Islamic schools across the country, though they were initially few in number.

A clash between the immigrant and African American Muslims was bound to happen. African Americans saw immigrant Muslims as hijackers of a faith in which they themselves had established roots more than two hundred years earlier. The newly arrived Muslims raised a question that has come to dominate Islamic history in the United States: who is a *real* Muslim? In the eye of the immigrants, the Nation of Islam and the American Society of Muslims, which Wallace Deen was determined to bring into conformity with mainstream Sunni Islam, were mere imitations of the true faith.

By the 1990s, the Nation of Islam had lost its luster and Wallace Deen had become disillusioned. He told me in 2003 that he was stepping down as leader of the American Society of Muslims because many of his prayer leaders in mosques around the country had refused to follow his example and master Arabic and embrace the teachings of the Koran. They were, he said, too locked into the separatist message of his father, Elijah Muhammad. Some prominent African American Muslims, such as the scholar Sherman A. Jackson, argue that the excessive focus on race among today's African American Muslims threatens to reduce their influence within the broader community of believers.

With the decline of organized African American Islam, the post-1965 generation has stepped in to offer the best hope to resolve once and for all what it means to be a Muslim in America. Many are working hard to create a multicultural Islamic community, one that is color blind. They are inspiring African American youth to join their schools and organizations, breaking with their parents' tradition of praying, marrying, and associating only with Muslims from their same ethnic background.

The creation of a distinct Muslim American identity has become more urgent than it was in the past. After September 11, Muslims were put on the defensive. Others were constantly defining their identity and their religion. Many Muslims told me that September 11 was a wake-up call: either embrace and explain the true faith or be lumped together with the suicide bomber in the Gaza Strip or the insurgent in the rutted streets of Baghdad.

As an Arab American who also woke up on September 11 to a new, imposed identity that is more Arab and less American, this work is also a personal journey. *Mecca and Main Street* takes a look at Muslim life, quite different from the perceptions, stereotypes, and clichés that have captured the American imagination.

New York   *February 2006*

ONE

Imams for a New Generation

In a moment he had never imagined, in a house he had never admired, Sheikh Hamza Yusuf was singing "God Bless America." It was a momentous occasion, so important that he had altered nearly everything about his appearance and demeanor. He had left his traditional tunics and skullcaps at home in California and packed a bundle of neatly pressed dark trousers and button-down white shirts. He had trimmed his minimalist goatee and tamed his tongue, trading his intellectual, introspective rhetoric for the simplistic language of television sound bites. And to stress that he was American, as well as Muslim, he introduced himself as Hamza Yusuf Hanson, using the surname that was his before he converted to Islam. The occasion demanded it; he was standing in the Oval Office, next to President George W. Bush, under the glare of television lights, with cameras capturing his every move. It was September 20, 2001, nine days after Muslim extremists had attacked the World Trade Center and the Pentagon. The president chose Sheikh Hamza to be the Muslim cleric photographed at the White House to show the world that America was not at war with Islam.

At the very moment that Sheikh Hamza was chatting with the president, the FBI was banging on the front door of his house in California and warning his wife, Umm Yahya, that he, and other well-known Muslims, could become targets of retaliatory attacks from Americans wanting to even the score. The agents were flabbergasted when Umm Yahya told them that Sheikh Hamza was at the White House.

As he posed for the cameras, Sheikh Hamza was worrying about a different kind of backlash, not from mainstream Americans, but from his own people. Some people in the Islamic community were angry that he had accepted this invitation to Washington. It was clear to Muslims that the president's intentions were less than sincere. Why, they wondered, was Sheikh Hamza helping the White House in a propaganda campaign designed to show America's tolerance for Muslims? Hamza knew his critics had a point, especially when he was asked to wear his Islamic cap, the one he had pointedly left behind in California, to a dinner hosted by First Lady Laura Bush that evening. The White House staff wanted to make sure the world would see a Muslim in the room when the cameras scanned the crowd.

Sheikh Hamza had his own reasons for accepting President Bush's invitation, an offer he surely would have shunned just weeks before. He knew that because of the events of September 11, life was going to be different for Muslims in America, and Muslims everywhere. Until this moment, he had been leading the scholarly life of an imam, speaking where he was invited and making his religious lessons and commentaries available on cassettes and videotapes. But that was over now. He had a forty-five-minute chat with the president, which the White House had arranged to avoid any impression that the retaliation America was planning against the Islamic world was directed at Muslims in general. Sheikh Hamza pre-

Sheikh Hamza Yusuf. (*Courtesy of Aaron Haroon Sellers*)

sented George Bush with two books. One was the Koran; the other was *Thunder in the Sky: Secrets of the Acquisition and Use of Power*, a collection of Eastern wisdom. The first book, Hamza reasoned, would teach the president about Islam's goodness. The second would show him that even the world's most powerful emperors can show compassion for humanity.

Sheikh Hamza has never revealed the details of their conversation, aside from saying that he tried to explain to the president that the terrorists were not true Muslims; when they hijacked the planes, they hijacked Islam. But when these few words leaked out, they were enough to transform his public persona from that of a contemplative scholar who offered private lessons to his students to a political imam whose every word would be examined for years to come.

History and circumstance cloaked him in this role, and he wore it well. He tried to protect the Muslim community from accusations of extremism. He toned down the sometimes-stinging public rhetoric that he had previously employed when talking about U.S. foreign policy. He tried to calm Muslim outrage against the United States by teaching the lessons of tolerance that are engrained in the Koran. And he toyed with the imagery used to stereotype Islam. If traditional Islamic tunics and caps were considered the indelible symbols of extremism, when in public, he wore suits and starched shirts. Hamza Yusuf, white-skinned with light brown hair and a neat goatee, came to be what the public calls a moderate Muslim.

After observing Sheikh Hamza at many of his public appearances over a few years and speaking with him briefly, I wanted a chance to sit with him for some time in a quiet setting. I felt there was no way to gain insight into his personality from a distance. Hamza Yusuf felt he had been misquoted everywhere—in newspapers, on television, and on the Internet—sometimes deliberately and other times simply as a result of the Western media's general ignorance about Islam. Now he was closely guarded, making it nearly impossible for an outsider like myself to get near him. I knew that could happen only by winning the trust of the broader Islamic community. After more than two years spent gaining that confidence, I received an invitation to Sheikh Hamza's house near San Francisco one morning in December 2005.

I walk nervously toward a stucco house at the end of a cul-de-sac hidden behind a few trees, still green under a chilly winter sky. The neighborhood is suburban, but not the generic kind of suburbia found in many American towns. The architecture of the houses, part Mediterranean and part Spanish, and the trees remind me of neighborhoods outside major European cities.

As I approach the wooden front door, I wonder if I should put on my black headscarf. I give the matter much thought. In the Islamic world, it would be unthinkable to visit a sheikh at his home without the scarf, but in America there are divergent views. I want to show respect to Sheikh Hamza, but on the other hand, he knows that I am not a Muslim. I do not want him to think I am somehow pretending to be a Muslim as a ploy to get information.

I knock on the door and a young voice shouts from inside the house, "She's here!"

Hamza Yusuf gently opens the door and immediately notices the head-scarf. "You don't have to wear that," he says in a cool, matter-of-fact tone. At that moment he seems like any other hip guy in northern California.

I take off the scarf and follow him into the living room toward two folding black chairs facing each other, about ten feet apart on the floor. Sitting on the floor is customary in Islamic homes; there is no other furniture in Sheikh Hamza's living room.

Umm Yahya, his attractive wife whose name was Liliana Trujillo before she converted, appears out of an adjoining room and greets me, as does one of their young sons. Then she disappears into the kitchen and emerges a few minutes later with a delicious fruit salad and freshly baked croissants served in cobalt blue dishes.

Hamza Yusuf expresses exhaustion at being the public face of Islam. He holds up a book just published in the Middle East in Arabic; its title in English is *This Is Islam*. The cover claims Hamza Yusuf as the author of the book, but he says he did not write it. The text contains inflammatory rhetoric and it is written in ungrammatical Arabic that the cultured Hamza Yusuf would never use.

"Do you see what I go through?" Sheikh Hamza asks me. "This is the latest."

His frustration is not just with having this book falsely attributed to him or with all the other distorted information printed and circulated about him on the Internet, but how public life has disrupted his work. "The center of my being is interested in philosophy and theology much more than politics. My public talks represent a small percent of my ideas," he tells me.

Sheikh Hamza is particularly concerned with how he is perceived by other Muslims. Since September 11, when he began editing explicit criticism of U.S. foreign policy out of his public speeches, some Muslims accused him of betrayal.

"I have done my best under the circumstances for the Muslim community," Hamza says. "If they disagreed with me and felt I was being duplicitous for toning down the rhetoric, I was only speaking from my heart. If you want to get Muslims riled up, it's easy. But does that help their cause? I don't think so." Historically, Islam has placed a great deal of importance on safeguarding the broader community of Muslims. This is considered a duty for Muslims and particularly for religious leaders. Whatever his critics might say, Sheikh Hamza is on solid theological ground.

The heart is as important to Sheikh Hamza as the mind. In his book, *Purification of the Heart*, he notes that the Prophet Muhammad spoke of the heart as "a repository of knowledge." In many ways, Sheikh Hamza lives by this credo, as did many great Islamic scholars throughout history. This belief serves Sheikh Hamza well; he is an orator who speaks fluidly without notes precisely because he speaks from the heart. When he gives lectures, often thought provoking and passionate, his followers experience Islam in a new way.

The meeting ends after nearly two hours and I realize that Hamza's frustration illustrates a broader problem: in the eyes of most people, September 11 has transformed Islam from a faith into a political system, an ideology. For imams such as Hamza Yusuf, Muslims and non-Muslims must understand the difference between the political Islam of the extremists and the religion practiced by the 1.2 billion Muslims around the world.

Whatever his public and civic responsibilities might be, Sheikh Hamza is most comfortable teaching young Muslims about the faith. This is his natural environment, where he feels free to be himself. I wanted to hear the substance and message of his teachings and see how his followers responded to him. I had heard that they often ask him intimate questions about their lives. So I asked his handlers if I could attend one of the intensive religious sessions that he holds across the country. Soon, I was setting off for San Jose, California, where hundreds of young Muslims were expected to gather.

Sheikh Hamza walks into the madrassa, literally a Muslim classroom, from the men's section in silence. With a purposeful stride and unflinching gaze, he heads toward a stage in the back of the room. He steps onto an elevated platform positioned near a *mashrabiya* screen, a traditional Arabic wood

carving often used for decoration. Hours earlier, with help from his followers, Sheikh Hamza had created a Middle Eastern ambience in a few
sterile rooms in the Hyatt Hotel. A kilim of orange and red hues covers
the stage and an Oriental carpet hangs from the wall behind him under a
dim light. Wearing a robe, a maroon cap, and wire-framed glasses, Hamza
loosens his clothing and makes himself comfortable on the platform facing the students. In keeping with Islamic tradition, which frowns upon
looking directly into the eyes of women, Sheikh Hamza speaks directly to
the young men to his left, glancing only occasionally at the young women
to his right. His inner glow and passion permeate the room.

"Salam aleikum," he says, in a calm but energetic voice.

His followers return the greeting. "Wa aleikumu salam." [And peace be
upon you.]

The students shift in their portable chairs, anticipating a long lesson.
Sheikh Hamza peppers his rambling lectures with citations from the Koran, delivered in his impeccable Arabic. His rapid-fire pace, and the skirt-
ing in and out of two languages, intimidates his followers. Many have never
learned Arabic, a shameful hindrance on their new spiritual journey. Reading the Koran in Arabic, the language of the holy book that the angel
Gabriel revealed to the Prophet Muhammad, is as essential for devout
Muslims as praying five times a day.

Before Sheikh Hamza arrived, the young Muslims were a bit nervous.
Brass oriental pots filled with red roses kept the front door ajar, as young
women in colorful headscarves moved in and out of the makeshift madrassa.
They hugged and kissed one another with great affection. It has been
months since they last saw one another. Discreetly, they eyed each other's
outfits: pink and purple silk flowing tunics and matching headscarves from
Pakistan; Iraqi-style black *abayas*; and the more eclectic American-influenced
Islamic dress that combines headscarves with long skirts hidden underneath mod leather coats. The color and cut hardly matter as long as the
clothes disguise the curves of their breasts and hips, and cover their legs. As
they sit cross-legged in rows, balancing their computers on their laps, they
hear the young men chattering on the other side of the room. A large
mashrabiya screen separates the men and women.

The surroundings reflect the double life of many Muslim Americans.
The young doctors, lawyers, and teachers gathered at the madrassa often
chide themselves for not devoting enough time to their religion and for
focusing too much energy on their careers. They came to the madrassa to

experience an Islamic existence they have never lived and to absorb as much knowledge as they can during a weekend.

Outside the Hyatt, the West beckons with all of its splendor and temptation. It is fitting that the hotel lies in Silicon Valley, home to a different kind of god. The atmosphere pales in comparison to the madrassas in the Islamic world, many set in ancient buildings constructed around large courtyards and fountains near a mosque. Because the United States lacks a history of Islamic education, the madrassas that Hamza Yusuf creates are the equivalent of mobile homes for Islamic learning. Several times a year, he organizes religious sessions, importing Eastern and religious decor and turning modern hotels and restaurants in different parts of the country into temporary madrassas.

Hamza Yusuf struggles to keep up with the demand for his mobile madrassas. The need to create a well-defined Islamic identity is more urgent now that Muslims live under a microscope in post-September 11 America. Young Muslims eagerly seek help in understanding who they are in a new world that denounces them and their religion. A few times a year, Sheikh Hamza teams up with at least two other imams to hold intensive sessions of religious instruction. Young Muslim Americans desiring a classical Islamic education set off on a pilgrimage, some traveling great distances to learn how to be a Muslim in the West.

Often, before the start of religious lessons, Sheikh Hamza hosts a banquet for his students. This time is no different. The night before his presentation, Hamza and the other imams gathered the students at a local Pakistani restaurant to welcome them, and to celebrate the founding of the Zaytuna Institute, a religious center and school he created. Decorations transformed the restaurant's two large dining rooms from American suburbia to Eastern exoticism: green prayer mats were laid out on the rose-colored carpet, and chiffon cascading from the light fixtures recalled colorful Middle Eastern weddings.

After hours of speeches, the students indulged in a feast of chickpea soup, stewed lamb, Indian naan bread, and chicken curry, all served on silver trays placed on shiny, golden tablecloths. They returned for second and third helpings. No one seemed to recall the warnings about overeating that Sheikh Hamza often recited from a *hadith*, a sacred saying of the Prophet Muhammad, which is not part of the Koran but believed to be inspired by God. "In a true *hadith*, the Prophet Muhammad said: 'The worst vessel that the son of Adam can fill is his stomach.' And he also said, 'It is enough for the son of Adam to have just morsels that keep his back upright with. But if you have to eat more than that, then one third for food, one third for water and one third for air.'"

The next morning, the sleep-deprived young Muslims don't let their exhaustion dampen their enthusiasm. There will be at least three sheikhs or imams, depending upon how they choose to call themselves, giving complex lectures during the next three days: Sheikh Hamza; Sheikh Muhammad Yacoubi, an imam who lives in Damascus, Syria; and Imam Zaid Shakir, an African American convert to Islam. The students ready their notepads and laptops to begin their meticulous note taking.

Sheikh Hamza begins the lecture. "In the name of God, the Compassionate, the Merciful."

He addresses the students as if he is at a pep rally.

"Everywhere I go, I see Muslims. Go to the gas station and the airport. Muslims are present in the United States and that was not true twenty years ago. There are more Muslims living outside *dar al-Islam* [Islamic countries] than ever. So we have to be strategic in our thinking because people who are our enemies are strategic in their thinking."

After a short time, he knows his followers are eager to ask questions. They need practical answers to all the dilemmas they face trying to practice their faith in a secular society. "How can you go about your day when you pray five times a day?" asked one young man.

"The *ulama* [religious scholars] differ on the most important prayers. The ideal place to pray is the mosque," Sheikh Hamza tells them. "There is a sound *hadith*, 'Whoever prays in the morning is a protected person.' So this is an important time." He cautions the students, however, against believing that all prayers must be said in a mosque. While it is preferable in the mosque, especially on Fridays, prayers can be said at work, school, or at home, he says.

He then turns to one of his favorite topics, extremism in Islam. Since September 11, Sheikh Hamza has become convinced that Islam's worldwide credibility depends upon the Muslim leadership's condemnation of religious violence. When he opens a newspaper or turns on the television, all he hears is that Islam is a violent religion. The more the non-Muslim world can be taught that the nineteen hijackers do not represent Islam, the less Muslims will suffer. And the more Muslims are taught that such violence violates Islamic teaching, the greater chance that further violence will be prevented. "If you cut off people's heads," he tells his students, referring to Islamic extremists beheading their perceived enemies, "How do you expect Allah to show mercy on you?"

With these words, Sheikh Hamza exonerates his young followers and himself. Still, Muslim Americans feel the hijackers' influence. Everywhere they turn—at work, in their apartment buildings, and at local supermarkets—they are called upon to defend Islam, under assault as a perceived religion of hate. How can they explain that the hijackers' Islam is incompatible with the way they practice their Islam? For women wearing a headscarf, a *hijab*, it is worse. There are sneers and rebukes and false assumptions. Nearly every woman at the madrassa has a story to tell of the outrageous things Americans have said to her. "Muslim women wear headscarves only because of pressure from their husbands, their fathers, or brothers." "They cover their hair so they don't have to bother shampooing." "They cover because they are too unattractive not to."

The fear and intimidation Muslim women experience lead Sheikh Hamza to issue advice on wearing a headscarf. The day a Muslim woman decides to wear a veil is a significant rite of passage. In the West, it is a more difficult decision than in an Islamic country, where headscarves are the norm. As Muslims in the West face increasing hostility within the societies they live, imams and Islamic jurists have reached different opinions about whether veiling is wise.

After September 11, Muslim women looked for theological guidance to determine whether they must endure the harassment that comes with wearing a headscarf, or if there are exceptions. Islamic law allows a woman to protect herself if she feels she is in danger. Using as his guide a fatwa that was issued by one of his mentors, Sheikh Abdallah bin Bayyah, Sheikh Hamza advises women who feel threatened not to leave their homes. If they must go out, they should wear hats or not cover at all. This exception is allowed, Sheikh Hamza tells his followers, because, "Islam is an intelligent religion."

This flexibility is key to the new movement among young Muslim Americans, and it distinguishes them from their parents' generation. Young Muslim Americans don't want to practice their faith blindly; they want rational explanations for why behavior is acceptable or not. Almost alone among prominent sheikhs in America, Hamza Yusuf meets this need. He relies heavily on his classical education to ground his rulings and advice about contemporary issues in Islam's great intellectual tradition, often consulting the four established schools of Islamic jurisprudence called *madhabs*. He is determined to counter the new tendency among many Muslims to interpret the Koran for themselves in the absence of a legitimate imam. Unlike Catholicism, with its well-structured hierarchy of priests, bishops, cardinals, and pope, Islam places responsibility on the individual Muslim to decide which religious scholars to follow. This has become confusing in the modern age, as Islam has spread throughout the world. Are the extremists who distort the meaning of the sacred texts competent to give sound religious guidance? And what about the self-appointed sheikhs with no theological education?

"The Muslims of today are perhaps the most disunited and confused generation of Muslims in Islam's history," Hamza Yusuf asserted in 2001. Identifying and following the teachings of learned Islamic scholars is one way out of the confusion, he wrote.

A Rising Star

Determining who is qualified to interpret the Koran and the *hadiths* has been an important issue for Muslims throughout the ages. Scholars study for years, cloistering themselves inside seminaries and poring over ancient Islamic legal texts so they can give sound advice. They take their duties seriously. Interpreting the Koran is not an easy undertaking. Some verses clearly explain what is forbidden. But most of the holy book's meaning depends upon the interpretations of clerics who try to understand God's will, not by reading the written page, but by studying the work of all the theologians before them who analyzed the Koran and *hadiths*. Many verses must be considered in the context of other verses appearing throughout the book before an educated judgment can be made about their meaning. And some contemporary scholars seek to place Koranic teachings in their historical context before applying them to today's world. From studies in the Koran, many scholars move on to learning Islamic jurisprudence and the other Islamic sciences.

In the United States, there are only a few seminaries where a budding imam can receive a classical Islamic education. If an American-born Muslim aspires to become an imam, he must first learn Arabic in order to read the Koran and the original Islamic sources. The majority of the estimated two hundred imams in America come from Islamic countries in the Middle East and Africa and were educated at respected Arab institutions such as al Azhar, the ancient university and mosque complex in Cairo. Since its creation in A.D. 970, al Azhar, which in Arabic means "most shining one," has been a beacon of light for students aspiring to become qualified scholars. There is nothing resembling al Azhar in the United States, and imams such as Hamza Yusuf have urged Muslim leaders to build seminaries in this country to train imams who will be able to offer real-world guidance to Muslim Americans.

Many imams in the Islamic world question whether those few imams trained in America are qualified to give sound religious advice. They might honor some of the five pillars of Islam, fundamental practices required of every Muslim, such as going to the mosque on Fridays or paying *zakat*, the portion of a Muslim's income that is set aside for charity, but their knowledge is superficial. Only complete submersion and submission to God can make a Muslim a good imam, they argue.

The American imams question whether a sheikh from Egypt can counsel young Muslim Americans on how to deal with the social pressures in America in ways that do not violate Islamic tradition. For example, in the Islamic world, couples marry young, without much interaction before their union. But in America, Muslims marry later in life and want to get to know one another before making a commitment. What can they do when physical contact and even dating before marriage are against Islamic beliefs?

For nearly a decade, and particularly after September 11, Sheikh Hamza and other American-born scholars at the Zaytuna Institute in Hayward, California, near San Francisco have been working to come up with answers to this type of question. After all, young Muslims are part of America's *ummah*, the collective Muslim community, and caring for believers is enshrined in the five pillars of Islam.

From a stucco house surrounded by tall palm and olive trees, the Zaytuna scholars craft a way of life for their followers. Their reach extends far beyond California. Not only do they travel across the country to teach their followers, but scholars in other cities spread their ideas. In Chicago, for example, Dr. Umar Faruq Abd-Allah, one of Sheikh Hamza's mentors, heads the Nawawi Foundation. This institute, much like Zaytuna, teaches young Muslim Americans how to interpret the holy texts.

To apply Islamic doctrine to modern life, these scholars rely upon the Koran and the Sunnah. In this way, they could be called the new traditionalists. Their scholarship is based on the interpretations of respected scholars who lived in the early Islamic period, shortly after the time of the Prophet Muhammad's death in A.D. 642. They interpret the texts by engaging in *ijtihad*, or independent reasoning. *Ijtihad* allows the imams to reinterpret the faith for modern times while adhering to Islam's fundamental principles. The sheikhs carefully distinguish among the vast collected sayings of the Prophet, the *hadiths* that were handed down over the ages. The *hadiths* influenced the scholars who wrote the Islamic laws that dictate what is forbidden and permitted for Muslims. It is known that some of the *hadiths* were transmitted by reliable scholars, while others are considered "weak"; they were either handed down by unreliable interpreters or there were too many interpreters.

Young Muslim Americans can no longer rely upon imams stuck in the mentality of the Old Country, whom second-generation Muslims fondly call "the uncles." Every Friday, the uncles recite from verses in the Koran in the mosques. Few of their followers ever feel that the verses add meaning to their lives in the twenty-first century. And when they are not putting worshippers to sleep with verse, these imams are telling them that much of American culture is *haram*, forbidden in Islam. As Muslim communities expand in London, Hamburg, Paris, and San Francisco, the same questions arise: How do Muslims remain loyal to their beliefs amid the cultural practices in the West, where a Hyatt hotel is the setting for a madrassa? And who will be their spiritual guides?

There is a generation gap in America between the imams and many believers. The younger Muslims reject the Islam their parents practiced and the imams their parents admired, some of whom do not speak a word of English. Their parents practiced a faith heavy with ritual, tradition, and folklore, and lacked the time or interest to establish institutions, such as Islamic schools, that would provide opportunities to acquire a formal religious education. But their children are seeking not only faith but religious knowledge. While their parents never challenged an imam, who might tell them, for example, that setting off fireworks on the Fourth of July is forbidden in Islam, their children ask for religious proof in the Koran or the *hadiths*. While their parents were content to follow an Islam dictated by ethnic tradition rather than religious doctrine, the children make a clear distinction between the two.

The younger generation, unlike their parents, is interested in the symbols of belonging to an Islamic community, the *hijab* being perhaps the most powerful expression of this identity. The beard, generally worn long and untrimmed, is also considered an important expression of Islamic identity for Muslim American men, but is adopted with more reluctance than headscarves for women. There is more risk in growing a beard, because non-Muslims often interpret it as a sign of radicalism, not piety.

In the past, with the absence of religious authority in the United States, the older generation often looked to sheikhs in Egypt or Saudi Arabia for religious guidance. But Muslims who are now part of the new spiritual movement instead rely on imams who understand their life in America.

The imams' task should not be underestimated. Once the sheikhs interpret from the Islamic texts the teachings God revealed through the Prophet Muhammad, they must then apply these teachings to modern Muslim life in the West. For instance, Muslims often ask if taking citizenship in America, a non-Muslim state, is forbidden. After conferring with scholars whom they believe are learned and reliable, the Zaytuna sheikhs give their answer. Their advice is based on a *hadith* in which a man comes to the Prophet Muhammad and says that the people told him he must make the *hijra*, migration, to a land of Muslims, or he will be destroyed. The Prophet instructs the man to avoid evil and live wherever he finds good. From this *hadith* the Zaytuna sheikhs determined that Muslims are permitted to live in a non-Muslim land, as long as they can practice their religion freely.

From the start of his religious career in the United States, Sheikh Hamza portrayed himself as an antidote to the "uncles," an imam of the future. In just a few years, beginning in the late 1990s, he amassed a wide following, which is still growing. His influence extends across the United States to Great Britain, Canada, and Europe, where young Muslims all want guidance about living in the West. His taped lectures and books are also commonplace in the Arab world. But just as his followers at home searched for their place as Muslims in an increasingly hostile America, so has Sheikh Hamza embarked on his own journey to determine the future he would chart for himself.

The sheikh quickly transformed after September 11 from a figure satisfied to defer to older and wiser imams to an international star. When he appears in public, especially in large conference halls and hotel lobbies, he walks with an aura of importance. Sometimes, two bodyguards appear at his side to shield him from the crowds. In California, where he often lectures in the San Francisco Bay area, and in many other parts of the world, however, he is more at ease. There, he is open to anyone who might approach him.

Hamza Yusuf can't be placed in any one category. He is neither an imam out of touch with the material world, nor a hypocrite dressed in religious garb. He often tells his followers that he suffers from viewing Islam through the filters he acquired at birth, as a boy born into a liberal, academic family. Born Mark Hanson in Walla Walla, Washington, to Catholic and Greek Orthodox parents, he converted to Islam at eighteen after a near-fatal car accident. The details are murky; Sheikh Hamza often shies away from discussing this part of his life, perhaps in keeping with Muslim tradition that shuns anything that might smack of self-promotion or public introspection. But his spiritual journey to Islam surely began the day of his accident. He set off to study Islamic jurisprudence and philosophy with independent scholars in the United Arab Emirates, Saudi Arabia, Morocco, Algeria, and West Africa. His approach to Islamic education— he studied the formal Islamic sciences, including official Sufism—has made him vulnerable now to being labeled a Sufi. Sufism is a strand of Islam that is often associated negatively with mysticism even though it is in fact part of the broader Islamic tradition.

Some of the greatest Islamic masters were classical Sufis, including the revered Iranian poet Rumi; the Muslim philosopher Averroes, who transformed thought in the Middle Ages far beyond his home in Moorish Spain; and Muhammad al-Ghazali, a renowned Muslim theologian and philosopher who lived in the twelfth century. But, in contemporary times, the meaning of Sufism has often been distorted. It is generally associated strictly with mysticism. In the West, Sufism is perceived as gentle, touchy-feely Islam practiced by "good" as opposed to "bad" Muslims. Many Sufi mystics have described God's love as akin to the overpowering love Dante writes about in the *Divine Comedy*, "the love that moves the sun and stars." But in the East, some of the Sufis' most strident critics can be found among the Salafists, a movement that claims to practice Islam in the same way the first three generations of Muslims did, through literal interpretations of the Koran and Sunnah. They argue that Sufis dilute Islamic law and doctrine. Scholars have often criticized Sufis for their mesmerizing prayer services that renounce the material world and reduce Islam to a personal experience between the believer and God.

In traditional Islamic society, Sufis helped spread the faith. As the renowned philosopher and Islamic scholar Seyyed Hossein Nasr writes, "In Islam itself, Sufism has been over the centuries the hidden heart that has renewed the religion intellectually, spiritually, and ethically and has played the greatest role in its spread and its relation with other religions."

Sheikh Hamza's critics argue that his emphasis on the intellect as well as the heart could lead young Muslims astray, a common criticism of the Sufi tradition. If they become obsessed with their relationship with God and ignore all other aspects of Islam, how will they develop a holistic Islamic education and find harmony with the Western societies that are now their homes?

As his popularity grew, Sheikh Hamza started to distance himself in public from any association with Sufism, even though he continued to uphold the tradition. During a speech on May 4, 1997, at Stanford University, he defended Sufism, saying misguided followers are giving Islam a bad name by associating esoteric doctrines with Sufism.

Sheikh Hamza has also become a target for his public criticism of some aspects of the contemporary Islamic community. In an interview with the *Manchester Guardian* held in London a few days after the September 11 attacks, he issued a warning to British Muslims: "I would say to them that if they [extremists] are going to rant and rave about the West, they should emigrate to a Muslim country."

His critics seized upon these words, giving him the title the Great White Sheikh. Even though he was referring to extremists, his critics claimed he was suggesting that all Muslims who criticize the West should leave for the Islamic world. One critic claimed Sheikh Hamza appeared to be defending "pick-up driving, flag-waving, good ole boys yelling, 'America: love it or leave it,'" said the popular Web site IslamOnline. To such critics, here was Sheikh Hamza, a white convert to Islam, denouncing the dark-skinned Muslims of Arab and Pakistani descent who helped catapult him to fame.

As his public speeches became more tempered, his critics threw him in the same lot with other imams and activists who emerged onto the public scene after September 11 to proclaim a simplistic message: Islam is a peaceful religion, but it has gotten bogged down with extremists. And Muslim Americans, unlike their unseemly counterparts in the Middle East who loathe the United States, should be grateful to live in a country where they can practice their religion freely.

Some of these imams hosted interfaith gatherings at their mosques and invited local rabbis and Christian clergy to open houses to see the real Islam, a religion of tolerance. But Hamza Yusuf began to move in another direction, strengthening his Islamic credentials. He clarified his earlier opinion given shortly after September 11 excusing women from wearing headscarves and suggesting that they wear a hat or nothing at all to cover their heads if they were being harassed. Few sheikhs anywhere in the Islamic world agreed with Yusuf that devout women should not wear headscarves, but Sheikh Hamza had issued the advice because of the tense times after September 11. Sheikh Hamza also retreated from his blanket condemnation of militant Muslims and began to place Islamic violence in context, noting some of the causes for militancy. "The modern Muslim has learned well the lessons of his counterpart," he wrote in the journal published by the Zaytuna Institute. "American military action rarely distinguishes between combatants and civilians. The Pentagon callously refers to them as 'secondary effects' or 'collateral damage.'"

As noon shadows fall on the Hyatt courtyard, the students leave the study session. The winter sun has wrung the moisture from the air and the morning mist has evaporated. Walking in bare feet a few steps to two adjoining rooms—one for women and another for men—where coffee, tea, and Danish pastries are set out on a white tablecloth, the students find that the adrenaline rush inspired by Sheikh Hamza's lecture is fading into early afternoon lethargy. There are no chairs in the rooms; the women sit cross-legged and mingle on the red carpets. Expressions of anguish and regret fill the room. Sheikh Hamza's lecture has overwhelmed them. How can they carry out his wishes to create positive images of Islam in the world when there were so many negative opinions about their faith?

"We don't want to practice watered-down Islam," a middle-aged African American woman blurts out, shattering the coffee klatsch chatter. "But this is what many people want us to do. They think Muslims shouldn't be seen or heard."

I ask her why she came to the madrassa. She is much older than many of the students, and had once been a member of the Nation of Islam, the black separatist movement considered heretical by mainstream Sunni Muslims. I realize she must be pretty determined to reach a new understanding of Islam.

"I came here because there is no Power Point presentation," she jokes. "But seriously, Zaytuna presents Islam in its traditional clothing. They are not trying to modernize Islam, but teach us what is permitted considering that we live in the modern world."

Rejecting the Temptations of the West

Muhammad Yacoubi's long straggly beard, compared with Sheikh Hamza's carefully manicured goatee, is a small detail that speaks volumes about their differences. Sheikh Muhammad, as the students fondly call him, had arrived in San Jose the day before the session started from his home in Damascus. He is not part of the Zaytuna Institute, but is often invited by Sheikh Hamza to give lectures. For reasons unknown to him and other Muslims, he was one of the few foreign imams the U.S. government allowed into the country after September 11. His floor-length *gallabiyya*, or tunic, and white skullcap, along with his Syrian passport, would surely raise suspicions at any airport. At times, he thought his pale white skin, green eyes, and ginger-colored hair confused the zealous security officers on the lookout for dark Middle Eastern men.

Sheikh Muhammad has just taken a nap to prepare for the long day ahead. He has cultivated such a following in the United States that he stays up for days without sleep to privately counsel his followers during his brief visits. When I met him a year earlier, he had not slept for two or three days, a testament to his immense self-discipline. When he is called upon, his advice ranges from cautioning young men to treat their wives with respect to instructing women to maintain conservative Islamic tradition by staying away from the mosque while they are menstruating.

As soon as he mounts the podium and squats on the floor, and even before he begins his lesson, he announces the news: "Sister Miriam in our community has just put on the *hijab*. Praise be to God."

"Taqbir," the crowd replies, using the Arabic word for extolling God's greatness.

Sheikh Muhammad has always touted his traditionalism. He was born in Damascus to a family whose lineage can be traced to the Prophet Muhammad and to Mawlay Idris al-Anwar, who built the imperial Moroccan city of Fez. The sheikh often tells stories of his own life to inspire his followers. Under the strict guidance of his father who was also his teacher, Ibrahim al-Yacoubi, one of the greatest religious scholars in Syrian history, Sheikh Muhammad began studying classical Islamic texts at age four. By the time he was seven years old, he was teaching the Koran at the Darwishiyya mosque in Damascus. At fourteen, he gave his first sermon in a mosque. And when he turned twenty, the religious sermons he gave on Fridays in the mosques were broadcast live on Syrian radio.

During the lesson in San Jose, Sheikh Muhammad ruminates about his childhood devoted to serious study, and makes it clear that he expects the same from his students. He reprimands them for devoting too little time to Islamic education. Over twenty years, Sheikh Muhammad tells them he has studied five hundred books, many of them complex theological texts.

Sheikh Muhammad makes no apologies for his approach, which is more conservative than Sheikh Hamza's. He doesn't have to; there is a natural affinity between him and the students. He is known for prescribing that Muslims should reject the temptations of the West. Often he tells stories about the life of the Prophet Muhammad to compare the perfection of the past with the imperfection of the present.

Sin in the modern world riles Sheikh Muhammad. "The first success is the success of the family," he says to the young Muslims at the madrassa. "There is no greater reward than raising a Muslim child." And he cautions the young professionals, "There is no reason to delay in getting married because there is so much temptation in the world. All you need to do to get married is change your bed from a single to a double."

He tells the crowd that in Western society there is *fitna*, an Arabic term meaning chaos borne from an imbalance in the social order. Some Muslim scholars believe sexual desire causes this chaos, and this drive can be curtailed only through marriage. "Buying a house and getting married is a Sunnah," Sheikh Muhammad advises, referring to the text that is one of the sources of Islamic jurisprudence. "Some people come to the United States and they can't resist watching pornography, so it is important to get married young."

"If you go to bed at 11 p.m.—and this should be the maximum—you should get up at 4. If you are sleeping seven to eight hours straight there is something wrong with your mind and body."

Once he has covered their personal lives, he moves on to their careers and dietary habits. "It is dangerous to study in Western universities. They teach what some Western scholars wrote doubting the virtues of Islam. And when you seek knowledge, don't eat a lot. If you eat a lot, you sleep a lot and you miss a lot."

The students chuckle. Sheikh Muhammad's charm lies in his ability to mix strict religious teaching with a bit of comic relief. Even though he is not much older than Sheikh Hamza, to the students he is more of a father figure. Sheikh Hamza appears Americanized, despite his perfect Arabic and knowledge of the Koran. But Sheikh Muhammad has a Middle Eastern mystique; he rarely tells the students what they expect or want to hear, and this has made him a revered authority. As far as he is concerned, Muslim youth living in the West waste too much time. Not only do they devote scant time to religious learning, but they watch too much television and indulge in materialism.

"Americans spend thirteen years of their lifetime watching TV. If you speak on the phone one hour per day, which is probably the least, with cell phones everywhere, and each hour of activity requires one hour of rest, so if you live sixty years, you will spend five years of your lifetime on the phone."

"Allah has given you everything you want. Why are you not turning to the *deen* [religion]? All you have to do is just study a little more and just try a little bit harder."

Nearly every phrase Sheikh Muhammad utters poses a challenge. The main reason Muslims should live in America, or the West in general, is to convey the message of Islam, not to adopt a Western lifestyle. Most customs and habits of American society should be rejected, for they undermine Islamic principles. In other lectures, Sheikh Muhammad has contrasted the Muslims' desire to spread the word of Islam with the U.S. government's determination to impose its idea of democracy around the world. The Muslims' effort is based on the divine, he said. But the U.S. government's will is motivated by greed and the drive for power. His ideas resonate with many of his followers. As Americans, they were angered by the U.S. invasions of Iraq and Afghanistan, and the United States' new agenda to impose its values on some countries in the Islamic world.

A shared rejection of America's foreign policy in the Islamic world is the foundation of the bond that forms among the students at the madrassa. They have traveled to San Jose not only to seek knowledge but to gain strength in their resolve to live as Muslims in America, not as Americans who happen to be Muslim. Some who were raised in religious families rejected Islam as adolescents, but then returned to the fold when they entered universities and began friendships with devout Muslim students. Once they were ready to embrace their faith, they needed a different approach from that of their parents. Their Islam would be free of national and ethnic identification. They wouldn't consider themselves Palestinian Muslims or Pakistani Muslims, but simply Muslims. These sentiments are so common that the Zaytuna sheikhs call these young Muslims the rejectionist generation.

This was why Rehan Seyam has come to the madrassa. With her large dark eyes and arched eyebrows, her milky-white face, and slim five-foot nine-inch frame, Rehan stands out in the crowd. Before she became a practicing Muslim, Rehan thought she led a depraved life. Her Egyptian parents from Cairo wanted their daughter to lead a strictly religious life, even though there were temptations all around. Her family lived in Islip, Long Island, and Rehan's public school friends indulged in drinking, drugs, and premarital sex. At different times as a teenager, she drifted further from Islam than her parents would have liked.

But her desire to become a devout Muslim lingered, as she watched her mother become more observant. Her mother started wearing a *hijab* when she was thirty-four, a bold decision at a time when few Muslim women in America were wearing headscarves. It was the late 1980s, and she was impressed by her close relatives in Egypt who were joining the Islamic revival. One sign of Egypt's increasing religiosity was all the women who began wearing the *hijab* for the first time.

Rehan was six years old, and her mother's *hijab* made a big impression. The day her mother first put on the headscarf, she took Rehan and her cousins to a water park on Long Island. "I will remember this day forever because I thought, wow my mother can wear a *hijab* and still have fun, even though her *hijab* is getting all wet."

The image stayed with Rehan, but it was not strong enough to persuade her to start wearing the *hijab* when she reached adolescence, as many Muslims girls do. She watched her mother read from the Koran, but the shopping mall, the teenage parties, and fashionable clothing were also calling her. The more her parents banned parties and the prom, the more Rehan rejected Islam.

By the time Rehan entered Stony Brook University on Long Island, a forty-five-minute drive from her house, she was torn between her deep devotion to Islam and her desire to acquire some of the freedom her parents denied her in high school. She protested her parents' decision forcing her to live at home, rather than in a campus dormitory, but it did little to change their minds. Still, underneath all her defeat and frustration, she was changing.

"I still had love for Islam in my heart," Rehan recalls, sitting in the lobby of the Hyatt hotel during a break in the study sessions. "My closest friends were four Muslim girls that weren't necessarily practicing. I wasn't too comfortable with them because of the guilt I felt from straying from my religion."

Rehan's older sister decided to start wearing the *hijab* shortly after September 11, as an expression of Muslim solidarity in the face of the widespread criticism of Islam in the United States. Suddenly, Rehan realized that she was a minority in America, a feeling she had not experienced before. Her sister tried to draw Rehan into her new world. "She told me, 'Your clothes are too tight.' I said, 'I don't want to hear it.'"

But the message did have an effect, and Rehan became more conflicted. She began attending mosque prayers on Fridays and lectures at the nearby Islamic center at night. In February 2003, when a close college friend put on a headscarf, Rehan decided she should do the same. After two years of feeling the spotlight was on her as a Muslim in America, Rehan wanted to defend her religion.

"After I covered, I changed. I didn't want to hang out with the night people anymore. I felt I wanted to give people a good impression of Islam. I wanted people to know how happy I am to be a Muslim."

Doing her part to change the image of Islam was harder than Rehan had imagined. Once she covered her hair, she laid herself bare to public opinion. "One day, I went to a supermarket and I was buying a tomato. The man next to me in the vegetable section said, 'You'd be so much more beautiful without that thing on your head. It's demeaning to women.'"

The supermarket incident, and many similar ones, made Rehan feel she needed to learn more about her faith. She decided to go wherever she could to become more educated. One of her first stops was a Muslim leadership conference in Princeton, New Jersey. Rehan felt proud to be part of the new religious revival, and she confidently sat in the front row of the women's section. She didn't know it at the time, but an Egyptian optometrist was eyeing her from across the room. Staring at a member of the opposite sex is considered taboo among practicing Muslims. Instead of flirting with her, the young man, Ramy, pursued her the Islamic way. He asked his sister to contact Rehan's sister to find out Rehan's e-mail address. For three weeks, they exchanged messages.

"I knew from the first e-mail that I would marry him. I had been so turned off by the men outside the Muslim community. They were so aggressive and bold. But the e-mails Ramy wrote were so modest and humble. His first comment was that he liked the way I interacted with my friends at the convention. He didn't mention anything about my looks until much later, and that really impressed me."

After three weeks, Ramy visited Rehan's family's house in East Islip. Rehan quivered with nervousness. After building such huge expectations, there was always the chance she wouldn't be attracted to Ramy, once they met face-to-face.

But when she saw Ramy, tall, dark-skinned, and muscular, she had to fight her feelings. "We were so attracted to each other, but we decided not to touch until our wedding day."

At a ceremony, called the *katbil kitab*, literally the writing of the book, a couple makes a promise to one another before a sheikh and their families. The *katbil kitab* is the actual marriage contract and is normal practice in the Islamic world. In America, however, it is becoming popular for another reason: couples are signing the contract but waiting to consummate the marriage in order to date and get to know one another before a second, final ceremony. In the Islamic world, the two ceremonies often occur on the same day, but in America the two ceremonies can happen as far as a year or two apart. If problems arise after the *katbil kitab*, the couple can break off the marriage. Though this is considered a divorce, the woman has a better chance of finding another husband if she is still a virgin.

Rehan wore a flowing champagne-colored gown to the ceremony held at a mosque in a Long Island suburb. In keeping with tradition, the sheikh had a private meeting with Rehan's father and Ramy to explain the religious and social commitments of marriage. As something of a test, he asked Ramy to explain the duties of a husband to his wife. The sheikh then described his idea of marriage, as Ramy and Rehan stood facing one another.

Young Muslim couples are convincing their parents, who never had a *katbil kitab*, to allow it in order to prevent them from sinning. These couples are reaching back into history and resurrecting an old tradition, created when the Prophet Muhammad married his third wife, Aisha. She was considerably younger than the Prophet, and the *katbil kitbab* seemed a more proper way to ease into marriage. For young Muslims in America, torn between human urges and the Islamic tradition, this old approach is slightly new again.

"If a woman wearing a *hijab* is out alone with a man and she hasn't had the *katbil kitab*, it looks bad. But as long as the couple has made a promise in the mosque, it is okay," Rehan explained.

Rehan wouldn't allow her newfound religiosity to slip. She wanted the Zaytuna sheikhs to teach her how to cope with her new existence as a practicing Muslim. She and Ramy had looked forward to attending the madrassa in San Jose for months. They had listened to Sheikh Hamza's dozens of taped lessons, sold across the world, as they commuted between Ramy's home in New Jersey and Rehan's on Long Island. Like many other students at the madrassa, Rehan's religious identity was suddenly the most important aspect of her life. What does Islam or the *ulama*, the religious scholars, say about whether a woman should make dinner every night for her husband? What does Islam say about the time a woman should devote to her husband if she has a career?

Sheikh Muhammad Yacoubi wants nothing more than to prescribe a set of rules for Muslims like Rehan, torn between their devotion to Islam and their need to integrate to some degree into American society. The first step is to change the false perception some Muslims have about an ancient idea that divides the world into two spheres—*dar al-Islam*, the house of Islam or the house of peace, and *dar al-harb*, the non-Muslim world, literally in Arabic, the house of war. Islamic scholars are in great disagreement over what constitutes this house of war. Some say it is when the ruling government is not Islamic. Others say, if Muslims are safe and protected in a country then it is not part of the house of war. In recent years, extremists have tried to recruit young Muslims living in the West by convincing them that the United States, Great Britain, France, Spain, and the Netherlands are part of the house of war and are therefore legitimate targets of attack.

The Zaytuna sheikhs oppose this extreme view and offer their followers another path. There is a third, forgotten universe, they advise, called *dar al-ahd*, the house of treaty. Abu Abd Allah ash-Shafi, a scholar whose book *Risalah*, published in 817, earned him the title "father of Muslim jurisprudence," developed this idea. The house of treaty is a place where an agreement allows Muslims to practice their faith without making compromises that violate Islamic tradition. In return, Muslims do their best to abide by the laws of their adopted land. The sheikhs refer to a saying of the Prophet Muhammad: "Do not enter the house of Christians nor eat any of their fruits except with their permission."

During his lecture at the makeshift madrassa, Sheikh Yacoubi's guide to living in America is strict and specific. Be a serious student; keep away from other activities. Don't socialize too much. "If you want to be promoted at work, don't attend parties," he lectures. "Don't use credit cards excessively to the point of humiliating yourself. People in America want to have everything. There is greed in every home and soul. Don't fall into this trap."

The point of this exacting talk is to caution young Muslims about America's cultural and social norms. A practicing Muslim must be fully engaged with the religion, Sheikh Yacoubi insists, not just on a weekend retreat or on Fridays at the mosque. That kind of part-time religiosity should be left to other faiths.

In Sheikh Muhammad and Hamza Yusuf, the students at the madrassa seemed to find a way to fill in the missing pieces of their spiritual journey. They had an authoritative imam, descending on his flock from a remote corner in the Middle East, and a modern imam, who, like them, had struggled as a typical American to discover the faith. Imam Zaid Shakir represented the third face of Islam in America, one most of the young Muslims at the madrassa had not encountered before. Imam Zaid was not blessed with Hamza Yusuf's family wealth. Nor does he enjoy Sheikh Muhammad's family pedigree. Like many black Americans seeking the social mobility often denied them, Imam Zaid turned first to the military and then to higher education. He joined the United States Air Force in 1976, and later became a student at American University in Washington, D.C.

Imam Zaid pulled himself out of the ghetto, but his past influenced his future. When he looked for religious guidance, he discovered Malcolm X, an influential member of the Nation of Islam. Like Malcolm X, Imam Zaid believed Islam was the solution to ending racism against blacks in America. But unlike Malcolm X, and perhaps other African American leaders who converted to Islam, Imam Zaid moved beyond viewing Islam through the prism of black oppression. He didn't share the resentment felt by some African American Muslims who believe that immigrant Muslims from the Islamic world have stolen the identity "Muslim American" from them, the first Muslims in America. Sheikh Hamza described him once as an imam who has transcended his blackness to a colorless Islam.

A tall, soft-spoken man, an artist and a published poet, he adds a different dimension to the new movement among young Muslim Americans. While Hamza Yusuf plays the role of the intellectual, Imam Zaid is an activist. While Shiekh Hamza speaks without notes, Imam Zaid is a measured and less passionate speaker. As I followed his appearances across the

Imam Zaid Shakir. (*Courtesy of Aaron Haroon Sellers*)

country, I noticed that he has a more entertaining speaking style with younger audiences and a more sober one with older groups. Over time, I asked his followers how they distinguish him from Sheikh Hamza. The answers I received were positive, yet extremely different, reflecting the different aspects of his personality. One university student said:

"Imam Zaid touches your heart too, but in a different way. You won't necessarily cry when he is speaking, like you probably will when Sheikh Hamza speaks, but just the overall vibe he emits, this feeling of serenity, peace, wisdom, that Islam is simple, not hard like we want to make it. It really touches your heart. I just love him and I never like talking about our sheikhs because I never do justice to their greatness."

As I followed him around the country, I noticed that only when he talks about U.S. foreign policy does he get a bit edgy. At times he said the government "doesn't care about babies dying in Palestine," and the government "cares about one thing, holding on to power, even it means raping the entire world." After September 11, Imam Zaid gave frequent public lectures about how the attacks hurt ordinary Muslims. The attacks called into question whether Islam has humanitarian qualities, he preached. Some Americans used September 11 to reaffirm the existing perception that some Islamic states and Muslim groups care very little for human rights, particularly those of women and minorities living in their midst.

But he didn't place all the blame on Islam's critics. He chastised the Muslim community for its failure to effectively explain that human rights exist within their faith. The Islamic community must speak a language the West can understand, he asserted, rather than simply stating that human rights exist in Islam because Muslims believe in God's existence and God requires human rights for all.

For Imam Zaid, it is just as important to educate Muslims about the faith as it is to teach them how to correct misunderstandings about Islam in the non-Muslim world. One necessary step is to correct the understanding of jihad, now part of the lexicon non-Muslims associate negatively with Islam. Popular wisdom has defined jihad as everything from a Muslim's perpetual, violent struggle against the non-Muslim world to a crusade specifically against the United States. These definitions assume that Muslims carry out jihad against the West even when there is no imminent threat. Imam Zaid, citing a litany of Koranic verses, makes the point that the ninth chapter of the Koran, the "Verse of the Sword," infers that jihad is restricted to the fight against polytheists, not Christians or Jews. He also likes to cite another Koranic passage:

God does not forbid you from being kind and equitable with those who have not fought you about religion and have not driven you out of your homes. God loves the equitable. (The Noble Quran, 60:8)

Before the students, Imam Zaid is unassuming. He adjusts his black tunic as he takes his place and begins to talk about intellectual honesty in Islam. To acquire this honesty, it is necessary to distinguish between the sayings of the Prophet that are "weak," or transmitted unreliably, and those that are sound. Muslims get into trouble by believing that the Prophet said something he probably never said.

The students take notes. Imam Zaid leaves an hour later. The madrassa is ending. Soon, all the students will return to their homes across America. They will report to their jobs, and tend to the practicalities of daily life, but they know that something has changed. In the new America, they now wear a new label, "Muslim."

TWO

The Child-Bride of the Dix Mosque

⮞

Shortly after her fifteenth birthday, Sherine's parents decided she should marry. She had no say in the matter. The time seemed right; a man her family knew from northern Yemen was about to visit their small Muslim enclave in Dearborn, Michigan. In their eyes, his arrival was a godsend. They were concerned that Sherine* was growing too old for traditional Yemeni suitors. In the Southend neighborhood, a young girl was looked upon with suspicion if she were still unmarried when she reached sixteen. The Muslim neighbors might start to gossip. They might think that Sherine had lost her virginity, making her off limits to a Muslim man. Sherine's parents wanted none of this shame.

On a warm afternoon, when the fog mixed with thick smoke rising high above the Ford manufacturing plants, Sherine met Ahmad, who was exactly twice her age. She sat on the brown sofa in the family's living room, clinging to an armrest, as Ahmad studied her carefully, from head to toe. Sherine refused to look directly at him. She preferred to get a glimpse of him from the corner of her dark almond-shaped eye. The thought of his

---

*Sherine is not her real name. Due to the sensitivity of family life in the Yemeni community of Dearborn, she and those in her circle would only speak to me on the condition that I change their names to protect their privacy.

scrawny frame next to her pubescent body repulsed her. She wondered how a couple could marry with no love, and only a few spoken words between them. She was troubled that life in Dearborn in the middle of America was as restricted as if she were living back in Yemen. On most days, she was either helping with chores at home or praying at the Dix mosque, a few blocks away.

It is easy to forget that the Dix mosque, formally known as the American Muslim Society, lies in a small corner of America. Hidden in the bowels of the manufacturing district in south Dearborn, the mosque's green minaret with a crescent atop stands out along the horizon. Five times a day, the melodic muezzin's call to prayer breaks the silence of the neighborhood. Bearded men in *gallabiyyas*, white, ankle-length tunics, and white skullcaps leave their houses nearby and walk to prayer. Such scenes are commonplace in the Islamic world, where the mosque, often located near a bazaar, forms the centerpiece of the neighborhood. But in America, Muslims tend to live miles away from their mosques and attend communal prayers only on Fridays.

Worshippers at Dix enjoy a rare privilege. They can hear the muezzin's call. Local governments have banned the call in nearly every other American city. It's considered too disruptive to the majority of non-Muslims living nearby. In Manhattan, it is common to see a muezzin, cloaked in a long white tunic, stepping out of the mosque onto the pavement and raising a megaphone to his mouth to call the faithful, hoping to be heard above the street noise. But in Dearborn the Yemenis bought all the houses, some wood-frame, others brick, within a few miles of the mosque. The only people living around the mosque are Muslims.

Life in Dearborn wasn't always this way. Most of the first Arab immigrants were Christians, a fact that greatly eased their assimilation into mainstream America, and those immigrants who were born Muslims generally came from elite secular families in their home countries. But during the last twenty years of the twentieth century, more and more Muslim immigrants to the Dearborn area hailed from the "peasant class." Those who settled in the Detroit area from Iraq and Yemen sought jobs in the auto and shipping industries, planning to earn money and then return home.

Sherine wanted to be liberated from the Old World lifestyle of the Southend. The struggle she faced as a Muslim girl in a traditional community reflected a greater tug-of-war within America's Islamic community: Who is a proper Muslim? The Muslims of the second generation, far removed from their parents' countries of origin? Or what Arab Americans in Detroit call boaters, recent immigrants such as the Yemenis at Dix? Sherine wasn't interested in such questions; she merely wanted to enjoy the full freedoms of living in America. "American girls lose their virginity at eleven or twelve, but we don't. American girls do what they want, but by the age of twelve, every Yemeni girl has to cook and clean," Sherine told her parents, protesting the marriage they had arranged for her.

It did no good. Ahmad and Sherine were married all the same. After their wedding, Sherine, a terrified bride, did anything to escape her husband. She slept in another room or at her parents' house a few blocks away.

Sherine's parents warned her not to leave him. Everyone in the community thought Sherine should remain married, despite her revulsion of Ahmad. She searched desperately for comfort. She thought she might find it among her girlfriends, who secretly ridiculed the community's traditions, which were usually justified under the banner of Islam. But they were too afraid to rebel and simply did as they were told. The sheikh at the Dix mosque, Imam Mohammad Musa, a burly man schooled in the classical Islamic tradition in Cairo, advised Sherine against divorce, or *talaq*, in Arabic. In Islam, divorce, though not a sin, is considered frowned upon by God.

"In this community reputation is more important than life itself. They'd rather have you dead than have a bad rep," Sherine thought.

All the pressure made Sherine angry. For most of her adolescence, she had avoided the wrath of neighborhood gossips by wearing her *jilbab*, a long tunic Muslim women use to disguise their curves, to school. When she reached her locker she would remove it until she left for home again. Living that lie was the only way she could live at all.

Most of the time, Sherine was just sad. She had been handed an adult life at fifteen, but was deprived of the freedom that usually comes with maturity. Instead, she was a child-bride suffocating under the weight of marriage to a man she didn't love. Eight months into her marriage, she left Ahmad, thinking, "I don't want this anymore." Of course it created a scandal. She was one of the few girls in the community to ever say she didn't want a man and then act upon it.

Sherine's divorce may have caused her family to lose face in the Southend, but the fact that she had kept her virginity made her feel better. Among traditional Muslims, divorce itself is not taboo, but because, in most cases, a divorced woman is no longer a virgin, remarriage is difficult.

Two years after she left Ahmad, Sherine remarried, this time to another man chosen by her parents but one whom she liked more than Ahmad.
Hasan was only eighteen, a year older than she was. Sherine was by now
wise enough to know what was missing from her first marriage. Hasan had
come to the United States a few years before they met to help his brother
run a liquor store in Manhattan. Hasan seemed more modern than Ahmad,
a trait Sherine thought might give her a greater chance to live like a Muslim in America, rather than a Muslim woman who might as well be living
in remote north Yemen.

Hasan paid the family twenty thousand dollars for Sherine, a small bride-
price in the Islamic world, but no paltry sum for the Southend. The whole
idea of paying for a bride was repugnant to Sherine. For many Muslim
women, the bride-price is akin to buying a slave. But Sherine decided not
to complain. Her father used three thousand dollars to buy her a car. He
spent a bit more on furniture for her new apartment with Hasan, and kept
the rest for himself.

This time around, Sherine felt more comfortable with her arranged
marriage, down to the most important detail. On their wedding night, she
and Hasan disappeared into a private room to consummate their vows. A
few minutes later, she returned with the coveted goods for all to see, a
soiled bed sheet. Even if a traditional Muslim bride manages to convince
everyone she is a virgin, a spotless sheet can raise all sorts of doubts. For
many brides, the fear of a clean bed sheet on their wedding night is nearly
as great as their fear of sex.

Hasan and Sherine made a pact. She dutifully gave him a child, con-
ceived on her wedding night. Every night she made the home-cooked
meals her young husband craved: Arabic rice with lamb or beef. She dressed
in her finest clothes and sweet-smelling perfumes inside the small wood-
frame house they rented in the heart of the Southend not far from her
parents. In return, she expected him to get a job at one of the local auto
plants, where Arab immigrants had found employment for decades.

She was soon disappointed. Hasan's English was too elementary to pass
a basic written exam. In fact, much of the English he knew, Sherine had
taught him. Then she hatched a plan. One day she accompanied Hasan to
the exam and pretended she was applying for work, too. Before they had
completed their tests, Sherine and Hasan switched test papers. Soon, Hasan
had a low-level job at Ford, making minimum wage.

For a time, she tried to make it work. Then, days after her high school
graduation in 1997, she discovered that Hasan was planning to return to

Yemen to marry a wife even more conservative than the women of the Southend. Traditional men in the Islamic world often marry more than one wife. It is an accepted practice, as much as the women may dislike it, as long as the men provide for each household equally, in keeping with Koranic doctrine. In order to assure equal treatment for all, the men alternate sleeping with their wives, moving each night from one house to the next.

Hasan went through with his plan to marry a second wife, and he found her back home in Yemen. Sherine turned to an imam at the Dix mosque, Sheikh Abdul Wahab, a small, sensitive man who was also a distant cousin. She pleaded with him to help her divorce Hasan. She could have filed for divorce in civil court, like any other American wife. But, if Sherine ever hoped to preserve some dignity in the Southend, a sheikh would have to give his approval. In many Islamic countries, it is very difficult for a woman to initiate a divorce unless her husband has committed violence against her or if he is unable to support her. This was essentially true in the Southend; only a favorable verdict from a sheikh would give a woman the right to leave her husband in the eyes of her fellow Muslims. Sheikh Wahab never gave his approval, but Sherine left Hasan all the same.

Sherine wanted to live as a Muslim woman in America, not a woman living in America bound by Yemeni custom. Her tight blue jeans, black turtleneck sweaters that revealed the curves of her breasts, and black scarf she tied tightly around her head, a style popular among African American Muslim women, symbolized her determination to break with tradition.

Unable to support her child on the meager funds Hasan sent her way, Sherine got a job at a local hospital working as a lab assistant from 5:30 in the evening until 2:00 in the morning. This schedule immediately fueled rumors throughout the community. Few women ever went out at night, and no woman she knew was permitted to work until the early morning hours. Some people called her a whore because of her hours.

Ever since she was young, Sherine had been the subject of vicious gossip. But the rumor mill reached a new crescendo when Sherine announced her desire to marry Rasheed, a Muslim from Ghana whom she had met at the hospital. This time it wasn't just a few men chatting idly in the neighborhood's Islamic food market. Her announcement infuriated the entire community. In their minds, Sherine was marrying an *obeed*, a racist Arabic term for a dark-skinned person. Muslims from the African continent were not real Muslims in the eyes of the Yemenis at Dix; they were just blacks.

Sherine's father had a similar response, even though she reminded him that one of the earliest converts and the Prophet Muhammad's first muezzin, Bilali, was a black man. When Rasheed came to the house to ask for Sherine's hand, her father quizzed him about Islam. Sherine again turned to her cousin, Sheikh Abdul Wahab at the Dix Mosque for help. She simply said, "You have to marry us, no one else will." But Abdul Wahab was unwilling to take such a drastic step. He knew in his heart it was the right thing to do, but aligning himself with Sherine meant siding against the community.

The hostility seemed to come from all directions, with the exception of the house across the street from Sherine's parents. Leila Fattah, her sister, mother, and brother dared to be different. They had lived in the Southend for nearly two decades, since the day Mrs. Fattah divorced her husband, an Oxford-educated physician. He settled in Florida, and she took their three children to Dearborn, where she thought they could keep up their Arabic, their religion, and Yemeni culture. Mrs. Fattah became very involved in the activities at the mosque; she taught Arabic classes to children and once a year organized an Islamic fashion show for the women and girls. Yet, Mrs. Fattah disagreed with much of what went on in the mosque, from the segregation of women to the Friday sermons that refused to address real life for Muslims in the West. She even suggested to Sheikh Abdul Wahab that he join a weekly discussion group with women in the mosque to talk about women's rights. He agreed, provided he could talk to them from behind a curtain. Mrs. Fattah thought this defeated the purpose.

Mrs. Fattah stayed in the community, despite her disagreements with the men at the mosque. She had bought a modest house for thirty thousand dollars years before and now she couldn't afford to move. To buy another house, she would have to take out a loan from a bank and pay interest. Paying interest to a bank, known as *rebah* in Islam, is considered a violation of Islamic doctrine.

Mrs. Fattah's eldest daughter, Leila, who was Sherine's age, spent the school year in Florida with her father and summers with her mother, until she turned eighteen and moved to Dearborn permanently. She was even more dismissive than her mother when it came to the mosque mentality. Thin as a rail, Leila had no qualms about wearing low-cut shirts. Like Sherine, she favored an unconventional headscarf, which she tied tightly around her head like a bandana. "My mother raised me to know the real Islam, not the one they preach at Dix," Leila explained to me one day.

"Where does it say in the Koran that women have to be thrown in the basement to pray? The purpose of the mosque is to practice your religion. They have it all mixed up."

The Fattahs' conflicted relationship with the mosque made it easy for them to sympathize with Sherine when she fell in love with Rasheed. Sherine's parents were shocked by her choice, and this time she knew she might be crossing the line of no return. In June 2004, she left her parents' house and moved in with the Fattahs. Word quickly got out that the family without a man running the household had taken in the wild girl who planned to marry an *obeed*. The pressure was relentless.

"Two young neighbors came to our house one day," Leila recalled. "We never associated with them, but my mother, who always welcomes everyone, let them in. They went down to the basement where Sherine was staying and yelled at her, 'Why are you marrying that nigger!'"

Six months later, Sherine convinced a sheikh living across the river in Windsor, Canada, to marry her. Then she left the Dix community for good.

At first glance, the neighborhood around the Dix mosque seems no different from an Arab village. A half dozen Islamic grocery stores and cafés, with signs written in Arabic, line two blocks of Dix Street. But there is an unusual twist: in many Arab countries, outsiders are generally welcomed into close-knit communities, but this is not true in the Southend. During the years that I worked as a journalist in the Middle East and visited impoverished neighborhoods and pre-modern villages, I was always greeted warmly. People were curious. But, because the Yemenis living in the Dix community interact every day with mainstream America, outsiders are not intriguing; they are necessary intruders. When I first visited the mosque, it was difficult to convince the worshippers, particularly the men, to speak with me. At La Friends, a dark, three-room restaurant and café with drawn blinds, women do not dare enter. I didn't know this at first. When I tried to order a Coke there, the men sitting on the worn plastic chairs delivered only deadly stares. Not surprisingly, my Coke never appeared. As I left the restaurant, I could feel the same stares drilling holes into my back.

These men are experts at spending entire days in cafés; they lingered in teahouses long before they ever came to the Southend. From Cairo to the Yemeni capital Sanaa, drinking tea in a café is not merely a pastime for a traditional man; it is the way he interacts with society. And, as in Middle

Eastern cafés, no woman should disrupt the men's tranquility. The intimidating atmosphere inside La Friends reflects perfectly the restrictive society of the Old Country where the men of the Southend came from.

Whether in cafés or any other public place in the neighborhood, the mosque sets the bar for what is considered acceptable social behavior. Only men are allowed to climb the steps of the mosque's entrance leading into the main prayer hall. The women enter around the corner on Woodlawn Street. A green-and-white sign, written in English and Arabic, hanging near the alley proclaims, "sisters' section."

The barefooted men often gather in the main entrance amid the pile of shoes that they've removed to keep the floor leading to the mosque clean. At the mere sight of a woman, they shout in Arabic that the sisters' section is around the corner, and then peer out the door, and point in the direction of the green-and-white sign. Women and girls known as *hijabat*— those who wear the veil—stroll down the alley and enter the mosque through a steel door. Once inside, they walk down a long hallway and up a flight of stairs that leads them to a prayer room that is closed off from the men's section.

Women never see the sheikh. They only hear his voice over a speaker system. When they pray, they face a wall decorated with a *mashrabiya*, a wooden, latticework screen. The semitransparent wall separates the women's prayer room from an empty section in the mosque, adjacent to the men's section. When women want to talk to men, they call them from their side of the *mashrabiya* and speak through the openings in the latticework.

The men running the mosque believe that Islam requires the sexes to be separated during prayers. But such strict separation is actually rare in much of the Islamic world. Women in Arab countries, for instance, generally pray in rows behind men, in the same space. The Koran makes no mention of separating the sexes during prayers. In Mecca, during the annual Muslim pilgrimage to Saudi Arabia, men and women pray together.

Many Dix women actually enjoy the separation because they feel it gives them privacy. They are bothered less by the limited contact with men than by the idea that Yemeni traditions are confused with Islamic practice. Many accept the mosque's decision to carry on these traditions in the heart of America. But they can't accept calling them "Islam."

The role of women in American mosque communities provides the central battleground where the universalist message of Islam clashes with the forces of local culture and practice. In America, the struggle is felt so acutely because believers must balance Islamic values with those of a mainstream society many deplore. But the problem of how to find a balance between local culture and Islamic doctrine is hardly confined to America. This tension has bedeviled Muslims throughout the ages, beginning with the founding of the religion fourteen hundred years ago and accelerating with the rapid spread of the faith across much of the known world. As Muslims conquered non-Muslim territories, they allowed their new subjects to preserve their beliefs and cultural traditions. Likewise, Muslim converts were allowed to retain their diverse languages and habits as Islam moved from Arabia to Africa and beyond. Ibn Batuta, the well-known fourteenth-century world traveler, noted that Muslim societies from China to sub-Saharan Africa were not forced to surrender their languages for Arabic nor persuaded that their cultural traditions violated Islamic doctrine.

Historically, Muslims have sought clarification from Islamic jurists and theologians on the role that culture properly plays in religion. Most point to the determination of the Prophet and his Companions not to declare different cultures good or evil but to accept those that did not violate the central tenets of the new faith. The story of the sons of Arfida, as the Ethiopians were known among the Arabs, is testament to the Prophet's notion of the place culture holds within the Islamic tradition. In the story, African converts celebrating an Islamic religious festival beat leather drums and dance with spears to honor the Prophet. Umar ibn al-Khatib, one of the Prophet's most influential Companions, moves to stop them on religious grounds. But the Prophet interrupts him and says the sons of Arfida are not his people, and therefore, should be allowed such wild dancing. In one account of this story, the Prophet encourages the Ethiopians to keep dancing, saying, "Play your games, sons of Arfida, so the Jews and Christians know there is latitude in our religion."

"Everyone Was Born a Muslim"

Many young American Muslims I met are interested in developing their Islamic identity as part of a broad religious community, whether it is with other Muslims on their campuses, in their Islamic centers, or in the mosques. This community provides a feeling of solidarity and offers a clear antidote to mainstream America, where they often feel uncomfortable. Yet the Yemenis of Dix cling to tradition, and often they confuse those traditions with Islamic doctrine. The first generation of Muslim immigrants to America generally did not concern themselves with distinguishing between tradition and religion. Their main goals were economic

survival and social mobility for them and their children. But the second
generation now faces a greater challenge: how to create a unified Islamic
community in the United States in face of the ethnic and racial barriers
that divide them.

Like Sherine and Rasheed, her Ghanaian husband, young American
Muslims are increasingly open to the possibility of marrying outside their
own ethnic group, as they work to create an indigenous Islamic identity that
is compatible with modern American society. For them, this does not mean
total assimilation into American culture, but rather a unified and strong
Islamic community that is not split along ethnic lines. But it is difficult, for
example, for an Arab woman to convince her parents that marrying a Pakistani man is permitted within the Islamic tradition. It most certainly is, but
this idea is foreign to the experience of their immigrant parents.

Islamic scholars sometimes harshly criticize Muslim Americans for the
importance they place on their ethnic identities. One such scholar is Dr.
Umar Faruq Abd-Allah, of the Nawawi Foundation, who has lectured and
written extensively on how some mosques, Islamic centers, and Muslim
Students' Associations on university campuses not only segregate Muslims along ethnic lines but isolate them from broader American society.
Many scholars agree that it is impossible for Islamic practice to be completely free from cultural influences, but they stress that Muslim Americans must learn how to distinguish between the two.

Separating culture from religion is perhaps more difficult in Detroit
than it is in any other part of the United States, because the large number
of Arab Muslims provides a critical mass of ethnic and historical tradition.
For the last thirty years, southeastern Michigan, including Detroit's metropolitan area, has had the highest concentration of Arabic speakers outside the Middle East. According to Detroit's leading Arab American
association, there are 490,000 Arabs in the metropolitan area, and Arabs
make up one-third of Dearborn's total population. The majority of the
Arabs in the Southend are Yemeni and Iraqi immigrants, while the more
affluent Lebanese have settled in other areas of Dearborn. An estimated
thirty thousand Yemenis live in the Detroit metropolitan area, and Iraqis
number around fifty thousand.

The story of the modern-day Dix mosque began when a Lebanese and a
Yemeni founded the American Muslim Society in 1937 in an old pool hall.
It took them until 1952 to establish a more proper house of worship, erect-
ing a green dome and two small minarets on the roof. For many years, the

former pool hall was more a place for social gatherings than for worship. The 1952 renovations extended the mosque from a few thousand square feet to more than twelve thousand.

With the 1965 repeal of the national immigration quotas, the Yemeni population of the Southend began to swell. Over time the newcomers announced they wanted their conservative ideas to govern the entire local Muslim community. They closed the mosque and declared they were taking it over from Lebanese-Syrian immigrants who had once been the majority. Soon, the Yemenis controlled Dix completely, and life was turned upside down. The Yemeni takeover and the patriarchal community they created filled a deep need for a traditional mosque community. A few of the Yemenis who led the effort were so proud of their new creation that they kept parts of the original pool hall—mostly wooden doors and knobs— as souvenirs to make sure they never forget how far they have come.

The unique situation of Yemeni immigrants and their strong attachment to the ways of the Old Country have shaped every aspect of life at the Dix mosque. Yemeni arrivals are overwhelmingly young men who arrive with little or no education or job skills. Few intend to settle in America permanently, and many keep wives and families back home, visiting periodically and sending funds whenever possible. With no personal investment in a Western future, the Yemenis are strongly resistant to compromise with contemporary American life. They often struggle to make a living wage, with some estimates putting the median household income in the Southend at $20,125, less than half the national average among Muslims. Approximately one-third of the population has never learned English and many first generation immigrant women are illiterate. Any concession to a new identity, say that of Muslim American or even Yemeni American, is often fiercely resisted. Daily life revolves around work, the traditional teahouse or café, and the Dix mosque.

The pace of the Yemeni population growth in the Southend increased after the uneasy unification in 1990 of formerly communist South Yemen and Islamist North Yemen, a process that effectively placed the entire country in the hands of religious conservatives. The North had a long history of theocratic control, extending formally until 1962. Islamic law provided the basis for all legislation. Polygamy was accepted practice and men could divorce without their wives' consent. With the departure of British colonial forces in 1967, the North soon found itself in direct competition with its southern rivals, now aligned with the Soviet Union as the Arab world's first communist state.

When the Soviet Union invaded Afghanistan in 1979, the North's rulers seized on the opportunity to embarrass the Communists in the eyes of the Islamic world by actively supporting their Muslim brethren, the mujahideen fighters, in their battle against the infidel invaders. Legions of Yemeni men joined the ranks of the mujahideen and became among the most intrepid Arab fighters against Soviet rule. North Yemen gave a heroes' welcome to the returning fighters after the defeat of Soviet forces ten years later. As in other Arab countries, these mujahideen fighters, now fired by the radical Islamic ideology common to many of the so-called Afghan Arabs, quickly spread their ideas within Yemeni society, contributing to an Islamic awakening. The fighters' power and influence was further enhanced in 1994, when civil war erupted between secessionists in the south and the unified government based in the north. After nine weeks, the north emerged victorious with the help of the veterans of Afghanistan. Such is the world that has shaped most Yemeni immigrants to the United States.

Many of the immigrants who stay in the United States still have their eyes fixed on Yemen. They make frequent trips home, not only for themselves but to give their children an authentic taste of their culture and religion. They fear the next generation will be corrupted in America and will adopt behavior that is unacceptable for Muslims. As more Yemeni men and women moved to the Southend, the community became more conservative. Some of their imams, including Sherine's cousin Abdul Wahab, came to the Southend after studying in Saudi Arabia, where Islamic scholarship is generally conservative.

As a result, the Yemenis of Dix are more isolated than most Muslim enclaves in America. In fact, in America—unlike in Europe, where Muslims often live in urban ghettos—more and more Muslims are moving to the suburbs and fewer are settling in densely populated areas such as Dearborn. Once in the suburbs, they build mosques, Islamic schools, and community centers, and leave their old urban mosques behind. The tight-knit community around Dix is something of an exception. Yemenis live so close to one another that they can socialize simply by going from house to house with friends or relatives they knew from their villages back home.

The new masters of the Dix mosque wasted no time establishing their conservative agenda. The board invited a young, Saudi-trained Yemeni imam to lead the worshippers. They opened the mosque every day, not just once a week. The prayer area on the first floor was set aside for men and the basement, once a social hall, became the designated prayer area for women. All women were to wear headscarves and enter the mosque, not through the main entrance, but the side door on Woodlawn Street. They were told not to enter the mosque at all when they were menstruating, a common taboo among Muslims in the greater Islamic world. Weddings and social celebrations were no longer permitted at Dix. "There will be no singing or dancing in this house of worship," the new imam declared.

He also ended coed Islamic classes and segregated the sexes in all other mosque activities. He advised the community not to have dogs as pets, in keeping with an Islamic tradition dating back to the Prophet's time that declared dogs unclean. These changes were unusual for Dearborn at the time, even though they reflected commonly held traditions in much of the Islamic world. The Yemenis felt the mosque, for years run by Sunni Muslims who had been separated from their native Lebanon for two generations, had become too Americanized. Their detractors argued that the Yemenis used Islam to justify their fears about sexuality, the role of women in society, and the threats posed by life in a new country filled with many temptations and social ills.

Faced with Yemeni supremacy at Dix, the Lebanese worshippers gradually drifted away, and by 1983 they had established their own religious community called the American Bekka Lebanese League, named for their native Bekka Valley. They turned a building that had been a social hall in the heart of Dearborn's Lebanese district along Chase Street, about eight miles from Dix, into a storefront house of worship. With time, the Bekka League came to resemble a more traditional mosque. From the outside, the brown brick building with a low roof looks like it could be a funeral home or a doctor's office. But inside, the men's prayer hall is bright, with clean white walls and grey and green carpet. The women's prayer hall, segregated from that of the men, is a much smaller room down the hall.

Dix, meanwhile, flourished under its Yemeni leaders. At the time, Saudi Arabia was pouring funds into mosque construction projects in the United States and actively supporting Muslim Students' Associations on the nation's university campuses. Eventually, the Dix mosque doubled in size to twenty-four thousand square feet with help from the Saudis.

Each year during Ramadan when the donation basket is passed around, the women at Dix give their gold bracelets and necklaces, their prized possessions from Yemen, for the upkeep of the mosque. They never know exactly how the money will be used, but they place their trust in the imams and the men on the mosque's governing board. So much gold was collected that the men were able to renovate and expand the mosque yet again in 2004.

A large chandelier with sparkling crystals and gold trim hangs in one of the entrances. The walls of a spacious office, where Imam Aly Leila, the head sheikh, and Abdul Wahab sit each day to counsel worshippers, are decorated with large photographs of the grand mosque in Mecca. Green and beige wall-to-wall carpet woven with designs of minarets covers the floor.

Dix worshippers had complained for years that time had stood still at their mosque. Before the expansions, the sheikhs greeted the visitors or worshippers who came for advice in a small, dark, dusty office that resembled a storage room. Only a desk and a few chairs could fit inside. They wondered when their mosque would grow, particularly because during Ramadan so many men came to Friday prayers that some had to stand outside in the parking lot. They watched as other mosques in Dearborn underwent facelifts: drab minarets were dotted with gold; the prayer rooms benefited from clean carpets; the plain windows were replaced with stained glass. For two years, the talk around Dearborn was about a $12 million Shiite mosque under construction about six miles from Dix. The Shiites at the Islamic Center of America were trading in their modest mosque, built in the 1950s and located in a commercial district, for an ostentatious mosque of gold and Italian tiles, spectacularly visible from the well-traveled freeway.

Everyone in Dearborn could see the budding mosque as it sprouted along the highway, one piece of gold at a time. The imam, Sheikh Hassan Qazwini, was a smooth talker with the polished manners characteristic of the Shiite clerics of Iran, where he had received his theological schooling. Qazwini could charm anyone. He did all the right things to achieve prominence in the community, from organizing lavish fund-raising dinners to appearing on religious television programs.

The Dix community, however, didn't want a famous imam or an elaborate mosque. The men simply wanted their house of God to be a little less rundown; the women were happy just to have toilet paper in their washroom, the place they cleansed their hands before prayers. It took September 11 to propel the community into action. After the attacks, zealous newspaper and television reporters descended upon the mosque in their frenzied search for snapshots of "radical Muslims." Anyone would do, provided they had the proper dress. The Dix men in their long *gallabiyyas* and the women in dark headscarves and *jilbabs*, ankle-length dresses, fit the stereotypes perfectly. Their pictures were splashed across the evening news to incite fear that there were Muslim extremists on American soil. The news stories created a bad reputation for the mosque, and the men in charge launched a public relations campaign to repair the community's image.

A few years later, after thousands of worshippers had pooled their donations, the mosque sparkled with new chandeliers, renovated classrooms for children learning Arabic, and a community room for hosting dinners and lunches. The mosque held two open houses after the renovations were finished. The worshippers gave visitors what they call a *dawah* package, from the Arabic word meaning the call to Islam. Manila folders were filled with an introductory booklet about Islam and information about the history of Dix.

Sheikh Abdul Wahab hoped the literature would not only give outsiders an accurate picture of Islam, but draw some to the faith. "Everyone was born a Muslim," Wahab often says, repeating an idea held by some conservative Muslims. The tradition can be traced back to the Prophet Muhammad, who, it is said, was asked about the offspring of pagans. The Prophet said, "No child is born but has the Islamic faith, but its parents turn it into a Jew or a Christian."

Imam Aly, a tall, handsome imam educated in the classical Islamic tradition at al Azhar in Cairo, arrived at Dix just as the mosque's latest facelift was getting underway. Sheikh Aly was approachable, true to the Egyptian reputation for charm and lightheartedness. He was far more open than the Yemeni imams who grew up in America. He looked women directly in the eye, unlike many men in Dix who lowered their gaze. Sheikh Aly is not afraid to express his view of the community. "Most of the people came here twenty years ago and they are not so educated. They are not integrated into American society. They speak weak English. I was invited to a wedding and nearly all of the one hundred people there were from the same tribe in Yemen," Aly told me during one of the few times we met.

It took a newcomer like Sheikh Aly to talk openly about the difference between culture and religion. "My ideology is to try to make a difference. People have many questions. 'How do you treat your husband or wife? What does it mean to be a Muslim?' How they raise kids back home doesn't fit here." At least this was the message he espoused shortly after he arrived. But Sheikh Aly gradually became less critical of the Dix community; he realized, as imams had done before him, that his survival depended upon the backing of the men running the mosque. The revolving door of imams at Dix is well known. Imams come and go; most worshippers never know why, and those who do, do not talk openly about the disagreements.

The presence of the Tablighi Jamat, literally the "proselytizing group," an archconservative Islamic group that originated in India, is a sign of this diversity. The Dix mosque is one of their regular stops on their tour of mosques across America. Dressed in white *gallabiyyas* and skullcaps, with their long beards and aloof demeanor, the Tablighi Jamat seem daunting. Inspired by the mysticism of Sufi Islam and the more rigid side of Sunni Islam, the Tablighi are officially apolitical. Their stated mission is to spread the *dawah*, the Islamic message, which they believe anyone can do. Unlike orthodox Sunni Muslims, the Tablighi dismiss religious scholarship and believe anyone can preach, even those without a classical Islamic education. They advocate veiling for Muslim women, oppose coeducational schools, and try to limit their contact with non-Muslims. While on tour, they sleep in mosques around the country as part of their missionary zeal. They rarely speak to women, in keeping with conservative Islamic views on interaction between the sexes.

One day in October 2003, the men at the mosque advised Abdullah, a Tablighi member and an engineering professor at the local colleges of Wayne State University, to speak to me about the community. The men knew I was trying to learn about the Dix community, and Abdullah seemed like the perfect person to represent them. He often gave non-Muslims tours of the mosque, especially after September 11, when many people in the Dearborn area became curious about the Muslims living in their midst.

Abdullah was reluctant at first; perhaps, I thought, he was uncomfortable at the prospect of being alone with a strange woman. But Faisal, a member of the mosque's board, worried I might be offended, and encouraged Abdullah to make an exception. Abdullah, his body hidden beneath his *gallabiyya*, escorted me into a room across from the mosque's administration office. It was a dark, cluttered storage area. Abdullah motioned for me to sit on a chair; he then sat down across from me, after making a point of leaving the door ajar. At first, I expected him to talk in slogans the way some conservative Muslims do in the Islamic world when they meet strangers. But I was pleasantly surprised. Abdullah's intelligence and candor were apparent from the moment we began talking.

"The most important thing is fear of God—*taqwa*. The more you take this seriously, the more of a strict Muslim you are. On a *taqwa* scale of zero to ten, some people try to be at five or six. The Prophet was at ten."

Abdullah wasn't always God-fearing. He was raised in an affluent Detroit family. None of his family members made religion an important part of their lives. But, as he got older, Abdullah wanted to find a new way: He married a woman who converted to Islam, and he inspired her to go to Damascus to study the faith and learn Arabic. Abdullah stayed behind and taught his children Arabic. Even in small ways, the family tried to recreate the Arab tradition in their daily lives; they stopped eating at a table and instead served their meals on the floor. The children were not allowed to watch television. Developing a strong belief in Islam was important to Abdullah, and he wanted the same for his children. He quoted from Umar ibn al-Khatib, one of the prominent Companions of the Prophet, who famously said that believers could never move from darkness to light until they developed "the sweetness of the faith."

Abdullah tells a story. There was once a French model. He read about her in the newspapers. She had a brain tumor and gave up modeling and started reading the Koran. Then the brain tumor disappeared. Anyone can find a cure for their ills, says Abdullah, if they find Islam. And once people find Islam, they grow more devout over time. "Repentance to Allah is always open and available. What is happening now at places like Dix is that if Muslims find an Islamic environment, they become more Islamic. The main thing in Islam is to work on people. In this country, temptation is great."

"Different Mentalities, Different Visions"

Under the Yemeni influence, a certain philosophy took hold of the Dix followers: the community consensus, not individuals or their families, determined proper moral and religious behavior. This gave the mosque, the center of life for the Yemenis, far more authority over people's lives than in other Islamic communities in America. This meant the imam at the mosque had to reflect the general ideas in the community, or he wouldn't last there very long. And that's why one imam was forced to leave.

Imam Mohammad Musa, the bubbly cleric who had once counseled Sherine against divorce during her unhappy first marriage, left Dix after twenty years for a ritzy mosque in the affluent Detroit suburb of Bloomfield Hills. Like Sheikh Aly, Musa received a classical Islamic education from Cairo's al Azhar. And, like many imams in the United States, he also studied in Saudi Arabia. As Dix grew more conservative, Imam Musa became more controversial until his differences with the mosque's board were irreconcilable.

More than two years after leaving Dix, Musa is still reeling. He sits in his well-appointed office, his dark-blue tunic perfectly pressed, with a box of expensive chocolates on his desk. His lifestyle is clearly more luxurious at his new mosque, but he is troubled by the war of ideas at Dix—a battle he decidedly lost. Remembering his days in the Southend, Musa tells me stories. I ask him how the Yemenis took control of the mosque.

"Muslims in the United States live freely to practice their religion without being bothered by anyone. But the men at Dix didn't understand that. They talked against America and put others down who didn't. This happened even before September 11. I told them, 'Don't try to create hatred in the hearts of Muslims about others. Teach us about religion.'

"But the board came to lead the community, and they tried to control the imams. But an imam has his own vision based on the Koran and the Sunnah, and they are supposed to accept that. The men on the board don't even have Islamic degrees, but they still questioned me, 'Why do you say that and this?' No imam would accept this."

Musa was appalled that the men on the board dared to challenge his religious authority. In Islam, a certified theologian who is an imam at a mosque generally has final say over disputed religious issues. He is held in such high regard that sometimes when a man addresses the imam, he places his hand over his chest to display reverence. Musa received little such respect. The story he often tells to illustrate the cause of his outrage concerns a disagreement over whether the mosque should invite Sheikh Omar Abdul Rahman to give a lecture. It was in the early 1990s, before the sheikh was sent to jail in New York for inspiring the Islamic radicals who attacked the World Trade Center in 1993.

Sheikh Rahman was the spiritual guide of the Gamaa al-Islamiya, a militant group in Egypt that tried, unsuccessfully, to overthrow the Egyptian government. The U.S. government had been building a case against Rahman but it was anything but solid. Yet Sheikh Musa felt Rahman's venom against U.S. policies in the Middle East would draw attention to Dix. The mosque board overruled him, however, and the sheikh spoke before hundreds of worshippers.

"Why did you object to Sheikh Rahman so vehemently?" I ask him.

"There is a *hadith*, the teachings of the Prophet," he replies. "It teaches me that because I am not an American citizen, I can't fight America. Because I must respect the law of the country where I live. This is why I left Dix. We have different mentalities, different visions."

Musa didn't realize it at the time, but the Yemeni triumph at Dix foreshadowed the Islamic revival that was coming to Dearborn and the rest of the United States. In the years that followed, the conservative takeover of mosques became more widespread, as Muslims became more involved in their faith and increasingly influenced by Islamic practice in the broader Muslim world.

Around Dix, the stories about Sheikh Musa's differences with the mosque board are still alive. Depending upon who is talking, he is either a savior or a misguided soul. The young women have fond memories of him as the imam who tried, but failed, to persuade their parents to give them more freedom. Enjoying the luxury of his new, upscale mosque, Musa clearly has traded in the conservatism at Dix for what he calls modernity.

When we meet, he explains that he is taking his new mosque in a different direction. Women hold seats on the governing board, and the community decides if non-Muslim women visiting the mosque should wear headscarves.

"Last week we discussed if women come to the mosque for open house, do they need to wear the *hijab*? I said, 'let's place some *hijabs* in a basket for them to wear and let them decide.' Even in a mosque, you shouldn't force non-Muslims to wear a *hijab*. We can't force someone to practice something they don't believe."

Musa's words were shocking; in nearly every mosque in America and the Islamic world, all women, even non-Muslims, are required to wear headscarves. "Many ladies decide in America to wear *hijab* after many years without it. One husband tried to convince me to tell his wife to take off her *hijab*. But I told him that it is her choice." The *hijab*, says Musa, is a sign of civilization. "Humans used to live like animals. But then they covered their private parts with leaves. The more civilized they became, the more they covered."

Young women at Dix were the ones most saddened by Musa's ouster. Muslim American life is not as clear cut for the children of Dix as it is for their elders. With one foot in Yemen and another in America, practicing their faith is not so simple. Even for those who prefer minimal exposure to American life, the public schools force them to confront American values. The young women felt that Musa helped them straddle these two worlds. After he was gone, they were on their own. They think the advice from their parents and the Dix imams is too conservative, so some of the girls and young women formed a *halaqa*, Arabic for "study group," that meets in the mosque each Sunday at one o'clock. They sit in a circle, and their teachers, who are older members of the mosque, alternate on different Sundays to lead the lesson.

One Sunday in the dead of winter in 2004 some girls have difficulty traveling to the mosque. The streets running behind the mosque, home to many Dix worshippers, are covered with deep snow. Drivers trying to inch out of the neighborhood form a long line at the stop sign. Snowplows seem to work in Detroit, and even in Dearborn, but not around the Dix mosque. The Muslims say the city has no interest in plowing the streets where they live, and there seems to be truth in that. Still, several young women manage to reach the mosque to attend the *halaqa*.

As is true on most Sundays, the lesson is about one theme: faith and behavior. Why should Muslim girls wear headscarves? Why shouldn't Muslim girls talk with boys? Why should Muslim girls obey their parents, even if they disagree with them? The topics reflect the difficult questions the mosque has faced over the last half century, as imams came and went and a younger generation grew up in America. Many have been coming to the *halaqa* for years. It is their safe haven from a world outside that challenges their beliefs. During the study session, the girls don't talk directly about their lives or their families. But once the *halaqa* ends and the teacher leaves, they sit together cross-legged on the carpet, unaware of their grace and beauty.

Speaking with me is a bit difficult for them. I had been to the *halaqa* several times, and only when I became a familiar face were a few young women willing to take a chance. Their memories of the aggressive journalists who came to Dix after September 11 still linger, and discussing with an outsider what they truly feel about the imams and the traditions in the community seems like a betrayal. But, finding safety in numbers, three young women decide it is better to talk to me than risk leaving me with the wrong impression. They begin revealing bits and pieces of their lives.

Hayat, a twenty-five-year-old psychologist, is the sister of Afrah, a strong-willed teacher who often leads the Sunday *halaqa*. Afrah has left her mark on the girls. Although she wears a long headscarf and full-length skirt covered by a tunic, her conservative dress does not mean that she is a submissive Muslim woman. Her ideas and goals are no different from those of a liberated non-Muslim woman in America. She juggles motherhood, a full-time job as a schoolteacher, and her mosque activities.

Hayat and Afrah's parents have several things in common with the other Dix families. They moved to the community in the 1980s from North Yemen. Their mother was illiterate in Arabic and English; their father worked at the Chrysler plant. Afrah veiled in the tenth grade, in 1985, when there were few Muslims at her public high school. For Hayat, ten years younger, veiling was easier because she had far more Muslim peers by the time she reached high school. But their parents stood out from the other Dix families in one important way: "It was always normal for females to go back to Yemen to marry and not to go to college," Hayat says. "It is Yemeni tradition to oppose girls going to college, but this isn't Islam. My father, thank God, was different. He swore he would provide his children with the life he never had."

When Hayat was a student at the University of Michigan in Dearborn, she joined the Muslim Students' Association (MSA). It was the first time she was surrounded by Muslims who dared to show they were proud of their religion in a non-Muslim setting.

Ismahan, sitting to the left of Hayat, is a thin and unemotional computer scientist. She believes the MSA on campuses should segregate the women from the men in keeping with Islamic tradition. When Ismahan went to elementary school in the Southend, she felt pressured to fit in and show that she was like everyone else. But, as an adult, she is more determined to display her Muslim identity.

"Now, I know my rights and I know I don't have to fit in. I don't think Muslims have to assimilate. We are not treated like Americans. At work, I get up from my desk and go to pray. I thought I would face opposition from my boss. Even before I realized he didn't mind, I thought, 'I have a right to be a Muslim and I don't have to assimilate.'"

Telling her coworkers that she is a Muslim shields her from exposure to language and behavior that might make her uncomfortable. "Now, they know me well at work and know what bothers me. Just two days ago, someone cracked a dirty joke and said, 'Oh, I'm so sorry.' It's not because I'm oppressed that I don't like dirty jokes. I find them offensive."

Fatma, a twenty-three-year-old third-grade schoolteacher, becomes vivacious and talkative once the others lead the way. Her father, one of the Dix founders, came to the United States in the 1970s. He spent two years in California before moving to Michigan. Like many Yemenis, he knew about Dix from his relatives and wanted to raise his children there, so his daughters would wear headscarves and memorize the Koran. "Some Muslims do anything to fit in. They drink. They date. My biggest fear is that I might assimilate into the American lifestyle so much that my modesty goes out the window," says Fatma.

All the girls want to marry and have children. But unlike other Muslim women in other parts of the United States, the Dix girls want to stay connected to the mosque in order to raise their children there. They worry that attending university and developing their careers have made them too old for marriage. They also hint that time will take care of the older men at Dix, and the mosque will be easier for their children. "Even if I am married and have my own family, I would want to have that feeling in my heart to come to the mosque," says Fatma. "What made me sane during years of public high school was coming to the *halaqa* every Sunday."

Some outsiders who pray at the mosque do not share the comfort these women from the Southend feel there. Muslim women who didn't grow up in the community try to blend in. Some give up right away, after climbing the big steps at the front entrance, not knowing that the women's section is around the corner, and hearing the men's alarmist shouts in Arabic.

But Aliciajewell Bayi, a vivacious woman in her twenties, stuck it out longer than most. An African American born to a Baptist minister father, religion was nothing new to her. By the time she became a student at the University of Michigan in Ann Arbor, she was searching for a new faith. When she met her future husband, Omani, a Muslim, she found Islam. When the two finished their studies, they moved to Detroit and discovered Dix.

Aliciajewell was excited about becoming a member of the Dix family. It was her first mosque, and the place where she made *shahada*, the profession of faith that makes one a Muslim: "There is no god but God, and Mohammad is his Prophet." She was drawn to its insular nature; she thought it was a place where she could make a difference. She started attending the Sunday *halaqa* and met Fatma, Ismahan, and Hayat. She joined the outreach committee, the group created after September 11 to improve the mosque's public image. When she attended the first meeting, she was shocked and disappointed. The members, all men, sat in a U-shape in a drab room inside the mosque. They talked to her only while looking into space to avoid eye contact. "I started refusing to answer when they did this. I said, 'He is not talking to me if he is facing the opposite direction.'"

Then she tried to join the mosque governing board, but women were not allowed. "No woman ever complained about it because they were afraid they'd get a bad reputation. The women don't want to become active in the mosque because their parents might find out they attend meetings with men in the room," she says.

Aliciajewell soon found herself cut off from almost everyone at Dix, including the women in the *halaqa*. Sherine was among the few friends she made. For her, Sherine was living proof that even a woman who grew up in the Southend might not ever be happy there.

A year after Aliciajewell and her husband found Dix, she sat in a chic modern condominium in downtown Detroit, taking care of her young son, Mohammad. The dark clouds outside threatened to dampen the cheer created by the apartment's blue walls and large windows. Aliciajewell and her husband bought the apartment in an up-and-coming section of downtown, but it was at least fifteen miles from Dix. The mosque now was too far for them to travel for prayers. But like Sherine, she no longer had a reason to go to Dix. She would find another mosque closer to home.

Aliciajewell's idealized image of what it is to be a Muslim was shattered. As I met her periodically over a year, she became hardened, more cynical as time went on. She had chosen the wrong mosque to begin her Islamic journey, she thought.

The men at Dix probably were not aware of the effect their words and actions had on outsiders, and even on the members of their own community. In their hearts they wanted to attract newcomers like Aliciajewell to the faith. They wanted to make all the worshippers in the community, including the women who grew up there, feel comfortable. But the convictions driving them to recreate the life they had left behind in North Yemen were at cross-purposes with their desire to preserve the mosque for the next generation.

THREE

The Roots of Islam in America

On October 3, 1965, the White House advance men had every reason to be pleased. They had carefully positioned President Lyndon B. Johnson on Liberty Island in New York City's harbor, in the lee of a single American flag. Beyond, the towering Statue of Liberty provided an irresistible backdrop for a photo-op, just as they knew it would. Busloads of grateful immigrants, including a group of thirty-five Slavs shipped in from nearby New Jersey, cheered the proceedings. One of their number, Adam Lech, of Somerset, gushed to a reporter minutes after shaking the president's hand, "What a country!" A crowd of others from around the globe, including some recent arrivals to America's shores, scrambled for one of the many presidential pens used to sign the first major liberalization of the nation's immigration laws in more than four decades.

Plenty of overheated rhetoric was used to commemorate the occasion. "Today we can all believe that the lamp of this grand old lady is brighter and the golden door she guards gleams more brilliantly in the light of an increased liberty for people from all countries," said President Johnson, in a nod to the Statue of Liberty behind him. The president and first lady then left the island by helicopter and flew to Manhattan for a dinner at the Waldorf Astoria.

Despite the hoopla of that day, most supporters of the new immigration rules, including the president himself, saw them as little more than a useful if unremarkable building block in the administration's Great Society legislation. Advancing civil rights was the order of the day, and immigration reform was simply part of the package. Cold War symbolism also played its part. Supporters argued that America could not retain its place as the head of the free world if it continued to determine who it took in and who it turned away on the basis of national origin. "The bill that we will sign today is not a revolutionary bill," LBJ told the crowd on Liberty Island. "It does not affect the lives of millions, it will not reshape the structure of our daily lives or add importantly to our wealth and power."

Nor, he might have added, was it particularly controversial. Three past presidents—one Republican and two Democrats—had all pressed for elimination of restrictive immigration quotas based on national origin, essentially unchanged since their enactment in 1921. LBJ signaled his own determination to open up immigration more than a year earlier, calling for reform in his 1964 State of the Union address. With the economy roaring along, organized labor and African American leaders had dropped their earlier opposition to this potential new source of economic and social competition. Most commentators predicted only a modest change in immigration patterns, perhaps a slight shift in numbers from Western Europe in favor of Asia and Latin America, with little or no real increase in the total number of new arrivals each year.

Even traditional defenders of the old immigration limits, including the Daughters of the American Revolution and other so-called patriotic societies, put up only half-hearted and disorganized resistance. Like the bill's supporters, they largely accepted the experts' predictions that the overall number would change little. Bitter opposition among congressmen from the Deep South, fresh from their dogged but doomed defense of Jim Crow, swayed no one. The Senate approved the bill by 76 votes to 18, while the House voted 318 to 95.

The president's signature, appended on that warm, sunny day on Liberty Island, effectively abolished the 1921 National Origins Act and the related Asiatic Barred Zone, an immigration regime designed to ensure that America's ethnic make-up remained essentially northern European, particularly German, Irish, and British. Italians, Greeks, Slavs, Asians, and Arabs, to name just some of the nationalities that had poured into the country since the 1880s, were no longer welcome after 1921. Syrian immigrants, for example, who had once arrived at a rate of nine thousand or more per year, were soon reduced to just a few hundred under the new quota system. Public opinion surveys after World War II consistently supported the national quota system, and Congress reaffirmed the regime in 1952, although it did lift an explicit ban on Asians at the time. Yet, within little more than a dozen years, the entire system was abandoned.

A number of trends conspired to distort the stated goals of the new policy from the very outset. First, a series of upheavals around the world created a huge pool of would-be immigrants, abetted by increased mobility and more efficient global transportation links. Worldwide estimates put the number of migrants at 75 million in 1960, a figure that would reach 175 million by 2000. The U.S. share of this mobile population dwarfed that of other countries, with an estimated immigrant population of 35 million at the end of these four decades. Second, the crafters of the immigration reform had sought clues to the road ahead by looking in the rearview mirror, relying on the past as a measure of what the future would bring. They were in no position to make accurate predictions about how the world's increasingly mobile population might respond to changes in American law. A rich and prosperous Western Europe was no longer a steady source of would-be immigrants. Meanwhile, family reunification, central to the new U.S. policy and today the primary driver of the swelling number of foreign-born residents, was hardly a factor in the decades before the 1965 reforms.

It should come as no surprise that the demographic and social effects of immigration reform shaped largely by such disparate forces as America's civil rights movement and the Cold War bore little or no resemblance to the original intent of its backers—or even to the darkest fears of its most strident opponents. Both sides in the political battle over the 1965 reforms failed utterly to envision the America of today that they helped create. Nor could they have foreseen perhaps the single most profound change set in motion by the new immigration regime: the permanent introduction of Islam, the third great monotheistic tradition, into American daily life.

Forty years on, America features a flourishing Muslim community, estimated to be six million strong and representing at least eighty different countries of origin. Only the annual hajj, the pilgrimage to Mecca, brings together more Muslims from more countries than live in America today. A recent survey by researchers at Georgetown University found that about two-thirds of Muslim Americans were born outside the United States. Of these immigrants, 34 percent came from South Asia, 26 percent were Arabs, and 7 percent were Africans. Meanwhile, African American Muslims, both converts and those raised as Muslims, represent about one-fifth of the total Muslim American population. The Georgetown survey also found that the American Muslim community was better educated, better off, and younger than the nation as a whole. Muslims tend to graduate from college at a rate more than double the national average, with half enjoying an annual household income of at least fifty thousand dollars. Three-quarters of adult Muslims are less than fifty years old.

Mosque life in America has grown along with the steady increase in population. The Mosque Study Project 2000, the largest such survey ever conducted in the United States, found regular attendance at Friday communal prayers almost doubled between 1994 and 2000, with the number of Muslim Americans actively associated with mosques up four-fold to two million during the same period. Like the population at large, the congregations at America's mosques are ethnically diverse; 90 percent of mosques feature mixed congregations of Arabs, South Asians, and African Americans, and only 7 percent are attended by just one ethnic group. Conversion rates among nonimmigrants held steady for the period, while the ranks of immigrants continued to swell. As a result, American Islam increasingly reflects the immigrant population, at the expense of African Americans, Latinos, and other native-born believers.

From about the eighth century, the great Muslim empires and states of the Old World, from China to the Iberian Peninsula, produced great science. Even as Christian Europe descended into the chaos, ignorance, and intellectual torpor of the Middle Ages, the Muslim world took classical learning to new heights. Muslim scholars made huge advances in astronomy, mathematics, and geography, as well as in their more practical stepchildren, navigation, engineering, and cartography. By the time the Muslim and Christian forces clashed during the First Crusade, in 1096, the Islamic soldiers were aghast at their new foes' barbarism and lack of even basic science and technology.

One byproduct of the Islamic intellectual revolution was an impulse toward naval exploration, now abetted by such navigational devices as the astrolabe and increasingly sophisticated maps and charts, and backed by growing military and mercantile power. Classical Muslim geographers and historians, including the renowned twelfth-century Arab authority al-

Idrissi, recount their co-religionists' exploits crossing "the Sea of Darkness and Fog," a contemporary reference to the Atlantic Ocean. More than a century earlier, the scholar al-Masudi noted the adventures of Khashkhash ibn Saeed ibn Aswad, of Córdoba, who returned home in A.D. 889, after crossing the Atlantic. Al-Masudi's map of the world includes a large, unidentified landmass in the Sea of Darkness and Fog. This great sea, he reported, was believed to be "the source of all oceans and in it there have been many strange happenings."

Arab explorers were, of course, not the only ones drawn to this vast ocean and the rumored riches that lay on its opposite shore. The glory of claiming to be the first voyager to the New World has also been advanced on behalf of the king of the gold-rich Muslim empire of Mali, who is said to have sailed there in the early fourteenth century. Chinese imperial fleets, under the Muslim admiral Zheng He, may have successfully crossed the Atlantic seven decades ahead of Columbus. Some have sought to buttress these accounts with linguistic and cultural evidence of pre-Columbian contact between the Americas and the established Muslim world, but modern experts remain deeply divided on the question.

There can, however, be no doubt about the next wave of Muslims to reach American shores—these Muslims were caught in the brutal slave trade that linked West Africa and the new colonies, by way of the dread Middle Passage across the Sea of Darkness and Fog. Islam had taken root in northern Senegal and Mali, carried across the Sahara by Arab and Berber merchants from the north, well before the first slaves were shipped to the New World, in 1501. The faith, popularized by local rulers, clerics, and traders, spread to the shores of Lake Chad and into northern Nigeria. West African Muslims soon became active participants in the global community of believers, establishing commercial, cultural, and diplomatic ties that reached into North Africa and beyond. African pilgrims on the annual hajj to Mecca, one of the five obligations of the faith for any able-bodied believer, further strengthened the region's bond to traditional centers of Islamic learning, as did the exchange of scholars, jurists, and clerics.

By the time European slavers had set up their bases of operations in the so-called Senegambia supply zone, the area had a large Muslim presence; those who were not themselves Muslims were at least familiar with Islam, its teachings, culture, and values. Among those values was an emphasis on literacy, study, and scholarship. The Prophet Muhammed once said of the pursuit of knowledge, "Seek for science, even in China." And the Koran is explicit about the need to study the teachings of the Holy Book. Education was highly prized in West Africa, and local Muslim rulers built numerous schools, many open to women and girls. In this vast area with no written language of its own, Arabic became the language of education as well as the language of faith. Some local languages were later written in Arabic script.

The inclusion of a significant number of Muslims among the slaves bound for America was not simply an accident of geography—the tragic intersection of European traders with a region undergoing profound religious conversion on a large scale. The rapid spread of the faith since its revelation in the seventh century led to severe social and political dislocation among West Africa's rival empires and kingdoms. Slavery in West Africa was a frequent consequence of defeat in battle, a phenomenon accelerated by the upsurge in war and violence that accompanied the rise of militant Muslim states. One contemporary Western account notes the disbelief and horror the local Africans expressed when told that Europe's battles generally ended in the deaths of thousands of soldiers, rather than in the mass surrender to a life of enslavement by the victors. These tumultuous times produced a ready supply of African captives, many of whom were sold off to European slavers for transit to the labor-hungry plantations of the New World. Islam's emphasis on learning and religious knowledge also produced in West Africa a local class of mobile scholars, who were easily caught up in the chaos of war and unrest and thus easy targets for capture and sale to European slave traders.

Estimates of the number of Muslim slaves, sketchy at best and based on the total number of slaves sent to America from those regions of West Africa with at least some experience of Islam, run into "tens of thousands." While always a distinct minority among the early American slave population, the signs of this Muslim presence were everywhere—if one knows where to look. Runaway slave notices, a regular feature of newspapers in the Deep South, read like a Who's Who of traditional Muslim names, although the derivations may have escaped many of the slave owners: Bullaly (Bilali, the first black follower of the Prophet and Islam's first muezzin); Boccarey (Abu Bakr, the first Muslim caliph); Mamado (Mahmud); Mahomet (Muhammad); Walley (Wali, a legal guardian or protector under Islamic law); and Sambo (or "second son" in the language of the Muslim Fulbe people).

Fellow slaves, owners, missionaries, and other observers also recorded behavior that was clearly Islamic, although they may not have recognized it as such. Anecdotal evidence, for example, mentions slaves who would not eat pork, forbidden under Islam. A slave narrative from 1837 written by Charles Ball, a non-Muslim, tells of one resolute captive who manages to observe Islam's five daily prayers despite his bondage: "In the evening, as we returned home, we were joined by the man who prayed five times a day, and at the going down of the sun, he stopped and prayed aloud in our hearing, in a language I did not understand." Ball noted that he had seen others throughout his long life on the southern plantations "who must have been, from what I have since learned, Mohammedans, though at that time I had not heard of the religion of Mohammad." Others described slaves who bowed in a particular direction, presumably toward Mecca, women who covered their heads and hair, and men who wore skullcaps and manipulated prayer beads when making their devotions. Few seemed to know the significance of what they had seen.

The presence of Muslims, particularly literate, well-educated ones, among the American slave population posed some serious challenges to an institution that cloaked its economic interests in morality and religion. After all, Africans were considered morally and intellectually inferior to whites, an understanding used to legitimize their enslavement. This assumption was hard to maintain when faced with a West African Muslim who could read and write Arabic, could quote from the Koran, and was versed in religious law and other learned disciplines. Second, converting the slaves to Christianity, although initially frowned upon in some of the colonies, was generally extolled because evangelization was part and parcel of the whites' justification for the slave trade. Converting Muslims, whose faith and religious training made them both familiar with the general outlines of Christian doctrine and well armed to resist any appeal it might offer, was problematic. For Muslims, Muhammad was "the seal of the prophets"—literally the last in a long line of holy figures that included Moses and Jesus—and Islam had addressed once and for all the shortcomings of the other monotheistic faiths.

Omar ibn Said, captured in 1807 in present-day Senegal, embodied these challenges to the Christian world to which he was so abruptly deported. He was born into a wealthy West African family around 1765, and lived the life of a scholar for twenty-five years, making the pilgrimage to Mecca in keeping with his faith and his exalted station in life. Omar became a teacher and a merchant, but he later found himself on the losing side of a religious war fought against a large non-Muslim army and was sold into slavery. He arrived in Charleston, South Carolina, after a passage of six weeks. Four years later, Omar attracted considerable local attention in Fayetteville, North Carolina, where he had been jailed as a runaway slave after taking refuge in a church. Townspeople were astounded that this middle-aged slave could write petitions for his freedom on the walls of his cell in Arabic, and they were impressed by his bearing and dignity. Omar was auctioned off to a prominent local family, headed by General Jim Owen, to pay for his jailhouse upkeep, but his new masters demanded only relatively light duties as a house servant and gardener.

It was during his time with the Owens family that Omar agreed to produce a brief autobiography and other documents, the earliest known examples of Arabic text written in America. Fourteen of his twenty-one works, all in Arabic, have survived to this day. Rediscovered in an old trunk in Virginia in 1995 and bought at auction by a prominent collector, Omar's original autobiographical sketch reveals much about the way his classical Muslim education and religious outlook served him during his hard life in a strange and hostile land.

Christian missionaries translated his work during his lifetime, and they were eager to see signs that Omar ibn Said—commonly known in white society as Moro, a corruption of his first name—had renounced Islam for Christianity. Omar may well have intended to give that impression, for his well-being was in the hands of his Christian masters. And there was always the possibility that he might win his freedom and secure passage back to Africa, as some other high-born Christian converts had done. Thus, in his writings, the author at times presents a modest portrait of his talents and abilities, apologizing that he has "forgotten much of my talk as well as the talk of the Maghreb," that is, the Arabic language.

Yet, a modern reading of the rediscovered manuscript paints a picture of a man who has retained his religious and intellectual essence, a man who is able to resist the culture and values of his captors, if only on the spiritual plane. He also clearly has a command of Arabic, which he uses subtly and with apparent ease. In one passage, Said seeks to ease the painful distinction between slave and master by invoking a famous verse from the Koran that reminds his readers that all men, even his captors, are ultimately slaves to God. Elsewhere, Said offers another telling verse, this time a declaration that Allah does not demand too much of Muslims living among nonbelievers. In all his writings, Omar opens with the traditional

Muslim invocation of Allah. Although baptized in 1821, he later openly declares his attachment to Islam. "I am Omar, I love to read the book, the Great Koran." Such sentiments prompted one Christian translator to note some years after Omar's death, in 1864, "It is a little startling to find that Uncle Moro still retained a little weakness for Mohammed."

Omar never did regain his freedom. But because of his learning he was granted special treatment, and he gained a certain celebrity through breathless newspaper and magazine articles about his life. Like other educated Muslim slaves who caught the public eye, Omar ibn Said was generally viewed not so much as an African but as a Moor, or simply a "Mohammedan." White newspaper readers were fascinated by tales of exotic African "princes" who had been sold into slavery, at times to be rescued by their exalted station and returned home, or at least treated as curiosities. Such fantastic stories skirted the inconvenient fact that there were Africans—black Africans—who clearly did not fit slaver owners' conception of them as uneducated beings suited only to manual labor and requiring the moral and physical protection of whites.

While Islam had equipped Omar ibn Said and many of his fellow Muslims with the spiritual means to resist some of the worst deprivations of their enslavement in the New World, it did not succeed in putting down permanent roots in antebellum America. There were simply too many obstacles to the establishment of the faith under slavery. The vast majority of slaves were males, and the common practice of selling off spouses and children made anything like family life, in which religious tradition could be passed along to the next generation, almost impossible. Conditions were harsh and few slaves lived a long or healthy life. Fertility was low and infant mortality was high.

For Muslims, the challenges were even more daunting. The odds that a Muslim male would find a Muslim wife were small. Islam requires time to pray, to study, and to learn Arabic. Copies of the Koran or other books in Arabic were not available. In a faith that effectively bars images and religious iconography, such as statues or church windows, the written word is crucial. Muslim slaves—often isolated from their co-religionists—were surrounded by the Christian culture of their masters. By 1830, conversion of the slave population to Christianity was almost complete. The final end of the trans-Atlantic slave trade three decades later cut off the supply of new African-born Muslims who could keep the faith alive. It is little wonder that only scant hints of this early Islamic tradition remain, such as the distribution of special sweets on certain days of the year in remote parts of Georgia or perhaps the practice of circumambulating the pulpit counter-clockwise in some black churches.

Ross, North Dakota, was little more than a lonesome railway siding when Hassen Juma arrived from his native Syria in 1899. Sam Omar joined him, and within a few years there were about two dozen families, all from two villages in a distant corner of the dying Ottoman Empire. The newcomers farmed the prairie like the other nearby settlers, primarily Scandinavians, but they also prayed five times a day and gathered for communal prayers on Fridays in one another's homes. Hassen Juma, Sam Omar, and his Syrian neighbors were all Muslims, part of the America's next significant encounter with the faith.

U.S. immigration and census records have never really kept pace with either the changing nature of immigration or with America's changing notions of ethnicity and race. Nor are they much use in determining the religious make-up of America at any given time. This is certainly true of a wave of immigration, running from around 1875 until 1912, from the part of the Ottoman Empire including modern Lebanon, Syria, Jordan, and Palestine. The vast majority of Arabs fleeing their troubled homeland for the New World were Christians. Yet among them were pockets of Sunni and Shi'ite Muslims, as well as members of the smaller Alawite and Druze sects. Whatever their religion, most of the new arrivals were eager to avoid the stigma often attached to Muslim "Turks" and simply called themselves Syrians. Official U.S. immigration records list them as people from "Turkey in Asia," or "Other Asian," making it impossible to quantify with any precision the number of Arab Muslims entering the country.

Members of this early wave often had little or no education. Some, such as Hassen Juma and his neighbors in North Dakota, took to home-steading. Others found work as unskilled laborers; some worked as peddlers before accumulating enough capital and enough local knowledge to become small shopkeepers or even successful large merchants. One colorful figure, known in America as Hi Jolly—a corruption of Hajji Ali, an honorific denoting completion of the pilgrimage to Mecca or a related honor—came from Syria as part of a short-lived U.S. Army program to deploy camels as military beasts of burden in the southwestern states, newly acquired from Mexico. He died in Quartzsite, Arizona, prospecting for gold. A commemorative plaque, put up by the state highway department in 1935, reads: "The last camp of Hi Jolly, born somewhere in Syria around 1828, died at Quartzsite December 16, 1902. Came to this country in February 10, 1856. Camel-driver – packer – scout – over thirty years a faithful aid to the U.S. government."

Many Muslim immigrants settled in the rural Midwest, where they formed some of the nation's first Islamic communities, although only some have survived until today. Detroit's fledgling automobile industry, with its demand for unskilled labor, gave rise to what became the large Arab and Muslim stronghold in Dearborn. Toledo and Chicago took their share. A cluster of Albanian Muslims settled in Maine to work at the mills, while Muslims from Lebanon moved to Quincy, Massachusetts, as early as 1875 to work in the shipyards.

In 1929, the believers of Ross, North Dakota, erected what is widely thought to be the first purpose-built mosque in the United States. Before that, America's Muslims had generally held communal prayers in private homes or rented halls and other public spaces. The North Dakota mosque was set into a shallow trench in the earth, more of a basement for a future structure than a finished work of religious architecture. It was used until the 1960s but never really completed, falling victim first to the Great Depression and then to the steady social and economic pressures felt by Muslims in the overwhelmingly Christian nation. This little community of prairie Muslims proved too small and too isolated to sustain itself; intermarriage and conversion to Christianity finally finished it off. By the time the North Dakota Historical Society got around to identifying America's first mosque as a site worthy of preservation, the building had been torn down. The old Muslim cemetery remains; its gate marked by a crescent and star.

Other communities fared somewhat better. An Islamic center was created in Michigan City, Indiana, in 1914 to serve local Lebanese and Syrian merchants. It later expanded as it attracted more and more Muslims and was renamed the Modern Age Arabian Islamic Society. Muslim peddlers and traders in Cedar Rapids, Iowa, held their Friday prayers in a rented hall until 1934, when they built what is now the oldest American mosque in continuous use. Forty-six years later, a minaret was added to the structure, a white-framed building with a green dome often referred to as the Mother Mosque of America.

Despite their successes, many of these early immigrant communities found themselves cut off from fellow Muslims and isolated in small cities

and towns in the American heartland. They often lacked the financial resources and social cohesion to build the mosques, Islamic centers, and
religious schools necessary to sustain and propagate the faith. The chaos
of World War I and the fall of the Ottoman Empire that had ruled over
much of the Arab world for centuries touched off a surge in immigration
from Muslim lands, but that was effectively halted by passage of the National Origins Act in 1921. With the supply of fresh Muslim arrivals cut
off, the long-term survival of many of these nascent immigrant communities was increasingly in doubt. Those that did survive, and even flourish,
did so not as part of a global or even American community of believers,
but as independent entities in which tribal or ethnic affiliation or place of
origin was more important than any universal Muslim identity. Islam had
again failed to take real hold on American soil.

Toward the Nation of Islam

The effective closing of America's borders to all but northern Europeans
after World War I coincided with a great internal migration of African
Americans heading for the industrialized northern states to work in the
region's factories, steel mills, auto plants, and slaughterhouses. Opportunities in the South, site of their former enslavement, and now home to the
so-called Jim Crow laws, were limited, and many sought the promise of
better jobs and a better life in the North. The loss of familiar settings and
culture, however hostile, were deeply wrenching. Cut off from their southern roots, including the ever-present black churches, many African Americans struggled to find a new identity and sense of belonging in the alien
surroundings. For some, this vacuum was filled by the rise of new social,
intellectual, and spiritual movements. The leader of one such movement,
which came to be known as the Black Islamizers, was Noble Drew Ali, who
like his followers had recently made his way north from the rural South.

Born Timothy Drew in North Carolina in 1886, he took the name
Noble Drew Ali and began to preach a message that African Americans
were a "Moorish" people, historically Muslim by culture and heritage.
Unlike Marcus Garvey before him, whose back-to-Africa movement had
decidedly Christian overtones, Ali invoked the language of Islam to foster
a sense of pride and focus blacks' attention on what they could achieve in
their families, communities, and American society at large. His Moorish
Science taught that African Americans had to free themselves of their slave

names and slave identities and revel in their great "Asiatic" culture. It is said Noble Drew Ali used to preach in a vacant lot in Newark, New Jersey, standing on a milk crate to attract attention: "Come all ye Asiatics, come learn the truth about yourself, that you are not Negroes, Black People, Colored Folks, Ethiopians and so called African-Americans." His followers were each provided with an official membership card. Men commonly adopted the fez and sported beards, giving them a distinct identity within the local black community. In one photograph, Ali, apparently at a conference of non-white activists in Havana, Cuba, a Moroccan flag draped over one shoulder and an American flag over the other.

Noble Drew Ali went further than simply preaching racial pride, personal betterment, and community development, all wrapped up in Islamic rhetoric. He praised Marcus Garvey for making blacks receptive to his own, divinely inspired message. He expropriated Islamic symbols for his own use, claimed he was a prophet of Allah (heresy for any true Muslim, for whom Muhammad was the final messenger of God), and produced a scripture that he called *The Holy Koran of the Moorish Science Temple of America*, an amalgam of scattered teachings from Islam, Christianity, Freemasonry, and other belief systems. He told his followers he had a mandate from the king of Morocco to instruct African Americans in the one true faith.

Ali founded the first Moorish Science Temple in Newark, in 1913, before moving his base of operations to Chicago, a hotbed of American spirituality. Moorish Science Temples were soon established in Detroit, Pittsburgh, and other major industrial cities, and the movement held its first national convention in 1928. Noble Drew Ali died one year later under mysterious circumstances, possibly the result of a police beating during an investigation into the fatal stabbing of one of his Moorish Science rivals. The movement continues to this day, but without its charismatic founder and leader it was unable to retain its early influence in the black community.

It is not clear where Noble Drew Ali first encountered Islam, although during his lifetime Islamic teachings and symbols had begun to gain some currency in urban America. This was partly the work of a white American convert, Muhammad Alexander Russell Webb, who became a Muslim in 1888 and actively propagated the faith in Chicago, New York, and other cities and towns across the country. A former newspaperman and later U.S. consul in Manila, Webb converted to Islam while in the East. He returned home to open a religious publishing house, establish an Islamic mission and mosque in New York City, and extol Islam's message of racial equality and social harmony. Webb, one of the first white Americans to convert, was something of a sensation at the World's Parliament of Religions, part of the 1893 World's Fair held in Chicago, where he presented what was for many their earliest introduction to the faith.

Chicago's civic and business leaders fought hard for the honor, and potential profit, of hosting the 1893 World's Columbian Exposition to commemorate the four-hundredth anniversary of Christopher Columbus's arrival in the New World. They raised five million dollars in seed money, and promised the U.S. Congress they would double that if chosen to host the fair. To their relief, the city was selected on the eighth ballot, and work began at once on the daunting enterprise, scheduled to open May 1. The Chicago World's Fair was a hit. More than fifty nations presented exhibits, and total admissions over its six-month run topped 27 million, equivalent to almost one quarter of the U.S. population. The fair also saw the introduction of such classic Americana as the Ferris Wheel, the carnival midway, Crackerjack, and Shredded Wheat cereal. Profits from the entertainment district—featuring the Orientalist fantasy, the "snake charmer's dance"—kept the entire thing solvent.

The exposition's leaders also organized a series of conferences to present the world's greatest thinkers on "the wonderful achievements of the new age in science, literature, education, government, jurisprudence, morals, charity, religion, and other departments of human activity, as the most effective means of increasing the fraternity, progress, prosperity, and peace of mankind." Of these, the largest was the World's Parliament of Religions, a revolutionary forerunner to today's interfaith movement. The gathering opened in September and ran for sixteen days. John Henry Barrows, a Unitarian who chaired the World's Fair religion committee, edited an illustrated volume to commemorate the Parliament. In a preface that captures the high-minded and optimistic goals of the time, he wrote:

> The faces of living men of all Faiths, the Temples wherein they worship, the record of their highest achievements, the reasons for their deepest convictions, and the story of their earliest meeting together in loving conference, are for the first time presented in one comprehensive work. The Western City which was deemed the home of the crudest materialism has placed a golden milestone in Man's pathway toward the spiritual Millennium.

Despite concerted opposition from the archbishop of Canterbury, the Muslim sultan of Turkey, and the Catholic leadership in Europe, the event drew a remarkable range of religious figures from ten of the world's most prominent faiths. The role of representing Islam fell not to an established religious authority from the Muslim world but to the convert Muhammad Alexander Russell Webb. His appearance at the World's Parliament, where he delivered papers entitled "The Influence of Islam upon Social Conditions" and "The Spirit of Islam," marked the high point in a vocation that never found much resonance with his fellow white, middle-class Americans during his lifetime.

Muhammad Alexander Russell Webb remains an important, if fleeting, figure in the history of Islam in America. In one of his writings, a text that in many ways still rings true today, Webb lamented the lowly state of Americans' knowledge of Islam and the Prophet Muhammad.

> Since my return to my native country I have been greatly surprised, not only at the general ignorance prevalent among so-called learned people regarding the life, character and teachings of the Arabian Prophet but also at the self-confident readiness and facility with which some of these same people express their opinions of Mohammed and the Islamic system.

Webb ascribed this ignorance to centuries of Christian hatred of Islam that dated back to the time of the crusades, as well as to the general inaccessibility of the Holy Book and other Islamic texts to those who could not read Arabic. But he also acknowledged a general distaste among his fellow Muslims for translating their sacred texts into an alien, Western tongue. "Therefore," he concluded, "the first purpose of this little book is to give to the English-speaking world a brief but accurate and reliable description of the character and purpose of Mohammed, and a general outline of the Islamic system."

After his conversion Webb traveled to India, where he became acquainted with the missionary movement the Ahmadiyya Association for the Propagation of Islam. The movement published the first English-language interpretation of the Koran aimed at the United States, and soon Ahmadiyya literature, including English commentaries on the Holy Book, was available in a number of American cities. Ahmadiyya missionaries, whose unorthodox views eventually caused them to be dismissed by most of the Muslim world as heretics, enjoyed some early success among the young African American communities now taking shape in the great northern cities, particularly in Chicago and New York. Webb's own books, lecture tours, and other religious work and his contacts with the Ahmadiyya made him something of a bridge between the Muslim world and his native land. He failed, however, to spread the faith among America's white middle class, and today his name is familiar only to scholars and some Muslim activists.

Noble Drew Ali was not the only disciple of Marcus Garvey to strike a chord among the new black communities of the North. Elijah Poole, a former autoworker and the son of an itinerant Baptist preacher, went on, as the Honorable Elijah Muhammad, to head the Lost-Found Nation of Islam in the Wilderness of North America, later shortened to the Nation of Islam. Like Noble Drew Ali, whose work later influenced him, Elijah Muhammad made his way north from the Deep South, first to Detroit, where he worked at a Chevrolet plant. He eventually settled in Chicago and in 1934 took over the Nation of Islam from its enigmatic founder, Wallace D. Fard.

Fard's origins remain something of a puzzle, as do the earliest days of his movement. A government file released under the Freedom of Information Act by the FBI, which for decades had targeted the Nation of Islam, says Fard was born in New Zealand in 1891 to a British father and a Polynesian mother. An anonymous FBI functionary could not resist a bit of bureau humor at Fard's expense, writing in a memo dated November 9, 1943, that the man known by his early followers as Allah and "the living God" had "proved to be very much of a human being because he has an arrest record in the Identification Division of the FBI." Fard disappeared from Detroit in 1934 and was never heard from again.

Nation of Islam teachings, like those of the Moorish Science Temple before it, borrowed heavily from Islamic symbolism, terminology, and history, while much of its actual religious practice resembled the traditions of black churches. Members sat on benches, sang, and listened to sermons on religious and topical themes of the day. At the same time, the Nation of Islam drew on a number of Islam's practical guidelines for virtuous living. Followers were enjoined to pray five times a day. Gambling, pork, alcohol, and drugs were all banned. There was a heavy emphasis on education and self-improvement, and Nation members were expected to give alms and support the movement with a portion of their income. These guidelines were all in keeping with established Muslim practice.

Elijah Muhammad, however, also established some decidedly un-Islamic notions, ideas that ultimately proved fatal for his vision of the Nation of Islam. He declared that white people were descendents of the Devil; W. D. Fard was a divine figure sent to usher in the Day of Judgment; he was a messenger of Allah; and blacks were the divinely chosen people, the long-lost tribe of Shabazz, discoverers of Mecca. Such teachings were anathema to orthodox Muslims. The *shahada*, the profession of faith that literally defines what it means to be a Muslim, proclaims, "There is no god but God, and Muhammad is His Prophet." For a human being to claim divine status, as Wallace D. Fard apparently did, was a sin of the highest order, and Elijah Muhammad's assertion that he was the last messenger of God also violated the most basic tenet of the faith. Moreover, the Koran and Islamic tradition stress that all races are equal in the eyes of God, a teaching that lay at the heart of Islam's phenomenal early success in creating a large, multiethnic community of believers that reached across much of the known world.

By invoking Islam and its culture, Moorish Science and later the Nation of Islam appealed effectively to their target audience, displaced urban blacks cut adrift from their southern roots. Here was an Eastern faith and culture that had evolved outside the now-dominant world of white Europeans. Its language was Arabic, a non-Western tongue written in a non-Western script. Arabs, Africans, and other people of color founded the grand Muslim empires. And it offered a simple and straightforward message of universal equality, as well as a social conservatism that matched many of the values of the traditional black churches. In other words, the Islam of Noble Drew Ali and Elijah Muhammad met the needs of the new converts, addressing their hopes and fears, explaining their present, and offering them a better future.

At its height, the Nation of Islam operated seventy-five temples and claimed one million members. It also maintained a strong presence in America's prison system, dating back at least to the 1940s, when Elijah Muhammad served time in Michigan for sedition, treason, and conspiracy after calling on Nation members not to fight in World War II, which he opposed on religious grounds. Zealous government investigators explored whether the movement had ties to America's wartime enemy Japan. Almost a decade earlier, Muhammad had been jailed for rejecting the public school system and demanding that his members' children have access to an education that reflected their religious and social values. These and similar experiences heightened the feeling among Nation of Islam followers that the white judicial system was out to get them. It also strengthened their standing within the urban black community.

Islam's historical lack of a centralized religious authority and its weak roots in America made it ripe for exploitation by Noble Drew Ali, Elijah Muhammad, and other Black Islamizers; there was simply no one in a position to challenge their reading of the faith, no matter how much they may have strayed. Only a challenge from within could shake the teachings of the Nation of Islam, and it came in time from two of the movement's luminaries: Malcolm X, once heir apparent to the leadership, and Wallace Deen Muhammad, the scholarly seventh son of Elijah Muhammad.

Malcolm X's world changed forever when he made his pilgrimage to Mecca, in 1964. Already, the charismatic public face of the Nation of Islam had privately begun to question some aspects of the group's teachings. Rumors of Elijah Muhammad's sexual improprieties only added to his disenchantment. The two men had clashed increasingly, most recently over the Vietnam War and the Kennedy assassination, which Malcolm suggested was a direct and natural byproduct of America's violent culture. Critics of the Nation took this to mean that Malcolm was sanctioning the assassination, and Elijah Muhammad banned his one-time protégé from speaking in public for ninety days. Soon Malcolm was removed as minister of New York City's prominent Temple Number Seven. At the same time, Wallace Deen Muhammad, whose mastery of Arabic allowed him to consult traditional Islamic sources, began to question central elements of his father's racist and separatist doctrines. Wallace was excommunicated in part for his increasing association with Malcolm, with whom he shared his doubts.

Malcolm set off on the hajj in a state of spiritual agitation and personal turmoil. After seventeen years in the Nation of Islam, he was completely unprepared for his first real encounter with the Muslim world. To his chagrin, Malcolm realized he knew virtually nothing of Islamic life, not even the basic prayers. In a brief letter home to his sister Ella, the former minister of New York's Temple Number Seven emphasized the need for proper knowledge of the faith: "Please give my best love and wishes for success to the believers there. All of them should learn the correct way that Muslims pray, and should learn the prayer in Arabic. It is a must, otherwise they will always be embarrassed at prayer time."

More profoundly, Malcolm's ritual walk seven times around the Kaaba opened his eyes to a new world, one defined by universal Muslim fellowship, not by race, skin color, or ethnicity. As Malcolm wrote in his famous "Letter from Mecca,"

> There were tens of thousands of pilgrims, from all over the world. They were of all colors, from blue-eyed blonds to black-skin Africans. But we were all participating in the same rituals, displaying a spirit of unity and brotherhood that my experiences in America had led me to believe never could exist between the white and non-white . . . You may be shocked by these words com-

ing from me. But on this pilgrimage, what I have seen, and experienced, has forced me to re-arrange much of my thought patterns previously held, and to toss aside some of my previous conclusions.

He signed the letter El-Hajj Malik El-Shabazz—a new name that reflected his new Islamic outlook.

Malcolm's trip to Mecca sealed his break with the Nation of Islam, an organization that had defined his life for almost two decades. He returned to America on May 21, 1964, with a new message of tolerance, one that repudiated the views of his mentor, Elijah Muhammad.

> In the past, yes, I have made sweeping indictments of all white people. I will never be guilty of that again—as I know now that some white people are truly sincere, that some truly are capable of being brotherly toward a Black man. The true Islam has shown me that a blanket indictment of all white people is as wrong as when whites make blanket indictments against Blacks.

Malcolm's relations with the Nation of Islam went from bad to worse, and at least one member of his own family publicly denounced his turn away from the Nation's teachings. Malcolm's house was firebombed on February 14, 1965, although no one was injured. Seven days later, the man now known as El-Hajj Malik El-Shabazz was gunned down while giving a speech in New York City's Audubon Ballroom. Three members of the Nation of Islam were convicted of the murder, although it later became clear that only one of them was involved; suspicions that the movement's leadership ordered the assassination have never been confirmed.

Malcolm was not the only influential voice from within the heart of the movement to question the Nation of Islam's doctrine. Wallace Deen Muhammad made his pilgrimage to Mecca in 1967; the experience helped prepare him to make the delicate but determined overhaul of the Nation that eventually turned the movement toward orthodox Islam. Wallace's chance to reform the Nation came in 1975, when he was declared the new supreme minister after the death of Elijah Muhammad. Perhaps mindful of the fate of his friend and spiritual companion Malcolm X, Wallace began his reforms with a series of cautious steps aimed at dismantling much of the Nation's ideology. He praised his father's leadership of the movement but also made it clear that Wallace D. Fard, the Nation's guiding light, was not divine. This in turn reduced the status of his "messenger," Elijah Muhammad, to that of an ordinary, fallible mortal. Wallace dismantled the Fruit of Islam, the Nation's security force, which posed the greatest threat of organized resistance to his new direction. He disentangled the Nation's varied business enterprises from its religious works.

These moves allowed for a more radical transformation of the Nation's core beliefs: whites were no longer seen as devils and were even invited to join the movement; black racial superiority and the call for a separatist state were no longer emphasized; and Wallace's former comrade, Malcolm X, was posthumously reinstated in the organization's good graces.

Although the Nation was now splintered into rival camps, Wallace took other steps toward what he hoped would be a final shift to Islamic orthodoxy. He changed the organization's name several times in quick succession—from the Nation of Islam to the World Community of Islam in the West to the American Muslim Mission—before proclaiming in 1985 that his followers no longer needed a separate, distinct identity. From this point forward, he said, they were simply members of the *ummah*, the world-wide community of believers. Along the way, Wallace Deen Muhammad changed his own identity as well, assuming the name Warith Deen Muhammad, literally "the inheritor of the religion of Muhammad." Meanwhile, Wallace's rival for leadership of the movement, Louis Farrakhan, sought to resurrect the legacy of Elijah Muhammad and keep the Nation of Islam alive. In recent years he too, has overseen a tentative movement toward some measure of authentic Islamic practice. However, many orthodox African American Muslims, as well as their co-religionists here and abroad, remain deeply skeptical of Farrakhan, despite his movement's good works combating drugs, AIDS, and innercity crime.

Farrakhan is not the only threat to Warith Deen Muhammad's power and influence. Many imams in his own organization, now broadly decentralized into more of a loose network, are affiliated to him in name only, and they often ignore his guidance to pursue their own visions. The result is a fragmented movement subject to attack on the one hand from Nation loyalists seeking to maintain its separatist mission, and on the other from orthodox African American Muslims demanding a faith grounded more precisely in traditional Islamic texts.

Warith Deen Muhammad has also come under attack for what some in the community see as his wholesale embrace of mainstream American society, in contrast to his father's aim to establish a separate state in the name of black rights and social and economic power. While Elijah Muhammad was once jailed for calling on his members to refuse to fight in World War II, W. D. Muhammad—himself a conscientious objector on religious grounds during Vietnam—decreed civic participation, such as voting and military service, acceptable. Although he is undoubtedly an elder statesman with no real equal on the scene today and up to fifty thousand followers, Warith Deen Muhammad exercises little direct control over the almost two hundred mosques tied to his network.

The phenomenon of black Islam, as expressed by the Moorish Science Temple and the Nation, had little to do with either Islam or Africa. It was, as the prominent scholar Sherman L. Jackson, an orthodox Muslim, points out, a product of America's racial politics and the failure of the black churches to meet the needs of southern black workers newly arrived in the industrial North. The early Islamizers, he writes, "were not so much *interpreting* Islam as they were *appropriating* it. . . . In fact, there is little evidence that Noble Drew Ali or Elijah Muhammad knew much at all about Islamic doctrine." Jackson also notes the complete absence among black Americans of any of the defining elements of African Islam—including its strong mystical tradition and its distinct school of Islamic law—and the lack of familiarity with its chief intellectual or religious figures.

It is often said that the experience of black Islam, whatever its theological deficiencies, helped pave the way for the eventual conversion of large numbers of African Americans to traditional Sunni Islam. Yet, as Malcolm X found to his dismay in 1964, black Islam was a self-contained, wholly American phenomenon with little or nothing to offer the broader Muslim world. There were few black Muslim religious scholars, no jurists, and no clerics capable of establishing their place in the worldwide *ummah*. Nor could black Islam really claim to have created an American Muslim identity, for its adherents were clearly blacks first and Muslims second—a reversal of the Islamic tradition that holds all believers as equals in the eyes of God and one another. As a result, African American Muslims were ill equipped for their first mass encounter with Islamic orthodoxy when renewed immigration from the Middle East and Asia began in 1965 with the collapse of America's long-standing immigration regime.

Muslim American Immigrants Today

Unlike the fleeting nature of American Islam under slavery, the tenuous hold of the prairie Muslims, or the theological ambiguity of Moorish Science Temple and the Nation, the new immigrant Islam had all the tools necessary to compete in the America's social, economic, and theological marketplace. Its followers were generally middle-class professionals—part of a "brain drain" that has plagued the developing world—seeking higher education and economic advancement in the West. The new arrivals had the financial resources and organizational skills they needed to pursue and perpetuate the faith. They opened mosques and Islamic centers, imported their prayer leaders and Koran readers from home, formed religious and Muslim professional associations, and generally set about re-creating much of the life they had left behind.

In theological terms, the new immigrants instantly became the religious authorities for the American *ummah*. Although African American Muslims challenged their knowledge, their beliefs and practice had a solid theological foundation. Unlike black Islam, which had sought first and foremost to defend its members from persecution by whites, the immigrant faith hinged on the traditional concerns of Muslims in the Middle East and Indian subcontinent. These concerns included the struggle against nonbelievers, the defense of religious and family purity, and the pursuit of distinctive, local cultural practices in the guise of universal Muslim religious observance. Even orthodox African American Muslims soon saw their concerns and influence pushed to the background by the commanding presence of the newcomers.

The 1967 Six-Day War in the Middle East; lingering effects of the partition of India, including strife in Pakistan and the creation of Bangladesh; the Iranian revolution; the Lebanese civil war; and the persecution of Arabs and Asians in East Africa set in motion huge swathes of humanity seeking improved opportunities and a respite from violence. Many saw the changes in U.S. immigration laws as the opportunity of a lifetime. The biggest groups of new Muslim arrivals were Arabs, Iranians, and immigrants from the Indian subcontinent, the last being the largest and fastest growing segment of all. The changing face of U.S. immigration was remarkable. Government figures show that Europeans made up 86 percent of all immigrants in the years 1901 to 1920. Asia provided just 4 percent of all immigrants during the same period, and Latin America 3 percent. However, from 1980 to 1993, Asia accounted for 39 percent of legal immigration. European immigration declined to just 13 percent. Many of these immigrants from Asia and the Middle East were Muslims.

Any portrait of Muslim immigration in America today must remain an incomplete mosaic. The Census Bureau is prohibited by law from asking about religious affiliation in its regular surveys of the American populace, forcing researchers to rely on a variety of techniques to approximate the numbers of adherents to different faiths. Identity politics and the competitive bid for political and social influence have also colored the effort.

However, most demographers accept a total of around six million Muslims, a figure that comes in well above that offered by several studies backed by Jewish organizations but below those of some Muslim advocacy groups.

A series of studies undertaken by Georgetown University sidestepped the question of the total Muslim population and focused instead on the specific makeup and social, political, and religious attitudes of the Muslim American community. Religion represents a significant element in the daily lives of America's Muslims. Georgetown researchers found that half of all Muslim Americans make the five daily prayers regularly, while another fifth make some of the five prayers each day, with women more likely than men to make all the prayers. Of those surveyed, 82 percent said both the role of Islam and spirituality in general were "very important" to their lives, with another 12 percent saying they were "somewhat important."

The latest survey, conducted in 2004, also found that American Muslims had reacted to September 11 and its aftermath by asserting their own unique social and political identity. Almost 70 percent told the researchers that being a Muslim was an important factor in their voting decisions, and 86 percent said it was important for Muslims to participate in politics. Beforehand, the majority of Muslims had generally preferred to maintain a low profile, seeking to blend into the diverse demographic landscape of contemporary American life. This shift was a direct response to sharp increases in discrimination, harassment by law enforcement, and racist rhetoric against Muslims in America sparked by the so-called War on Terrorism.

Among the most important factors in crystallizing the rise in Muslim American pride and collective identity was the passage, and selective enforcement, of the 2001 USA Patriot Act—an acronym for the Orwellian Uniting and Strengthening America by Providing Appropriate Tools Required to Intercept and Obstruct Terrorism—rushed to Congress by the Bush administration in the weeks after September 11. It was approved with little debate by lawmakers, many of whom later acknowledged they had not even bothered to read a bill that greatly expanded the powers of law enforcement to intrude on the daily lives of American citizens and legal residents. Among its most alarming provisions were the broad expansion of the definition of "domestic terrorism" to include some college protest groups; increased access by law enforcement to medical, library, financial, and sales records without a demonstration of probable cause; and the so-called sneak-and-peak authority to search someone's home without a warrant or even timely notification to the owner or resident.

Almost immediately, Muslims in America found themselves targets of law enforcement operations in the name of homeland security. Thousands of Arab and Muslim men were questioned and at least twelve hundred people—U.S. officials stopped reporting the figure after reaching this number due to what it called statistical confusion—were rounded up and detained under the new provisions of the USA Patriot Act, ostensibly for suspected visa violations. Reports by Human Rights Watch found that the men were held in what amounted to "preventive detention," something generally barred by U.S. criminal law. What's more, the detainees were held without charge, denied bond, and barred from contacting their families or legal representatives. The inspector general for the Department of Justice later noted many of the detainees were subjected to physical and verbal abuse while in custody. The roundup produced virtually no charges of involvement in terrorism, and most of the suspects were either deported or eventually released.

Suspected "illegals" were not the only ones to feel the sting of the Patriot Act. Attorney General John Ashcroft, a born-again Christian who led prayers in his government office and ordered that bare-breasted statues in the Department of Justice building be covered with curtains, directed the FBI to interview five thousand legal immigrants from Muslim countries, even though the authorities acknowledged that they had no evidence that any of those sought for questioning had any connection to terrorist activity or any knowledge that would aid their investigations. Federal agents fanned out to mosques, schools, Islamic centers, and private homes—often guided by nothing more than an anonymous tip or general racial stereotype. Ashcroft also ordered the special registration and fingerprinting of young males from twenty-five countries—with the exception of North Korea, they were all Muslim or Arab states.

In the months after September 11, Ashcroft or other senior U.S. officials regularly held press conferences to announce with great fanfare the latest terrorism related arrests. Virtually all these high-profile cases have since ended in quiet dismissal or reduction to simple immigration violations. A few select cases have found federal prosecutors stymied by an increasingly skeptical judicial system, wary that the executive branch has over-stepped its authority in the War on Terrorism. Meanwhile, Muslim Americans have no doubts that they are now the targets of vicious racial and ethnic profiling at the hands of their adopted homeland.

The atmosphere of official fear and hostility toward Islam created fertile ground for vigilante attacks and general hate crimes against Muslims and Islamic institutions. The FBI's Hate Crimes Unit recorded an astonishing rise in attacks on Muslims in the immediate aftermath of September 11, from 28 in 2000 to 481 in 2001. In the nine months after September 11, the Council on American-Islamic Relations noted more than 1,715 incidents of hate crimes, discrimination, and racial profiling, including 303 reports of actual violence against members of the Muslim community. One of the first deadly cases of anti-Muslim violence involved a man proclaiming to be an American patriot shooting a dark-skinned businessman wearing a turban in Mesa, Arizona. The victim was Balbir Singh Sodhi, whose traditional Sikh headdress, authorities say, led the shooter to mistake him for a Muslim. Other anti-Muslim murders were also reported in Los Angeles and Dallas.

At times, the violence against Muslims has been rhetorical, often led by allies of President George W. Bush. Reverend Jerry Falwell, whose evangelical zeal, money, and influence have greatly benefited the Republican establishment over the years, famously declared the Prophet Muhammad "a terrorist" on the CBS program *60 Minutes*, a little more than one year after September 11. Reverend Franklin Graham, son of the conservative icon Billy Graham, decreed Islam "wicked, violent, and not of the same God." And Lieutenant General William Boykin, who served George W. Bush as undersecretary of defense, only confirmed Muslims' fears when he defined the War on Terrorism as a war against Islam. Addressing Christian evangelicals, the uniformed general recalled taking solace in his faith during a firefight with a Muslim Somali warlord in 1993. "I knew that my God was bigger than his. I knew that my God was a real God and his was an idol." Boykin, the man charged by the administration with tracking down Osama bin Laden, told another audience, "We in the army of God, in the house of God, kingdom of God, have been raised for such a time as this." President Bush has never publicly disavowed any of these comments, and he himself famously declared a "crusade" against terrorism five days after September 11. After howls of protest from the Muslim world, all too aware of the lingering effects of the Christian crusades against Islam, the White House "clarified" his remarks.

Perhaps surprisingly, given the events of the last five years, a majority of those surveyed by Georgetown University say it is a good time to be a Muslim in America, despite their general unease with the country's foreign policy, the growing domestic pressure on them and their fellow believers, and their dismay at how their faith is treated by the media, in

Hollywood, and by mainstream society in general. Of course, any opinion survey offers little more than a simple snapshot, frozen in time.

My own travels through Muslim America have revealed a dynamic, active community determined to define itself in its own terms. This is particularly the case with the post-1965 generation, the children of the sweeping Muslim immigration that began four decades ago. They are seeking to understand the faith in both intellectual and emotional terms in order to apply its tenets to their daily lives. And they have largely broken free of the Old World practice of distinguishing one Muslim from another by race, skin color, place of origin, or even sectarian affiliation. While "slave Islam" was too brittle, the "prairie Muslims" too isolated, and black Islam too focused on race, the Muslims of contemporary America have finally managed to carve out their own identity, one that will shape the national landscape in new and challenging ways for the foreseeable future.

FOUR

Taking It to the Streets

ᴣᴕ

Rami Nashashibi wears his trademark baggy blue jeans, blue skullcap, and loose T-shirt to make the call heard throughout "the Hood." He clutches a small black microphone, raising and lowering his melodious voice to the rhythm of rap music blaring from a stereo system. From a makeshift stage, a two-foot-high platform Rami planted in the middle of a vacant parking lot, he scans the neighborhood inch by inch as far as his dark eyes can see. The midmorning scene gives him little hope. He wonders if the young black man, a pack of cigarettes in hand, strolling out of a corner grocery store across the street will answer his call and take a seat on one of the folding chairs set up in front of the platform. The two-lane street is otherwise deserted. The summer Chicago sun and high humidity alone are enough to keep people away. A few teenaged African American boys are gathering in front of the stage. Rami glances instead at some Muslim brothers unloading musical equipment from a truck and a sister nervously pacing the pavement, her cell phone glued to her ear. Bringing the microphone up to the tip of his round chin, he shouts as if speaking to a large crowd, "Listen up, brothers. There's going to be a big star here in under an hour."

Like the muezzin calling the faithful to prayer, Rami hopes to awaken the South Chicago neighborhood to his distinct vision of Islam. Days before this muggy Saturday, Rami hung posters on telephone poles and on bulletin boards in neighborhood stores announcing the arrival of Napoleon, a star from California who raps about his Muslim identity. Part social activist, part spiritual guide, and sometimes just an ordinary brother, Rami speaks the slang of the street, a bit removed from his other life across town as a Ph.D. student in sociology at the University of Chicago. There, he spends much of his time analyzing the role of Islam in the inner city.

With his lanky build and even his walk, the way he plants one of his big Timberland boots in front of the other, giving his stride a bit of bounce, Rami has become a symbol of hope in the neighborhood. His double life allows thirty-two-year-old Rami to traverse two very different worlds, and it has helped make him a familiar leader in Islamic circles across the country. Rami has a unique American Dream: the creation of a network of Muslim artists, scholars, and activists who will create a multiethnic and unified Muslim community. Fifteen hundred years ago, the Prophet Muhammad taught that Islam must form a collective community of believers, or *ummah*, composed of Muslims from many ethnicities. But this *ummah*, the dream of Muslims across a wide spectrum, has even now yet to be realized.

Rami thinks that Napoleon, a musician from the West Coast with the popular band Tupac's Legendary Outlawz, can inspire the youth. A Muslim recently returned to his faith, Napoleon flew in from Los Angeles to devote some time to Chicago's ghetto. He hopes to change the fortunes of the youth the way he changed his own, from drug addict and petty criminal to pious Muslim, from gangster rapper to socially conscious Islamic hip-hop artist and spiritual mentor.

It is rare for any kind of celebrity to venture to South Chicago, where last night's shooting is the subject of the daily chatter. Many of the Muslims born here never return once they rise to the middle class and have fled with their families to new homes in the suburbs southwest of Chicago. It isn't just the poverty or the vibrations of a dying society that keep them away. They simply don't like the ethnic mix. Once they retreat to the suburbs, the Pakistanis go to the Pakistani mosque, the Arabs to another mosque, and the Bosnians to yet another. The order created by these separate ethnic universes makes everyone feel comfortable.

History and fate determined South Chicago's ethnic landscape. It wasn't anyone's choice. After World War II, Arab immigrants trickled into the neighborhood, which was fast becoming white, working class, and at odds with the blacks who were migrating across Chicago's South Side. But, by the 1970s, the Palestinians outnumbered all others. The community was by then famous as the site of the race riots of the late 1960s and early 1970s. Marquette Park, the only green visible in the neighborhood, had been the scene of a violent attack on Martin Luther King Jr. in 1966. With the rising racial tension, the few whites still living in the area fled to the Chicago suburbs and the economy deteriorated. Now, neglect is visible all around: boarded-up windows, gaping potholes, and garbage-strewn alleyways.

Rami is honored that Napoleon has agreed to spend a few hours here. He is just the kind of role model who could inspire the youth with the vitality of Islam. At one point, Napoleon was just like them: a lost soul in search of something—drugs, crime, religion—to ease the pain of ghetto life. Standing alone in the parking lot dotted with potholes, Rami tries to remain optimistic. Over the last decade, he has seen locals turn to Islam under his guidance as leader of the Inner-City Muslim Action Network (IMAN).

Rami moved to America shortly after the end of the Persian Gulf War. He became an activist at DePaul University, the Catholic college in Chicago where he was an undergraduate. He joined the local chapter of the Palestinian Solidarity Committee, but he soon concluded he could have little influence trying to solve a conflict a world away. Instead, he devoted his time and his heart to the fight for civil rights for African Americans and Latinos. He led demonstrations on the campus and helped raise money for ghetto youth.

At the time, Rami was not a practicing Muslim. Just like the nonobservant African American and Latino youth he would later introduce to Islam, Rami was raised in a family where religion had no role. His father was a Palestinian from Jerusalem who attended graduate school in California and later became a Jordanian diplomat. Like many Muslims of his generation who had lived for a time in the United States, he resented American policies in the Middle East. Islam was nowhere in his psyche. Rami's mother identified mostly with American values and culture, right down to her love for peanut-butter-and-jelly sandwiches. His parents divorced when Rami was ten, and later as a high school student he roamed the world from Saudi Arabia to Italy. He shunned institutionalized religion, believing it was for weak souls, those seeking conformity in order to feel a little less lost in the alienation of the modern world.

From his own experience, Rami understood the youth he and IMAN were trying to educate about Islam, youngsters who either had never thought about religion or viewed it exclusively from an ethnic and cultural perspective. To reach them, he drew upon resources and ideas from his other life, the one rooted in the ivory tower. Over a decade, Rami worked to build a community in South Chicago with its own mosque, health clinic, after-school tutoring program, and even recreational events. Initially, other mosques and Islamic organizations in Chicago supported Rami's efforts with only meager donations. For all their talk about Muslim brotherhood, they left Rami out in the cold because his work was in the ghetto, not middle-class America. Over the years, Rami came to depend on the guidance of a few African American professors and the federal funding he sometimes received. But most of the time, he relied upon the good will of Muslim friends who were able to donate to his cause. But as time went on, and IMAN's credibility grew, some mosques and other wealthy Muslims began to contribute to his efforts.

Day by day, Rami set out to draw African Americans, Southeast Asians, and Latinos together with their Arab neighbors toward his particular vision of Islam. Rami's work tapped into the new urgency that arose after the attacks on September 11, 2001. When a growing number of Muslims became targets of everyone from the neighbor who confused the peaceful Muslim with the militant to the FBI and local police, they searched for sympathy among African Americans. With their shared experience of discrimination in America, some Muslims thought they could find common cause with African American Muslims. Relations between the two groups had been strained for decades, if not a century. African American Muslims reacted to the sudden interest in them among Muslims from the Islamic world with great suspicion. There was too much history dividing them, too many wounds. In its glory years, the Nation of Islam had had a magical appeal. By presenting Islam to African Americans, the Nation provided an alternative way of being black in America. African Americans in the Nation were expected to adopt Muslim names and ban pork from their diets. But, perhaps more significantly, the Nation eased the pains of ghetto life. In densely populated urban areas, such as Brooklyn and Chicago, the Nation offered social services and counseling about drug use, teenage pregnancy, and crime. Most of this activism had faded by the 1990s.

With the arrival of great numbers of Muslim immigrants from the Islamic world, beginning in 1965, the notion of Islam in America began to change for African Americans. African Americans were no longer the owners of American Islam; instead, the religion they practiced was overtaken by Islam defined in Saudi Arabia, Egypt, Pakistan, and Palestine. Suddenly, as Sherman A. Jackson noted in his latest book, *Islam and the Blackamerican*, black Muslims discovered they had moved from "the back of the bus to the back of the camel."

Traditional Sunni Muslims easily displaced African American Muslims because they never had a solid base in Islamic doctrine from the beginning. They devoted little or no attention to how Muslim communities outside the United States interpreted the most basic Islamic texts. The new wave of immigrants to the United States soon established their ideas of "true" Islam. Suddenly, there were authorities on Sunni practice challenging the prism through which African American Muslims viewed the faith. The Islam created in the United States could now be compared to a more authentic practice, putting African American Muslims at a disadvantage. When it was once easy for African American Muslims to ignore aspects of their culture that violated Islamic principles, by the 1970s these behaviors were publicly deemed un-Islamic. By the time Rami began working to create a multicultural Islamic community in Chicago, African American Islam had become further diluted through its own decline. Louis Farrakhan's Nation of Islam had lost its thunder, leaving as few as 200,000 to 500,000 members in the movement. Warith Deen Muhammad's American Society of Muslims, the movement he created after he split from the Nation of Islam, was also losing its luster.

September 11 solidified America's image of the modern Muslim—that of an Arab from the Middle East. This effectively obliterated any lingering awareness of African American Muslims. Deprived of their own group identity and lacking an effective, well-structured organization, African American Muslims were forced to search for an Islamic alternative, in order to avoid being overwhelmed by the immigrant wave. Yet, the failure of their movement cannot simply be blamed on the arrival of newcomers from the Middle East and South Asia. Sherman Jackson writes,

> As America strides toward its ever-elusive dream of eradicating the negative significance of race, or as national concerns such as the catastrophe of September 11, 2001, force race and related matters to the margins of the national discourse, Blackamerican Sunnis are likely to find themselves increasingly irrelevant to American public life.

Louis Farrakhan failed to spell out how African American Muslims should practice the faith in America. And although Wallace Deen Muhammad was among the first ever to articulate the need for a Muslim American identity, he was ahead of his time. It would take the second generation, the children of Wallace Deen's original followers, to try to find a way to be both black and a bona fide Sunni Muslim.

Rami is the perfect person to build a multicultural Muslim society. As a civil rights activist, while he was a university student, he worked for social justice for African Americans. As a Palestinian, he can relate to the Arabs in the neighborhood. He speaks their language; he shares their political views about the need for liberation for Palestinians living under Israeli oppression.

Rami teaches by example. On that day in June 2004, he saw in Napoleon an ideal success story to put on display for the community; here was a man who had returned to the faith, after years of straying, to find peace in his music and in the Koran. Napoleon believes that the courage he found to replace the marijuana he once carried around in his pocket with a miniature Koran is proof of God's existence. But once he made the transition, Napoleon didn't retreat into the self-satisfied superiority of a religious fanatic. Instead, he fused his personal history with his newfound virtues, reflected in the title of an album he made when he returned to Islam, *Scriptures from a Thug's Point of View*. Rami thought Napoleon's blend of gangster rap and Muslim cool would appeal directly to the neighborhood kids.

Napoleon's music is a strong part of his attraction. His CDs belong to the new genre of hip-hop, tunes that sound like African American rap music with lyrics that either allude to Islam or speak directly about being Muslim. Islamic hip-hop has been on the rise only since the late 1990s, as more African Americans have converted. The music is becoming so popular that bands such as Native Deen, a group of twenty-something African Americans from Maryland, are even debuting on commercial radio stations in New York City, Chicago, and Los Angeles.

As Napoleon's arrival draws near, Rami's call grows more insistent. He gestures with upturned palms, motioning to the crowd in the parking lot that has now grown to about a dozen young boys to come closer to the stage. His face shines with sweat. He smiles a half smile, showing the large white teeth that soften his expression. His voice grows louder to compete with the sounds from the street, now awakened from the Saturday morning torpor.

"We are encouraging everybody who is walking by to participate. It is a rare opportunity to get an autograph from Napoleon. He'll be here in a few minutes. It's a rare opportunity on the South Side of Chicago to meet a very well and established brother who is about to drop another CD. When Napoleon comes, the few of us here, I want to show him we have a lot of love from South Chicago. So give him a lot of love when he comes."

While those in the crowd take their seats, a few warm-up acts appear on the makeshift stage. Brother Big Move, an African American rapper in his twenties, reminisces about his childhood when the neighborhood was a safer place. "Back in the day, the kids wrestled on mattresses and chased the ice-cream truck for a fifty-cent cone." Rami interrupts the music to give the crowd a progress report: Napoleon has called in. He is on his way, "inshallah," God willing. His words are far from reassuring. Even those who don't speak Arabic know what *inshallah* means: Napoleon could appear in the next ten minutes or the next ten hours.

Still, Rami starts preparing the African American teenagers, their bodies hidden beneath big cotton shorts, baseball caps, and oversized T-shirts. When Napoleon arrives, each boy and teenager is to sign a summer pledge, a promise to stay away from violence, "stupid" violence, Rami tells them, that leads to prison, to getting shot, to death. Once they get an autograph from Napoleon, they must sign the peace pledge. There is an unstated pledge, too; once they shun violence, they should turn to God.

Napoleon finally arrives, more than an hour later, and takes a seat on a beige metal folding chair positioned behind a small table. With his slight stature—the inspiration for the nickname Napoleon, given by his fellow musicians—he appears formidable only because some of the boys standing in line in front of the table are quite young. But for the most part, he looks like everyone else in the crowd with his close-cropped hair, jeans, and billowing T-shirt.

One by one the kids approach, get his autograph, and happily sign the pledge. But Napoleon knows his signature alone can't possibly convince the kids to turn away from the crime they have been exposed to their entire lives. Some of their fathers are in prison, their mothers on crack. To expect them to take the next step and open their hearts to Islam seems unrealistic. They have to be inspired, and there is no better way to do that than to tell them about his life.

"This is my third time here, man. Came about a year ago and met Brother Rami. The Brother Rami told me he did a lot for the community and wanted to get me back here. I was born in New Jersey, man, by Muslim parents and at the age of three my father and mother were murdered in front of me. I got shot in the foot. My grandparents adopted me. My grandparents are Christian people, beautiful people. It doesn't matter what religion you are. I got caught up with selling drugs. At the age of sixteen, I met a guy named Khadafy. He took me, he embraced me in his home in Atlanta. The brother had a good heart. He took me out of the Hood. But we were living the fast life. He got murdered in Las Vegas. He was out there raising me and then I was on my own again. I was searching. I was in a studio and I met a Muslim brother. I told him I was a Muslim, but I had a drink in one hand and a weed in another. But the brother never judged me and eventually I went to the mosque. I never felt that kind of peace in my life. There is nothing like putting your head on the ground and praying to God.

"*Have Mercy* is coming out on a major label, inshallah. It's positive. There are no cuss words. Sometimes I might say 'nigger,' but sometimes you act like niggers. So that's it, man. That's my life."

There is silence. The beat of the neighborhood, the car horns and the pop music pulsating out of car windows, appears to come to a stop. The dozen or so kids expected Napoleon to perform his music. But instead they only got to hear him rap about his life and his CDs. They wiggle in the folding chairs, waiting for something to happen. They look at one another and then at Rami.

Rami steps up to the microphone. "Let's give it up for Napoleon," coaxing a round of applause from the audience.

"If you haven't gotten your autograph from Napoleon, we want your signature on the pledge for peace, and turn it into something positive, like spirituality. Before we listen to more of the CD, does anyone have a question for Napoleon?"

"Yeah," calls out a small voice from the back rows of folding chairs. "Can we break dance with him?"

Rami turns on Napoleon's CD just loud enough to be heard. At that moment, blaring music would be out of step with the dramatic end to Napoleon's monologue.

It is easy to see that any inch of progress Rami Nashashibi has achieved over the last decade in bringing Islam to the South Side is an extraordinary accomplishment. Many of the kids in the district have no interest in attending school or learning about anything—much less about Islam. Still,

Rami has succeeded in helping an unknown number of kids in South Chicago become educated about Islam. He shows them how Islam—often a religion stifled under the weight of Friday sermons delivered by the aging imams in the mosques—can do good deeds, whether it is through an afternoon concert or by providing health care for the needy.

Rami, the college-educated visionary, might seem an odd match with Napoleon, the streetwise Muslim from the ghetto. Ten years before they appeared together on that stage in South Chicago, Napoleon the drug addict and Rami the budding intellectual and student activist had little in common. Rami's journey to Islam was an intellectual one, while Napoleon found his inspiration in the street.

When a record producer named Mikal Kamil—the "Muslim brother" mentioned in his talk that afternoon in South Chicago—first laid eyes on Napoleon, the young man had a Colt 45 malt liquor in one hand and a marijuana joint in the other. Napoleon told him his real name, Mutah Wasin Shabazz Beale, given to him by his Muslim parents, and Kamil vowed to bring Napoleon back into the faith. Turning Napoleon, who openly admitted he was evil, into a devout Muslim seemed like a huge undertaking. But, in 2001, when Napoleon made his first pilgrimage to Saudi Arabia, one of the five obligations devout Muslims must perform at least once in their lives, everything changed. He soon gave up drugs and alcohol and began praying five times a day, often in a Los Angeles mosque. He also ditched the obscenities in his rap lyrics.

Napoleon's appearance with Rami that day on Kedzie Street reflected the two men's hopes, and those of many Muslims, for the future of Islam in the United States. The goal is to make Islam a religion in which African Americans, Latinos, and Arabs can share the same stage and the same mosque. There would be no difference between the Muslim from the ghetto and the one from the Ivy League. An inclusive approach is the key to spreading the faith, growing the number of Muslims in America, and making Islam a formidable force in society.

Rami had every reason to hope that the young break-dancers, seemingly unimpressed by his speech and Napoleon's inspirational stories of being born-again, would one day be praying in a mosque.

Napoleon left South Chicago that day a satisfied man. A few young boys followed him to the van that would take him to the airport. They watched some burly men load a big black case filled with speakers and

CDs into the trunk. Before Napoleon climbed into the passenger's seat, the boys reached out to him, hoping to clutch his hand so he might stay a bit longer. Napoleon gave them his signature handshake and promised to return. "As soon as the Brother Rami invites me, I'll be on the next plane."

Faith and Action:
The Inner-City Muslim Action Network

Within Muslim circles, Rami is open, charismatic, and even self-effacing. But at times when he deals with the outside world, particularly journalists, he becomes suspicious, overly sensitive, and guarded. His instincts tell him that anything written about him or the Inner-City Muslim Action Network is likely to be incorrect, oversimplified, and devoid of cultural and religious sensitivity. He also worries, almost to the point of obsession, about the public perception of IMAN. Like many other Muslims, Rami has had conflicts with journalists and other types of writers. But unlike other Muslims, who are often satisfied when an outsider comes to them with good references from within the Islamic community, Rami makes his own judgments about people wanting to know even the smallest detail of his life. He gets to know them before deciding whether to work with them.

This is what he told me when I first approached him in 2003. I explained that I was writing a book and thought IMAN provided an important illustration of the new direction young Muslims were taking in America. It wasn't easy to persuade him. Rami is the real thing, an authentic Muslim voice, which makes his views and his work so important. While he has reached out to exchange ideas with other faiths, he dislikes public recognition or publicity, even at times to his own detriment.

Several months passed, and I wasn't making any headway in persuading him to allow me to spend time with him and members of IMAN. Finally, one evening out of frustration I wrote him a letter as if I were applying for a job. In my most persuasive tone, I argued that he should agree to let me profile his organization. He finally consented. "Okay. But I need to get the approval of the staff. I will take your letter to the next staff meeting."

The outcome was mostly in my favor. Rami would talk and his acquaintances and friends would talk.

Even before he began transforming this patch of South Chicago, Rami Nashashibi transformed himself, as many other Muslims one day would, by returning to the faith. When Rami was a student at DePaul University in the early 1990s, he felt more comfortable with Latinos and Black Panthers than with Muslims. Then, Rami realized that some of the Black Panthers were drawn to Islam. One friend, Jaleel Abdul-Adil, an African American Ph.D. candidate, had already converted to Islam. Jaleel demonstrated the fusion of two worlds—black nationalism and Islam—that Rami had never fully encountered but had always assumed were mutually exclusive.

Even though African Americans had been converting to Islam in significant numbers since the 1970s, for Rami, this was an awakening. He soon began to view Islam in a different light. For years, he had believed his faith was stagnant; he thought it amounted to imams preaching verses of the Koran with no relevance to modern life. Like some Muslims living in Western society, Rami had chosen to minimize the role of faith in his life. But for Muslims the persistent pull of Islam is never far away. Even a nonbeliever remains in touch with the faith through occasional mosque attendance for social events and contact with other Muslims. Through his friendship with Jaleel, Rami came to see Islam as a religion that could turn the fight for equal rights and social justice into action. Rami realized he should embrace Islam, instead of trying to ignore his Muslim identity.

"When I met Jaleel and others who had made a spiritual transformation to Islam, they had adopted a spiritual discipline. When they asked me what I was, I was forced to say I was a Muslim. They were challenging me and it forced me to think. I asked myself, 'Will I answer that I am a Muslim? Am I going to disavow my faith?' After that, I started reading the Koran to refute Islam.

"I debated Jaleel for years. I remember I was much more attracted to black nationalism than Islam, but when I met black nationalists and they said, No, 'Islam has a much more emancipatory framework,' I started to reconsider. I confronted Jaleel about this and he was the first person I ever really had a serious conversation with about Islam.

"It wasn't an epiphany. It was a long process."

For Rami, becoming a devout Muslim meant significantly altering his life. At the time, he lived near Hyde Park, a middle-class area of trendy bars and restaurants and fifty-year-old brownstones. Like many typical young men, he thrived on the crude lyrics of rap music that was popular among his African American friends. But once he decided to get back in touch with his religion, he interrupted his daily routine for prayer five times a day, and drifted away from his non-Muslim friends.

The egalitarian idea of unifying Muslims of different races and ethnic and socioeconomic backgrounds first came to Rami when he was a student at DePaul and beginning to learn about the Prophet Muhammad's vision. He helped establish DePaul's Muslim Students' Association, a social and political organization that then joined forces with the Concerned Black Students. Together they staged a sit-in on campus in April 1995 and shut down the student newspaper, *The DePaulia*, over coverage they believed was racist. The student protest, reported on Chicago television stations and in city newspapers, was a dress rehearsal for Rami. He discovered the benefits of Muslims working with African Americans to fight injustice.

After he had become more involved in the Muslim Students' Association—named UMMA, like *ummah*, the Arabic word for the Muslim community of believers—Rami received a call from the Arab American Community Center on Kedzie Street in South Chicago. He was aware of the decades-long Arab presence in the neighborhood; his mother grew up there, and some of his Arab friends at DePaul lived in South Chicago. An organizer asked him if he wanted to help the young, poor kids in the area.

Rami agreed at once, but he wouldn't do it alone. He soon included other Muslim activists from UMMA. So began Rami's journey. He and the other DePaul students started tutoring kids on the South Side during the summer. They worked out of the Arab American Community Center, home to a staunchly secular group of Palestinian activists. The students from DePaul and the Arab community organizers had one profound disagreement; although their ethnic backgrounds were similar, if not identical, the DePaul students wanted their social work to expose the good deeds possible within Islam and draw non-Muslims and Muslims who were not practicing to the faith.

Rami recognized that the presence of an Islamic organization in South Chicago would be a departure from recent history. Like other Arab community groups, the Arab American Community Center, founded in the 1960s, had downplayed Islam and emphasized its Palestinian identity. Politics had displaced religion. The center raised money for Palestinians in the West Bank and Gaza City. Historically, Muslim identity in South Chicago was overshadowed by ethnic affiliations. Muslims were not Muslims so much as they were Palestinians, Syrians, Pakistanis, or Egyptians. Rami did not realize it at the time, but, in introducing Islam to the non-Muslim youth in the community and teaching the young Muslims living there to tie their faith more closely to the concerns of the modern world, he was helping to break the enduring link between culture and tradition.

For Rami, Palestinian activism was a prime example of how Islam became confused with politics and culture. Unlike the secularists at the Arab

American Community Center, Rami did not believe the Palestinian struggle for a homeland should be the central rallying cry for American Muslims. But this was a minority view in South Chicago, home to 10 to 15 percent of all Palestinian immigrants who have come to the United States since 1965. "The mosques and centers were so consumed in the political reality of Palestine that it was hard for the kids to see anything coming out of there as a pure expression of this new identity around a faith as opposed to the extension of a political movement. When it comes down to it, even the storeowner selling liquor that is forbidden under the faith would rather have his son learning about Islam than the politics of Palestine."

After less than a year of working in the community, Rami and a few friends decided to launch a new organization. With a handful of fellow students who had founded DePaul University's Muslim Students' Association, Rami opened a modest ground-floor office on Sixty-third Street. He called the new organization IMAN, the word for "faith" in Arabic and an acronym for the Inner-City Muslim Action Network. Instead of limiting prayers to Fridays in the half-dozen storefront mosques, where Arab imams refused to utter one word of English, IMAN would be different. The organization would bring former and future Muslims into the Islamic fold through good deeds, such as after-school tutoring programs, computer lessons, and health care. No other Muslim organization in the United States performed such a role, even though in the Islamic world it is common for Muslim groups to provide social services, including insurance, hospital care, and loans to fund houses, cars, and even weddings.

Just as Rami started to see his vision come to life, he received a scholarship from the prestigious and politically charged Beir Zeit University in the Israeli-occupied West Bank. In 1996, he left Chicago to spend a year there, and placed IMAN's fortunes in the hands of Mona el-Gindy, a fellow Muslim student at DePaul who was from Egypt. Mona was reluctant to take charge of IMAN. She feared she could not measure up to Rami's leadership skills and charisma. And, because IMAN had just been established, she knew it was a critical year for the organization. Mona, who went on that year to organize a large fundraising event for IMAN, was determined to show Muslims and non-Muslims in South Chicago that practicing Islam is different from being an Arab and from being involved in Palestinian politics.

"We wanted to separate ourselves from the very secular movement that existed, but we didn't want to alienate people," recalled Mona, who later became a teacher at an Islamic school in a Chicago suburb. "We wanted to work with different groups in the community but we also wanted people to know why we had come—to do things under the banner of Islam. Some people in the community at the time thought everyone who was a Muslim had to be an Arab."

The South Side was ripe territory for bridging the divide among African Americans, Latinos, and Arabs under the banner of Islam. Even those who knew next to nothing about the religion perceived Islam as a faith for the disenfranchised, such as the African Americans and Latinos living in South Chicago. And the Arabs, some of whom were recent immigrants, were attuned to the Islamic revival, either having witnessed it firsthand in their native countries or having heard about it from their relatives. This made them more receptive to the Islamic call.

The African Americans in South Chicago were also drawn to IMAN's Islamic message because they had grown up with at least a vague idea of the faith. Chicago had long been a hotbed of spirituality and religious foment. More than one hundred years ago, it hosted the World's Parliament of Religions, which first introduced Islam to many Americans, and it was once home to an early Muslim missionary movement from India. The Nation of Islam was headquartered in the city.

Some African Americans of Rami's generation who were seeking to convert tried to join the Nation, but they were discouraged by its radical ideas. And immigrant Muslims felt they were not welcomed because of their race. By the 1990s, the Nation and its leader Louis Farrakhan had mellowed; there was no more talk about whites being the Devil. But the movement was still more focused on African American rights and the plight of the ghetto than on religion.

African American youth growing up in the 1980s had at least heard about the Nation and Warith Deen's breakaway movement. Their greatest hero, though, was Malcolm X. Malcolm X's legacy differed greatly from his image during his lifetime. For the younger generation, Malcolm was a hybrid of Farrakhan and Warith Deen Muhammad—someone who sought to practice Islam within the tradition of orthodox Sunni Islam but who also championed African American rights.

Among the Arabs of South Chicago, the community gradually shifted from one that was decidedly Arabic to one that had a more general Islamic identity. Changes in the types of immigrants who came to the area contributed to this transition. Toward the end of the nineteenth century, Turkish, Syrian, and Lebanese immigrants began settling in Chicago. According to the 1910 census, there were 772 people of Arab descent living in Chicago. Immigration laws enacted in the early 1920s barred Muslims from entering the country, separating those who had settled a bit earlier from their families.

In Chicago, the new immigrants used their economic and social power to establish some of the first mosques in the city and surrounding suburbs. Proof of their Islamic awareness can be found in the organizations that emerged. The national Federation of Islamic Associations was created in 1953. The first ever Muslim Students' Association was founded in Illinois in 1963. In the 1960s and 1970s, the Muslims who arrived in Chicago established one of the most dynamic Muslim communities in the country. Islamic schools and mosques were built in the 1980s and 1990s. There are seven full-time Islamic schools, as well as specialized *hifz* schools, where memorization of the Koran is taught. The number of mosques, ranging from large formal houses of worship to mosques in homes, is estimated at one hundred.

When I first visited South Chicago, I couldn't help noticing its unusual ethnic blend. About 250,000 African Americans, Latinos, and Arabs live side by side in wood-frame houses. Sixty-third, one of the main streets running through the neighborhood, is lined with Arab groceries that are carbon copies of those in Cairo, Syria, and Palestine. The sweet smells of cardamom and other Eastern spices fill the air. But there is one important difference between the Arab stores on Kedzie Street, the main avenue that runs through the community, and those in the Middle East: next to the Arab groceries selling falafel and hummus is a taco stand or a hair salon selling African American hair-straightening products or a Hispanic supermarket offering specials on tamales. The police station on Sixty-third is perhaps the most prominent building in the area: dozens of white-and-blue police cars fill the parking lot each day. The station gives residents some comfort; it offers some protection from the Arab and African American gangs that occupy the streets at night, when the multicolored neon signs plastered on Mexican restaurants mix with the street lamps to distort what light there is.

The IMAN office on Sixty-third, known in the neighborhood simply as the markez, the Arabic word for "center," has a homey feel. On any given day, Rami might shuffle in, his backpack slung over his black T-shirt, and end up wrestling on the floor with young kids who are hanging out at the center. More studious young boys sit at the computers lined against a wall near the glass door. Some attend the computer classes IMAN provides.

Others drop in just to read their e-mail because they can't afford their own computers. It is clear that IMAN is an Islamic organization. Young women with headscarves meander in and out; posters with sayings from the Prophet hang on the lilac-tinted walls. Others spell out the principles of the faith: "What Do Muslims Believe?" and "What Are the Five Pillars of Islam?" The six-member staff works out of two rooms in the back. Several people share two desks in the small space, their lives organized only by the plastic mailboxes hanging on the walls with nametags for each employee.

While Rami is a steady presence in the IMAN office, the office's main gatekeeper, Adalberto, guarantees Rami's privacy: Adalberto knows that religious leaders from other faiths, with whom Rami has worked closely, are allowed direct contact with Rami, but others have to pass muster. Since September 11, 2001, Rami and most other Islamic activists are more reluctant to talk to outsiders.

Rami's skepticism about the media is different from that of the leaders of other Islamic organizations. He has no fear that the spotlight might trigger an FBI investigation of IMAN, or uncover alleged terrorist connections and result in his name being splashed all over the evening news. There is certainly nothing suspicious about IMAN's operations. The group's modest funding comes from private donations, and federal and city grants, not from Islamic radicals in Saudi Arabia or other Islamic countries that might spark a federal investigation. Rami worries instead about spin, the false images outsiders might attach to IMAN simply because it is an Islamic organization.

Creating a Multicultural Islam

Adalberto, exhibit A in the long line of IMAN successes, was the perfect liaison between IMAN and the outsiders phoning or dropping by the office. Like many whom Rami and a core group of young Muslims have inspired to join their faith, Adalberto discovered Islam through IMAN. He was quickly drawn to Islam and in a short time recited the *shahada*— "There is no god but God and Muhammad is His Messenger." This recitation is all that is required to convert to Islam. Becoming a Muslim does not require extensive study in a theological school; learning the ins and outs of the religion often comes later.

In many ways, Adalberto, a burly, easygoing twenty-five-year-old, was a prime candidate for conversion. He was born into a religious family, but struggled for many years to find the religion that was right for him. His spiritual search reflected an anti-authoritarian streak, as he rebelled against his Catholic family, a Mormon missionary, and an elder in the Jehovah's Witnesses in Mexico, all of whom tried to define his relationship with God. Having a taste of so many strands of Christianity, each proclaiming a monopoly on religious truth, Adalberto was left with an unmoving belief only in himself and his relationship with God.

Growing up in Autlan, the Mexican town that is home to the pop superstar Carlos Santana, with a Catholic father and a mother who was a Jehovah's Witness, Adalberto adopted his mother's faith. He followed an elder in the Jehovah's Witnesses who meant more to him than his father. The elder was the head of the town's small congregation and he taught Adalberto to proselytize. At fourteen, he was already counseling adults and giving sermons to the congregation. Adolescence had passed him by; he was living like an adult, even down to his white shirt and ties.

Then one day, he turned on the television news and learned that the elder, the mentor he had relied upon for spiritual and moral guidance, was having an affair with a young girl.

"I called this guy all the time, all day. I couldn't believe that he was sleeping with a young girl. He was married. He was thirty-six and the girl was too young. After the problem was on the news, when I knocked on people's doors to tell them about the Jehovah's Witnesses, they shut the door in my face."

Adalberto began searching for a new source of inspiration. He started reading about the Mormons and began to infuse Mormon thought into his lectures when he spoke to his Autlan congregation. After the elders found out, he was excommunicated from the Jehovah's Witnesses, and cut off from nearly all the friends and family he had in town. To be excommunicated meant that no Jehovah's Witness could speak to him, not even members of his family.

A few years after he was excommunicated, Adalberto decided to move to Chicago to live with his sister on the South Side. Eager to make money, he landed a job at a plastics-making factory. He inhaled plastic dust for five dollars an hour, all day long. Still searching for spiritual guidance, he saw a notice: the Mormons would pay him nine thousand dollars to become a missionary. After a year as an itinerant missionary traveling around the country and trying to convert people, Adalberto ended up back in South Chicago. One day he passed the IMAN office and saw signs out front with Arabic inscriptions. He decided to go inside to ask if the center offered Arabic lessons. In addition to his native Spanish he had learned English since coming to the United States, and Arabic seemed like a greater challenge.

When he entered the lilac-walled office, he met Reza, a soft-spoken Palestinian and recent graduate of DePaul University. There were no classes, Reza told him, but he could learn Arabic by reading the Koran. He gave Adalberto a Koran translated into Spanish and for four days straight he read it like no other book he had ever read. "I read it and never stopped. It wasn't like the Bible or the other books. It answered all my questions."

On the fifth day, Adalberto returned to the IMAN office to find Reza in time for the noon prayer, and Reza asked him if he wanted to walk across the street to pray in the Al Qasm mosque. It is the kind of mosque Rami says, dismissively, that's run by the "uncles," the aging imams who try to recreate in the United States the mosque community as it existed in their native Arab villages. In addition to the daily prayers, Koran recitations are the preferred activity; women have a small role in the mosque community; and the Friday sermons are in Arabic, not English.

Reza showed Adalberto how to make *wadu*, to wash his hands thoroughly before the prayer, a practice required in Islam to cleanse the faithful before their encounter with God. After the prayer, Reza asked Adalberto if he wanted to become a Muslim. Without hesitation, Adalberto recited the *shahada*. Sheikh Hassan performed a small ritual that to Adalberto's recollection happened with great ease.

The difficulty came when he had to break the news to his sister. He told her when they were working together at a car wash in South Chicago. "One day, my sister said, 'Why don't you go to church anymore?' I said, 'Because I became a Muslim.' Then she said, 'Why do you want to be with these people? They have more than one wife. They kill people.'"

Adalberto ignored his sister's remarks. He had found his spirituality, the gem he had searched for among at least three faiths and in two countries. Soon, he would begin his life's work. He started to bring Islam to other Latinos whom IMAN touched: kids from the neighborhood who happened to stroll into the IMAN office. When I last saw Adalberto he had organized a system to find jobs for Hispanic illegal immigrants. He called it "the day laborers' campaign." Every Saturday, he gathered Latinos in South Chicago and took them to paint houses or spruce up lawns. Adalberto's desire to convert Latinos to Islam was not part of IMAN's plan; it was his idea.

Adalberto's conversion and his attempts to spread the faith, however, reflect IMAN's goals, understood, but never articulated to outsiders. Adalberto's experience was representative of others who have either converted to Islam or were Muslims who rediscovered the faith through IMAN. For them, Islam was the answer to an emptiness in their lives that they never even realized existed until they visited a mosque or began spending time with Muslims.

Rami made no secret of his conviction that Islam could thwart the drugs, crime, and immorality of the inner city: if young boys devoted their energies to learning about Islam, they would shun the pervasive world of drugs and gang violence. Once they began reading the holy texts, they would understand the harmfulness of such behavior. That was the reason he formed a separate organization in South Chicago, apart from the secular Arab community groups that had existed for decades. But to suggest that IMAN's only purpose was to draw non-Muslims to Islam is to simplify the vision. Yet, that was often how outsiders saw it.

IMAN's efforts to create multicultural Islam first in South Chicago and then in other major cities, had many more dimensions than the narrow approach Adalberto had once employed as an elder in the Jehovah's Witnesses, or those a typical missionary uses to win over nonbelievers. Islam for IMAN was not just belief in a faith; it was a way of life, an answer to the social injustice suffered by those of different races and creeds. For decades, Islamists abroad, such as those in the Muslim Brotherhood in Egypt, have lived by this goal. One of IMAN's founders told me how the extensive writings of an Islamic thinker of the 1940s and 1950s had guided him to become a more devout Muslim.

The first time IMAN made public its desire for a unified Muslim community was in June 1997, when the group hosted an Islamic festival called "Taking It to the Streets." At Marquette Park, historically a hangout for drug addicts and the homeless, IMAN organizers spread their message by selling T-shirts that read, "What do you choose—God or Evil? Islam, a way of life." Perched on a stage, one IMAN leader explained the reason for the festival and IMAN's existence: "Islam encompasses many cultures. That is what we celebrate and mark here. In a moment when you see us pray together, you will see African Americans, Latinos, Arabs, and Indo-Pakistanis standing side by side."

By the summer of 2005, "Taking It to the Streets," now an event held every other year, lit up Marquette Park; IMAN's maturity and popularity were clear. Hip-hop artists took to the stage that was set up in the park.

The large, lively crowd drifted through several white tents spread out along several blocks of green grass. When they were not chanting along with the lyrics of the music, they were huddled inside the tents, discussing ways to create a Muslim American identity and to unify immigrant and African American Muslims.

At the time of the 2005 festival, Rami was applying for new state and federal grants to replace the expired ones that had kept the organization afloat. Rami and the other IMAM leaders had established a mosque in a neighborhood about ten miles from the IMAN office. They turned the front of a mom-and-pop grocery store along Justine—a small, tree-lined street with wood-frame houses reminiscent of the Deep South—into a community center, and converted the back of the store into their mosque.

On Sunday mornings at eleven, IMAN holds a food pantry at the new community center. As neighborhood kids play pool in the middle of the room, their parents or older siblings approach a wooden counter to ask for their groceries: brown bags filled to the brim with bread, cereal, powered milk, and other nonperishables. IMAN buys the food from the Chicago Food Depository, run by the city. Often, a city representative hands out the food alongside a member of IMAN. But the image that makes a big impression on the people of the neighborhood is the various women in headscarves who arrive each week to distribute the grocery bags. Next to the counter where they work is a poster similar to those in the IMAN office on Kedzie: "What Is Islam and Who Are Muslims?" Below the headline is an explanation.

Each week after all the food is distributed, Mona Martinez, an IMAN leader and graduate of DePaul University, gathers young girls from the neighborhood in a fenced area outside the building for a lesson in everything from nutrition to the basics of Islam.

One Sunday, dressed in shorts and colorful stretch pants, six African American girls ranging in ages from four to fourteen jump rope, their braided hair bouncing on their small shoulders. The girls assume the Sunday gathering is simply a play session; many had learned about it from Mona, who stands in front of the food pantry door and encourages anyone she sees to come by later in the morning.

That afternoon, Mona, a twenty-eight-year-old with a soothing demeanor and a full-length navy blue veil that makes her look like a nun, brought a box of dates and unsalted almonds with her. She tries to encourage the reluctant girls to nibble on the unfamiliar snacks and gives a brief history of their popularity in the Middle East. The girls are restless; they bounce up and down on the hard chairs, and their eyes dart across the yard. "Have you ever seen dates before?" Mona asks. "No," one girl answers. "But they look funny." Then Mona begins to tell them a few things about Islam. Their blank expressions say it all.

The next Sunday, Mona and her shy daughter, Amina, sit on a picnic bench and wait for the young girls to arrive. After thirty minutes, no one appears and she searches for the reason. Mona had sent a letter to the girls' parents the week before asking permission to take their daughters to a museum downtown. The letter also explained Mona's objectives; she wanted to educate the girls and expose them to Islam.

"Maybe that's why they didn't come today. I scared them off," Mona says, with a defeated look in her eyes that had not been there before. Were the young girls open to new ideas? Would they ever be open to learning about Islam?

"We are starting from the very bottom. Sometimes I think they don't understand anything. Most of these kids don't even go to school. When they come here on Sundays, they ask for hamburgers, steaks, and pizzas, you know, real meals. Most kids would ask for potato chips, but these kids ask for full meals because they don't get them at their own house."

Mona was clearly frustrated that her efforts to educate the young girls about proper nutrition and other life necessities were likely being ignored. She did not want to state the obvious; the girls' parents were willing to send their daughters to the Sunday gatherings for a free meal or even for an hour or two of free babysitting. But, once they realized Mona hoped to teach them about Islam, they were no longer interested.

Many months later, Mona's initial frustrations were a distant memory. The mothers in the neighborhood had grown accustomed to the Sunday ritual of picking up supplies at the IMAN food pantry, and bringing their daughters for lessons with Mona. Lessons about dates turned to elementary teachings about the Koran and Ramadan, the Muslim holy month of fasting.

The mosque IMAN created is also beginning to attract worshippers living nearby. It is the size of an average living room. Red carpet lines the floor and a small brown podium serves as the *minbar*, the place where an imam delivers the Friday sermons. A large chandelier hangs from the stained white ceiling. A white curtain separates the men's section in front near the *minbar* from the women's area in back of the room—a sign of a traditional mosque. Yet, IMAN establishes the mosque to offer believers a more modern interpretation of the faith.

One Friday at the mosque about fifteen minutes before the 1:20 p.m. Friday prayer, someone pulls back the white curtain so the women would be able to see the imam in front with the men. It is a test of one of the most hotly debated issues in American mosques. At many mosques, women are fighting to remove the curtains or other barriers separating them from the men. The separation had become a tradition among Muslim Americans. After a few minutes at the IMAN mosque, the women begin to arrive and squat on the red carpet. Before the prayer began, one of them steps forward and draws the curtain. The imam and the men are no longer in sight.

The voice on the other side of the curtain giving the Friday sermon is that of Abdel Malik, one of the IMAN founders. Abdel, a lawyer who often preaches at the Friday sermons, is not a learned theologian. Even though he may not be formally versed in the Koran and other holy texts, he does his best to offer guidance to the worshippers.

A Muslim convert who grew up Catholic in the middle-class Chicago neighborhood of Oak Park, he had little exposure to Islam before he met Rami at DePaul University in the 1990s. Before then, he had tried to join the Nation of Islam, but felt rebuffed because he was white. After he met the Muslim students who later formed IMAN, Abdel began reading the works of Islamic thinkers who have inspired moderate and radical Islamic movements for more than half a century. Abdel, like many young Muslims, turned to books from the Islamic world because there were no prominent Islamic thinkers in the United States.

"I was influenced about how you could change the world from a position of social justice," Abdel told me.

That day in the mosque, Abdel Malik, his thin body covered in a long tunic and balloon-shaped trousers, leans against the *minbar* and preaches that God expects the faithful to die in a state of submission.

When the sermon ends, two African American women step outside into the bright sunlight. They had traveled at least ten miles from their homes across town, passing several other mosques along the way to pray here. They know little about IMAN but have heard that the mosque offers a more modern approach to practicing their faith. At their traditional mosque downtown, women are forbidden from bringing their children into the mosque. They are told to stay away while they were menstruating, and to enter the mosque through a different entrance than the men. No matter the distance, they plan to pray on Justine Street every Friday.

Before driving away in a rundown Chevrolet, one of the women vows to return. "This is the first mosque we have been to where there is no discrimination because we are women or because we dare to pray with Arabs or because we wear our headscarves tightly tied to our heads," she says.

FIVE

Muslim Voices

ॐ

As Rami became better known in South Chicago, he began to realize he could expand his sights far beyond the neighborhood. There was one guaranteed way to attract youth interested in Islam from a greater swath of the city: Islamic hip-hop. If Napoleon could woo a small crowd of young boys to the middle of a parking lot, older music fans would attend an intimate concert in a café. The only problem was finding the right venue. There were no cafés around Sixty-third Street, at least none suitable for what Rami had in mind. But, just as the idea began to take shape, he learned that a few friends were opening a café called Ndiga, meaning "root" in Swahili, on Sixty-third—not far from the glow of the police station.

On opening night in December 2003, the crowd numbers a few dozen. Most are from the neighborhood, but a few non-Muslim university students have ventured across town out of curiosity. Although Islamic hip-hop's popularity is growing steadily in large cities, such as Chicago, it is just becoming fashionable among Muslim youth and is still barely known among non-Muslims.

As I enter the café, I am struck by the diversity of the crowd: Puerto Ricans, Palestinians, African Americans, and whites. The people congregate around a dilapidated beige sofa. Hamburgers, brownies, Cokes, and herbal teas are being served from a bar, but no alcohol. Ndiga is painted in psychedelic colors, perhaps more suited to Berkeley, California, in the 1960s than the African American and Latino culture of South Chicago.

When the concert begins, the crowd gravitates toward a stage on the opposite side of the café. Instinctively, the women choose the beige folding chairs on one side of the room and the men sit on the other side. They are so accustomed to being segregated in mixed company at Islamic gatherings, that they separate themselves automatically. David Kelly, an African American convert to Islam, a musician, and a lawyer, is hosting the show, the first of many in which he will serve as the master of ceremonies.

"Thank you all for coming out. This is the first community café. We're going to have a few bands tonight and then open mike. Anybody can come on up to the stage."

A thin man with a soothing voice and creamy light brown skin, David Kelly came to Islam through hip-hop, the way Rami hopes the youth in South Chicago will. David's parents raised him Catholic in one of Chicago's affluent southern suburbs and he attended Catholic schools. But Catholicism was always problematic for him. He didn't think Jesus was the Son of God, and he didn't like organized religion in general.

When he entered Morehouse College, the country's largest all male, traditionally black university, friends in his book club were reading an autobiography of Malcolm X, memorizing every aspect of his life. David wasn't as interested in Malcolm's political views as he was in his take on social justice during his years in the Nation of Islam. David was inspired by Malcolm's spiritual awakening after his pilgrimage to Mecca, and how he combined spirituality with politics. David decided to follow in Malcolm's footsteps and bought a Koran. But he knew Islam required discipline, the same kind of discipline needed to be a practicing Catholic. Over the next decade, David stopped reading the Koran but continued listening to Public Enemy, a hip-hop band that sang the virtues of the Nation of Islam.

Years went by. David met his wife, Zeenat Khan, a Pakistani Muslim from Birmingham, England. She encouraged him to pick up the Koran again. One day in 2000 he visited a mosque near the University of Chicago with the sole intention of finding out if music was banned in Islam. He had never been to a mosque before this day. He met a mosque leader who told him he must stop playing his music because a verse in the Koran says the human voice can be seductive. This was a major stumbling block; David had been playing for more than a decade in a hip-hop band he'd formed called All Natural.

David had discovered one of the greatest challenges facing young Muslim living not only in America but also those in the wider Western world. The absence of Islamic scholars educated and raised in Western countries has produced two choices: either young Muslims follow the religious guidance of the available imams, knowing it might not apply to their modern lives, or they interpret the holy texts for themselves, with the risk that their conclusions may distort Islamic doctrine.

David didn't agree with the mosque leader's interpretation of the Koranic verse referring to music. But he did not have another source for more reliable religious guidance. He was willing to give up his music in order to convert. He proclaimed the *shahada*, the rite of passage, and became a Muslim.

Several months later, David met Rami while he was having a conversation with a fellow Muslim. He asked Rami if playing music was against Islamic teaching, and Rami delicately told him it was an open question and suggested that David research the topic.

Not long after David met him, in June 2001, Rami held the Taking It to the Streets festival and asked David and All Natural to perform there. It was the first time David had appeared before an all-Muslim crowd. They were so receptive, and Rami was so welcoming that David started to think that playing music couldn't possibly be harmful.

Still, he remained conflicted about whether he could perform his music and remain a good Muslim. At first he put the issue aside. He had entered the University of Illinois law school in September and wanted to concentrate on his studies. But almost immediately, the attacks of September 11 turned his indecision into action. David felt that music had to become a voice of expression for Muslims, who in his words had overnight become America's new "bogeyman." Hip-hop could become a first line of defense. David had already used his music for political commentary; one of his band's early albums, *Insomnia*, sharply criticized U.S. foreign policy and American society. In the tune, "Culture of Terrorism," the band sings:

> I'm strictly off limits to the cotton-soft scented type
> who tip-toe and tread light and dread the sight
> of a kufi-wearing kid who's kicking science
> picking mental padlocks . . .
>
> The American economy's surviving off arms
> third world debt
> closing down farms
> promoting conflict and violent behavior

then using convicts 4 cheap slave labor
extending patents on the X Y chromosome
pushing drugs from crack down to methadone
drones to the metronome march along to the rhythm
of the free trade and forced patriotism

David's latest and perhaps most important transition from recent Muslim convert to outspoken Muslim musician was just one of the many personal transformations that were taking shape across the country in the
wake of September 11. Suddenly, the nation's hidden Muslims found themselves and their beliefs in the crosshairs of every radio commentator, newspaper pundit, and politician whose refrain became: "Who are these people?
And why do they hate us?" Such questions—framed in ignorance, bigotry,
and most of all fear—hammered the Muslim community from all sides.
Gone was the general sense of benign neglect that had largely shaped the
Muslim American experience for decades. Overnight, mainstream America
had imposed a stark choice on Muslim believers everywhere: disavow key
aspects of your faith and culture, or risk being lumped together with the
September 11 militants.

In the days and weeks that followed, many Muslim American leaders
who interacted with non-Muslim society took to the airwaves to assure
their fellow citizens that Islam was not a religion of violence and America
was not a breeding ground for Islamic extremists. Ordinary Muslims took
a less defensive approach. They began to realize it was up to them to define what it means to be a Muslim in the modern world, and more specifically, what it means in the new America.

Rami and David certainly weren't the first to use hip-hop for Islamic
expression, or what is known as *dawah*, spreading the faith. Hip-hop, now
estimated to be a $1.8 billion industry in the United States, first appeared
in the 1970s. Since that time, this unique brand of music, which has been
used to fuse the racial politics of African Americans with the religious and
cultural forces of Latinos, Arabs, and South Asians, has inspired the rise of
Islam among disenfranchised youth in America's inner cities. It is not primarily poverty that draws them to Islam; it's what Islam has to offer. Many
Westerners assume that desperation born from impoverishment inspires
people to turn to Islam. But for some, Islam is a refuge from consumer-
ism, immorality, and the intoxicating lure of Western culture. Since September 11, a new dimension has entered this movement—opposition to
U.S. policies around the world. The result is a powerful movement that
unifies black nationalism and Islam through hip-hop.

The first well-known religious organization to use rap-style lyrics was the Five Percenters. This sectarian, offshoot group split from the Nation of Islam in the late 1960s. The movement's founder, Clarence 13X "Pudding," known to his followers as Father Allah, differed with the Nation of Islam in one fundamental way: the Nation taught that God had appeared in Detroit in 1930 in the form of Farad Muhammad who passed on his teachings to Elijah Muhammad. But Father Allah believed that the black man collectively is God. His movement taught that 85 percent of mass society was ignorant and incapable of seeking truth. Ten percent realized the truth but used it to co-opt the 85 percent; and only 5 percent of humanity knew "the divine nature of the black man who is God or Allah."

The Five Percenters began preaching in the 1960s; they used African-American slang to create rhymes and attract urban youth on the streets of and around New York City. For mainstream Sunni Muslims, however, the notion that God's divinity is embodied in the collective identity of black men is blasphemy. Such thinking contradicts a basic principle of Islamic doctrine, *tawhid*, or the unity of God.

Despite their unorthodox theology, affiliates of the Five Percenters went on to inspire rap groups and were recruited by some bands that emerged in the 1970s. The rap bands from the 1970s, with their Afrocentric music, eventually contributed to the evolution of Islamic hip-hop in the 1990s. The message changed dramatically as the musical genre took root within some Sunni Muslim circles, and Islam became central to the music. Just as rap has empowered African Americans, Islamic hip-hop is inspiring young Muslim Americans. The ethnic diversity of these bands gives them even more historical importance, and allows them to appeal to Muslims of all backgrounds.

Recent groups, including Native Deen, MPAC, and Sons of Hagar, have left behind early lyrics about drugs, sex, and violence. Instead, they praise the Koran and the Sunnah. Native Deen, consisting of three African American rappers, promotes positive religious messages while appealing to Muslims of diverse ethnic backgrounds. In one song called "What We Go Through," Deen sings:

One billion strong, all year long,
Prayers to Allah even in Hong Kong.
Can never be wrong if we read the Koran,
Cause it's never been changed since day one.
Others may brag, say that we lag,
But they don't know all the power we had.

The power we had, the power we have.
So Muslimoon don't you ever be sad.
Take many looks, go read their books,
You'll see all the facts that your friends overlook.
"So always be proud, you can say it out loud,
I am proud to be down with the Muslim crowd!"

M-U-S-L-I-M
I'm so blessed to be with them . . .
M-U-S-L-I-M
I'm so blessed to be with them . . .

On their Web site, Native Deen made it clear that they saw themselves as members of the *ummah*, the worldwide community of believers.

Although we are Black, we are not part of the Nation of Islam or the Five Percenters. Not all Black Muslims follow Farrakhan. In fact, over a third of all Muslims in America are African-Americans who belong to the international community of Muslims. Some call this mainstream Islam, and it is this Islam that Native Deen follows.

In the lyrics of another band, the Sons of Hagar, two Arabs, one Irishman, and Korean convert to Islam portray Muslims around the world as a subjugated minority. The multiethnic nature of this group illustrates the growing cultural convergence between African American Muslims and their immigrant co-religionists who seem to have agreed, particularly since September 11, to place their Muslim identity first.

MPAC, or Muslim Produced Athletic Company, was created in 2001 by two African Americans and four Arabs, all of whom lived in Bridgeview, a predominately Arab Chicago suburb. The band quickly caught on, playing at large Islamic conventions and on college campuses. On a recent single, "Muslim American," MPAC sings:

How would you deal with being labeled as evil
To such an extreme point
You're no longer being labeled as people
These thoughts are lethal injections
Affecting cerebral connections, through media feeding projections
It weakens your brother
Turning Muslims undercover like sleeping through fajr (morning prayer)
We need to stand and stop being viewed as children crawling
We believe in peace not pieces of building falling
Its constant presence
They say we all strap bombs and arms to measure
Our commitment to our lord but Islam's a treasure
A religion based on truth. No room for terror to push them
Take a step into the world of the American Muslim

In explaining the lyrics of many of their songs, two MPAC musicians, Luqman Rashad and Jameel Karim, say their words are catharsis, a way of telling the world what Muslims are experiencing after September 11 and various conflicts around the world, from Bosnia to Palestine to Iraq.

A shared feeling of betrayal, of hurt, reflected in hip-hop lyrics is breaking down the ethnic divide among second-generation Muslim Americans. This sentiment convinced Rami that his community cafés would be a hit. After the first few concerts at Ndiga, the crowds became so large that Rami had to move the performances across town to the Spoken Word Café, a larger, more upscale venue near the University of Chicago. On the last Friday night of each month, David Kelly's voice projects from the stage. Bands from MPAC to Native Deen pump up the crowd. Even all-female bands, who would be discouraged from performing at many Islamic events simply because they are women, have become regulars—so much so that the crowd has memorized their lyrics. This new generation of Muslim entertainers has chosen the path of *dawah*, spreading the faith, but of all the words spoken during these evenings, no one has ever called it that.

Your Muslim Neighbor Is Your Friend

The Chicago traffic is more congested than usual one afternoon in September 2004 as I listen to a message on my voicemail, one hand on the wheel, the other grasping my cell phone. An afternoon rain is beating hard on my windshield, making the soft, serene voice on the message nearly inaudible. I struggle to listen to the lightly accented voice. It's Abdul Malik Mujahid, an imam, acquaintance, activist, and scholar.

By now I have to come to know the Islamic community in Chicago and in other parts of the country. I feel their frustrations of living in post–September 11 America. I share their determination to try to educate the public about their religion, however difficult that might be. If anyone can change the tide of this vast sea of nationwide ignorance, it is Abdul Malik. A poised, slender man, always impeccably dressed, he has the smooth, conciliatory skills of a diplomat, and the serenity of a theologian. He disagrees with anyone who might suggest that Muslims are the "other" in American society. Yet, he works to encourage a distinctive Islamic identity for all Muslims.

I struggle to hear his message, while trying not to lurch into the car ahead of me in the bumper-to-bumper traffic. "Hello, this is Abdul Malik. I am calling to let you know that Radio Islam will be on the air in a few days."

A few days? He is giving me short notice to convince my editors at the
Chicago Tribune to let me write a story. The first daily Islamic radio show
in the United States is certainly not front-page news. There are Hamas
bombings, and the Bush administration's threats of "regime change" in
Iran. There are the usual home-team sports sagas, which I ignore but which
are more important to the *Tribune* than the war in Iraq. Each time I watched
the newspaper deploy numerous reporters to cover the Chicago Cubs—
after all, the newspaper owns the team—I wondered why Americans don't
have more substantive ways to occupy their lives and why newspapers don't
have more enlightening subjects to fill their pages. Radio Islam would
definitely be a hard sell for all these reasons, not to mention that it would
be a positive story about Muslims.

Such pieces rarely generate much interest among the high-ranking
Tribune editors, who worry out loud in editorial meetings that the paper
would look foolish if favorable stories about Muslims appeared on the front-
page along with stories about Islamic militants beheading Americans in
Iraq. In their eyes, one Muslim is no different from the next. But somehow this logic is never applied to other faiths. Otherwise, the *Tribune* would
have to suspend its fawning coverage of Catholics—written to appease the
city's large Catholic population—every time the Irish Republican Army
set off a bomb in central London. Even so, I am determined to write the
story, even though I know it will end up buried inside the "Metro" section, a repository for articles more suited to small-town newspapers filling
space with reports on Sunday night bingo.

Abdul Malik's spontaneity is typical of Muslim Americans and Muslims
everywhere. I had asked him to give me plenty of warning about Radio
Islam's debut. It was unlikely a national newspaper would cover it, and the
Chicago Tribune was probably the best hope for any publicity. But self-
promotion is as taboo to Muslims as forgetting to offer a houseguest food
and drink. It is not only a cultural taboo, but a religious one.

That Abdul Malik is launching a radio station on a public frequency
accessible to non-Muslim listeners is already a significant departure from
the Muslim tradition of public reticence. But as he tells me, since September 11, Muslims are tired of everyone speaking for them and about them.
It is time for Muslim Americans to speak for themselves. Islam does not
condone terrorism; Islam is not at war with the West; and your Muslim
neighbor is your friend. This is Abdul Malik's message.

The night the radio program hits the airwaves, I am having trouble finding the building that houses the station. The entrance to the building at

the address Abdul Malik has given me is confusing. The front door with a sign that reads "Kasper Dance Studio" is located on a small street off a busy thoroughfare running through Chicago's Polish neighborhood. When I reach the door to the studio, I look around for evidence of the radio station, WCEV, which has agreed to sell Radio Islam an hour of airtime each evening from six to seven. I finally spot a half-hidden sign, "WCEV, We're Chicago's Ethnic Voice." Ethnic is the key word. For two generations, the Migala family, hardcore Chicagoans, have devoted themselves to giving a voice to minorities who were otherwise excluded from commercial stations. WCEV airs programming in Polish, Arabic, Bosnian, and a host of other foreign languages, including Gaelic. Now the time has come to add Chicago's vibrant Muslim community to the mix.

I ring the bell and pass through a door leading into the studio. Inside, Abdul Malik is supervising every detail of the preparations for the show. The studio is in a time warp, which gives it a special charm. A red light hanging from the ceiling outside the control room reads, "On Air." Everything else is brown: the carpet, the wood paneling, the curtains. The 1950s atmosphere seems particularly incongruous once the host takes his seat in the control room and begins the show.

Dressed in a long, white Islamic tunic, Altaf Kaiseruddin, a doctor and friend of Abdul Malik, sits in front of a large black microphone ready to greet his guests and callers. When the show begins, a loud, prerecorded male voice sounds a confident and purposeful chord. "Everyone is talking about Isl-a-a-am and Muslims. It's time you talk," he says, with the slight lilt of an African American rap musician.

The premodern equipment only allows one caller to hang on the line at a time; some callers abruptly hear a dial tone when they think they are on hold. But it doesn't matter because the callers are friends who have been asked to phone in. Who else could possibly know that the station is on the air? There has been little or no advance promotion, and most listeners only know to tune in by word of mouth.

Abdul Malik, the hosts, and producers struggle through the hour until the last guest is set to call in. "Hello, hello," says Kaiseruddin. For a few anxious seconds, there is silence. Has the line gone dead?

Then the guest, a comedian named Preacher Moss, sounds a loud "Salaam aleikum!" (Peace be upon you!)

Kaiseruddin breathes a sigh of relief through the microphone. The line isn't lost.

"So tell us about your national tour, 'Allah Made Me Funny.'"

"It is a thirty-day tour. It's a comedy," Moss says, before delivering the punch line. "I am only five-foot-five-inches tall. Allah made me funny because he didn't make me tall."

This remark is exactly what Abdul Malik envisioned when he first considered producing Radio Islam. He wanted the show to prove to non-Muslim listeners that Muslims are just like them, that their lives are not consumed with religious activities. They joke, and are even capable of making fun of themselves.

Abdul Malik's view about how Muslims should be perceived in America is just one among many diverse opinions within the nation's Islamic community. Many Muslims feel they are caught between competing demands: If they try to convince Americans that they are just like them, are they not apologizing for being Muslim and de-emphasizing the glorious qualities of their religion? But on the other hand, if they stress the differences between Muslims and non-Muslims, are they not encouraging some people's efforts to alienate them from mainstream American society?

Some Muslims deal with this dilemma through a bit of self-denial. They want to believe that Americans can distinguish between the Islamic militant profiled on Fox News and the peaceful Muslim living next door. They recall the time a neighbor did them a good deed, or when, after September 11, non-Muslims in different parts of the country linked arms around mosques to protect them from vandalism. But they minimize empirical and anecdotal evidence showing that for the most part, Americans have grown increasingly hostile toward Islam and Muslims.

There is yet another Muslim voice, one that has turned Islam into a commodity to be marketed shamelessly to non-Muslim America. After September 11, the community saw the emergence of the "professional Muslim." Suddenly there were lucrative opportunities to tell America what it wanted to hear about Islam, rather than challenging the nationwide consensus.

Irshad Manji, the author of *The Trouble with Islam*, is one of the most damaging voices for the Islamic community. Of all the professional Muslims to emerge after September 11, Manji won most attention from the non-Muslim world. Her book was an international bestseller; she became a television pundit, and an essayist on the editorial pages of the world's most influential newspapers. She earns thousands of dollars for speaking engagements on college campuses.

Muslims, as well as non-Muslim experts, around the world—particularly in Canada, Manji's home and where she hosted a radio talk show—condemn

her. First, most don't consider her a Muslim, even though she was born as
such. She identifies herself as a lesbian, and homosexuality is considered a
violation of the faith. Her political views are the antithesis of Muslim feeling about nearly everything, from her favorable attitudes toward Israel in
its conflict with the Palestinians to her support of U.S. policy in the Arab
and Islamic world. A scholar of Islamic studies who is a friend of mine calls
her a Muslim Zionist, a label Manji would no doubt accept. My own encounter with Manji was not encouraging; her opinions about Islam, she
offered when I interviewed her in 2004 for the *Tribune*, had no basis in the
teachings of the faith. As a result of her unorthodox views, many Muslims
believe she claims to be a Muslim only to sell books; a Muslim denouncing
the faith is a marketer's dream.

To many non-Muslims, however, she is the voice of "progressive" Islam. Why progressive? Because Manji's prescription for correcting the
"troubles with Islam" is for the faith to conform to the ideas of Western
philosophy. Essentially, Islam would cease to be Islam. Manji is neither a
scholar nor a theologian. Yet, she portrays herself as a savior and calls for
reforming the faith. Her market-driven campaign has become a problem
for Muslim reformers who now have difficulty convincing Muslim society
that their ideas for altering Islam are not the kind of reform Manji is prescribing. Manji quickly became the darling of the non-Muslim world because she reinforced what they already believed about Islam. She often
claims, for example, that the Koran condones violence against non-Muslims.
Muslims sometimes blame themselves for her fame; her voice stands out
in the absence of other Muslim voices willing to debate her views in the
national media.

The question of who is the authentic Islamic voice in America has always been a divisive issue among Muslims, but the debate became even
more heated after September 11. Who should it be? The Arab voice, the
Pakistani voice, or that of the African American believer?

Abdul Malik was sensitive to this debate, having spent so much time in
Chicago, in many ways the home of African American Islam. He was aware
that many African American Muslims resented the fact that the public
perception of Islam in America was shaped by the image of Muslims as
either Arab or Pakistani, but not African American.

When inviting Muslims to explain Islam, organizations across the country often approach Arabs, Pakistanis, and Indians, but rarely African Americans. Most Islamic leaders, such as Abdul Malik, believe that after September

11 Muslims must unify. And, although great tensions remain, September 11 did inspire at least some immigrant and African American Muslims to begin chipping away at an icy relationship that dates back decades.

Abdul Malik wanted Radio Islam to illustrate the diversity of the Islamic community, so he arranged for Muslim hosts of all ethnicities, including African Americans. Finding content for the radio program that would neither further divide Muslims from each other nor dilute their identity was the next challenge. In choosing the name Radio Islam, Abdul Malik considered this conundrum. Would listeners think it was a platform for proselytizing? In the end, he decided that the program should have two purposes. It should offer Muslims a chance to set the record straight about Islam, but should also host discussions about everything from the death of Pope John Paul II to the Cinderella story of the Boston Red Sox's 2004 World Series victory.

In practice, Radio Islam focuses most of the time on issues of particular concern to Muslims. One night in October 2005, Robert Grant, the new director of the FBI's Chicago office, was a guest. It was the holy month of Ramadan and the question posed to Grant was appropriate considering the time of year: how can Muslims be assured that when they donate to charities, they won't be hunted down by the U.S. government and ac-

Abdul Malik Mujahid. (*Photograph by Janaan Hashim*)

cused of raising money for Islamic militants? During Ramadan, it is especially important for Muslims to give to charity.

"Our investigations make a distinction," Grant said, between Muslims donating to charities and those donating to illegal causes.

"But how is this possible?" asked a caller. She wanted to know how the U.S. government could claim to know which charities, if any, might be fronts for Islamic radicals, and which were not.

Grant couldn't answer. Instead he tried to change the subject from fundraising for Muslim extremists to fundraising for the Irish Republican Army. The United States was not just singling out Muslims in its crackdown on fundraising, he suggested. Rather, agencies such as the FBI were scrutinizing all ethnic or religious groups that might give money to radicals.

"The IRA, a deadly organization, was funded through fundraising in the United States," he said.

In shows like this one, the conversation between Muslims and their neighbors, as Abdul Malik would say, was at cross-purposes. The Muslims wanted the truth, but, in this case, Grant's failing effort to improve relations was transparent. It was easy to hear the caution in his voice as he carefully constructed each halting phrase. The Muslim callers were unable to convince Grant that fighting terrorism was one thing, but violating their civil liberties was another. And Grant failed to persuade them that the new laws enacted after September 11, which made it difficult for Muslims to carry out their religious duties, were not aimed specifically at Muslims.

The host that evening, Frederick al Deen, could easily have pressured Grant to answer the caller's question. Al Deen was certainly not afraid to speak truth to power. For many years, he had been an imam at mosques belonging to the American Society of Muslims, the movement Wallace Deen Muhammad created after he split from the Nation of Islam. Al Deen, himself African American, was a seasoned activist, one seemingly unlikely to tolerate half-truths from an FBI agent.

But inside the studio, al Deen's face remained stoic, as he concentrated on taking callers' questions. He showed respect for Grant, and allowed him a graceful exit off the air. This was the Radio Islam way. Let the callers pressure the guests and let the hosts remain above the fray.

Al Deen's behavior was in keeping with Abdul Malik's idea of what Radio Islam should be. At heart, Abdul Malik never wanted to believe how negative public opinion was toward Muslims and Islam, and he didn't want the program to become a battleground between Muslims and everyone else. His early years in America helped shape his perspective. When he arrived at the University of Chicago in 1981 to study political science, he immediately joined a small community of Muslim intellectuals who made him feel at home. Fazlur Rahman, a world-renowned scholar of Islamic studies, taught there, and he became Abdul Malik's good friend and spiritual guide. He often led about ten Muslims, all from overseas, in Friday prayers held in the university chapel. At the time, there were no Muslim Americans at the university; all were foreigners. Abdul Malik's roommate, a Muslim from Malaysia, was the national president of the Muslim Students' Association. Associations like the MSA, which became more common on university campuses in the 1990s, and even more so after September 11, were at first created to foster a comfortable environment for Muslims from abroad.

Abdul Malik had intended to stay in the United States for two years and then move back to Pakistan. But, like many elites of his generation from developing countries, he never returned home. This was common not only among Pakistanis, but also Egyptians whose wealthy families could afford to send them to America for higher education. Unlike most, Abdul Malik didn't stay because he thought he could make more money in America. He worried, even during the 1980s, about the future relationship between America and Islam. He thought that if Muslims living in America could develop a healthy relationship with mainstream society, this would be important for Muslims across the world. America's acceptance and knowledge of Islam would be good for world peace. There would be a ripple effect; understanding at home would mean tolerance abroad.

Abdul Malik's visionary spirit did not change after he left the University of Chicago. In the 1980s on the Eid al-Adha, the feast day in the Muslim calendar that marks Abraham's willingness to sacrifice his son for God, Malik told a Chicago congregation that they should encourage their children to become journalists in order to correct public perceptions about Islam. Following his own advice, in 1988 he enrolled in a vocational school to learn how to become a broadcaster. Two years later, he finished a feasibility study and determined that it would cost $1.2 million to start even a modest radio station. It was money he didn't have. He had decided to give up the idea, when he came face-to-face with the type of ignorance he had hoped to change through just such a radio station. In 1990, when he went looking for a house, his real estate agent asked him, "What church do you belong to?" Abdul Malik said he didn't belong to a church, but attended a mosque. "What's a mosque?" the agent wanted to know.

Abdul Malik realized his calling: he would educate Muslims and non-Muslims about Islam. In 1988, he had started a company called Sound Vision, now the largest Islamic multimedia company in the United States. Sound Vision produces Muslim-based educational tapes, CD-ROMs, and videos, on topics ranging from reading the Koran to learning Arabic. A video series for children, modeled after the PBS programs *Sesame Street* and *Mr. Rogers's Neighborhood*, made Sound Vision famous. It's called *Adam's World*, and centers around a Kufi-wearing puppet. Adam has a friend, Anisa, and neither of them knows much about Islam or the West. But during the series they learn about pluralism and different cultures. In North America, live performances by the characters from *Adam's World* can draw a mostly Muslim crowd of up to ten thousand.

After Sound Vision became lucrative, Abdul Malik decided in 1990 to produce RadioIslam.com. With some inexpensive software and a high-speed Internet connection, Abdul Malik placed Radio Islam on the World Wide Web. It wasn't ideal, but it was a beginning. It took him years to find a commercial station willing to sell airtime to Radio Islam. Meanwhile Sound Vision became a media empire and, by the time Abdul Malik made a deal with WCEV in 2004, he was able to fund the show with profits from Sound Vision.

Eight months into the show, however, Abdul Malik needed fresh funds to keep the program alive. They were still airing only a few commercials, one possible way to raise money. So he did what is common within the Muslim American community: he held a fundraiser. Generally, fundraisers are used for the upkeep or expansion of a mosque, or to meet the imams' salaries and other expenses. In recent years, Islamic communities across the country have also collected vast sums for earthquake and hurricane victims. No matter the cause, the scene at fundraisers is usually the same: a large dining room in a five-star hotel, circular tables, no alcohol, and typical American banquet fare, such as salmon or baked chicken.

The Radio Islam day for giving is a bit different. It is held at a restaurant, not a hotel. And although the restaurant is located in a suburb, Bridgeview, it isn't a white-picket-fence suburb; it is home to, perhaps, the largest Muslim population around Chicago. There is also a PowerPoint presentation, not the usual parade of speakers.

Dressed in a modest, dark blue pantsuit, Janaan Hashim, a lawyer, takes the stage to make the case for donating money. Janaan, who invited me to attend, easily refutes the stereotype of a submissive Muslim woman. Like

the demanding schoolteacher she once was, Janaan commands the podium with her five-foot-three-inch frame. Muslims are familiar with giving money to mosques, but donating to Muslim media is something new
to them. In many of their countries of origin, there are only government-
run media outlets, not a commercially driven, independent press as there
is in the United States. Those who understand the free expression of ideas
are skeptical that a program on an ethnic radio station in Chicago can
possibly counter the continuous assaults on Islam on mainstream television, radio, and in the newspapers.

The way to soften this crowd, like any other, is to tell a few jokes. But
Janaan expects the guests to do more, to laugh at themselves as well. She
shows the first images in her PowerPoint presentation, revealing on a big
white screen a few remarks from callers who have phoned Radio Islam. "I
didn't know Muslims had such good American accents," says one caller.
And, "Where do you get those people who talk in such a normal way?"
remarks another.

"We were born in America!" Janaan replies, turning away from the
screen and facing the crowd. Her warm-up seems to be effective. The
audience laughs in a way that suggests that such awkward moments are
familiar.

Abdul Malik, executive director of Radio Islam and on this night chief
fundraiser, takes the stage.

"Who is going to give ten thousand dollars to Radio Islam?

"This is your station. It's the only daily Islamic station in the country. It
can't stay on the air without your support. If you can't afford it alone,
team up with others to make the donation. I'm looking for a show of hands."

As I glance around the room, I see no hands, only blank stares. Many
guests in the room, well-dressed doctors, lawyers, and professors, can afford to donate ten thousand dollars. I have seen them at so many other
fundraisers for Islamic causes, and they have surely made generous contributions in the past.

"Okay," says Abdul Malik. "Five thousand dollars. Who is going to give
five thousand dollars to your favorite radio station?"

Still, no hands. Janaan is sitting next to me and becoming more frustrated with each passing minute. Between helping to organize the event
and arranging the presentation, she is exhausted. "I knew this would happen," she mumbles under her breath.

The inertia and indecision within the Islamic community often frus-
trate Janaan. Of the hundreds of Muslims I have met across the country,

few match her energy and assertiveness, which serve her well as she attends law school at night and raises three children by day with her husband, Raid. Janaan feels that some Muslims have a tendency to let life happen to them, as if every event were predetermined and human intervention couldn't make a bit of difference. This tendency is rooted in the Islamic world, where the rhythm of life is much slower than in the United States. It is so common that they laugh about it among themselves.

Azhar Usman, a Muslim comedian who has become internationally known for his stories about Muslim life and Western reactions to it, tells a joke during his acts around the world that sums up the Muslim tempo. "When the Oklahoma City bombing happened, the first reporter on the scene said, 'This bombing has Middle Eastern characteristics written all over it.' What does that mean?" asks Usman, who with his intimidating long black beard and husky frame bears a strong resemblance to an overweight Osama bin Laden. "That the bombers were supposed to show up at three o'clock and came at six?" The punch line refers to the Arab penchant for arriving everywhere hours late; in my own Maronite household we called this Lebanese Standard Time.

On this night, however, it is more than passivity that prevents the Muslims from rising in their chairs to Abdul Malik's call. They can't make the cultural leap of faith from funding their local mosques or religious schools to keeping their local radio station on the air. On the surface, the idea is simple enough; here is a rare chance to control both the medium and the message. Muslims for once can choose for themselves how to portray their community to one another and to their non-Muslim friends and neighbors.

As I sit at the dinner, I recall an encounter I once had with a wealthy Iranian woman during my time in Tehran. Her father had bequeathed a large sum to a rural religious school for orphans, and the local cleric told her at the dedication ceremony that the children would pray for her every day of her life in return for her father's gift. Such an exchange is a normal part of life for many affluent Muslims, but where is the heavenly reward for keeping Radio Islam on the air? The doctors, lawyers, accountants, and other professionals around me understand that the media, any media, is a force of nature. But, for them, it is something with which they have almost no experience and little access. They are beginning to adjust but it will take time. Abdul Malik's grand idea is indeed ahead of its day. More than a year later, in January 2006, Radio Islam has raised more than $170,000.

Making Their Voices Heard

To understand why Muslim Americans need their own media, take a look inside the newsroom of nearly any American newspaper. The Islamic community's relationship with the *Chicago Tribune*, by far the largest newspaper in the Midwest, is a good example of the difficulties they face in trying to correct misguided and inaccurate stories written about them. Of course, it is important not to over-generalize the media's portrayal of Islam. Television news is far more biased than print media. But I offer the *Tribune* as a good example of how attitudes about Muslims and Islam are institutionalized within some media circles.

In the spring of 2004, some of the people who attended the Radio Islam fundraiser paid a visit to the *Chicago Tribune*. A group of about twenty, including a doctor, a schoolteacher, and the president of the board at the Bridgeview mosque, came to complain about an article the newspaper published concerning the mosque. The *Tribune* had unleashed a team of ambitious, hungry reporters on the mosque, having decided after September 11 to launch a series of articles they called "The Struggle for the Soul of Islam."

When I joined the *Tribune* as the religion writer in August 2003, reporting and research for the series had been underway for nearly two years. At first, the editors asked me to serve as something of a consultant to make sure the terminology and contemporary Islamic history in the series were correct. I quickly realized that the reporters and editors had neglected to educate themselves about Islam. The project had been underway for many months, yet the editors and reporters were still trying to figure out basic information, such as the difference between Sunni and Shi'ite Muslims, or the bare-bones history of the Muslim Brotherhood in Egypt, the single most important Islamic movement of the twentieth century.

The stated purpose of this series was to educate readers about Islam around the world. But, behind closed doors, it was clear there was another motivation: to write primarily about the extremists, the militants misrepresenting the tenets of the religion and giving Islam a bad name. The *Tribune* editors and reporters on this particular project were not interested in enlightening readers about how the majority of Muslims practiced their faith. They wanted only to make sensational headlines by writing about the fringe. One reporter on the team, in fact, was an ambitious Muslim who despised those Muslims she perceived to be too conservative. The Muslims she interviewed later told me countless stories of how she deceived them to gain entrance to their homes and mosques. Their first impulse was to trust her; she wears a headscarf and they thought a Muslim reporter would accurately represent their lives and views. But, for this reporter, the series of articles on Islam allowed her two interests to converge. Through her work on the story, she would please the paper's top editors, and, as part of her personal crusade, she could condemn Muslim traditionalists. From the paper's point of view, her presence on the team served an important purpose; she gave the newspaper cover. Surely, a Muslim involved in the project would give the stories credibility, no matter what was written. After September 11, in fact, the *Tribune* displayed posters of her around Chicago, a marketing gimmick designed to convince readers of the paper's authority on the subject.

The *Tribune*'s zeal was also motivated by hopes the series would garner a big prize for the paper, which labors under an abiding sense of inferiority before more decorated newspapers, such as the *Los Angeles Times* and the *New York Times*. A careful, thoughtful explication of Islam worldwide, with all its nuances, or so went the thinking in the executive suites, would not bring the *Tribune* any glory. Instead, it had to uncover a story that would reaffirm readers' impressions of the faith after September 11. An exposé on homegrown Muslim extremists in the American heartland would definitely fit the bill.

The reporters' original aim in writing about the Bridgeview mosque was to show how Muslim moderates had been chased out of the community, after Islamic extremists took over the mosque. The paper also hoped to prove that these extremists used donations worshippers gave the mosque to help Hamas, the Islamic Resistance Movement, carry out militant attacks against Israel. But, after two years, they still hadn't discovered the incriminating evidence they were convinced they would find. Instead, they published a story about radicals' takeover of the mosque and merely implied that these radicals raised money for terrorist organizations. "Hardliners Won Battle for Bridgeview Mosque," read the headline on Sunday's front-page.

When the article hit the newsstands in February 2004, the Islamic community in Chicago was dismayed, and angry. They disagreed with the article's premise that radical Muslims had succeeded in their hostile takeover of the mosque. The *Tribune* claimed they were radical Muslims because the women wore headscarves and the imam preached against the policies of the U.S. government and Israel. The story asserted,

Among the leaders at the Bridgeview mosque are men who have condemned
Western culture, praised Palestinian suicide bombers and encouraged members to view society in stark terms: Muslims against the world. Federal authorities for years have investigated some mosque officials for possible links to
terrorism financing, but no criminal charges have been filed.

This paragraph, appearing at the beginning of the long piece, begged
an obvious question. If the U.S. government had probed the lives of mosque
leaders for years and come up dry, what right did the *Tribune* have to try
to convince its readers that the mosque is a breeding ground for radicalism? In August 2004, months after the article was published, the U.S. government did charge Muhammad Salah, a man who worshipped at the
Bridgeview mosque, with laundering and disbursing more than one million dollars to support Hamas. But no one within the mosque leadership
was named in the case.

The *Tribune* story also angered the community for another of its assumptions, one that is common in the American media and public opinion. The *Tribune* suggested that the Muslims fell into two categories. "Bad"
Muslims are practicing Muslims; they attend prayers on Fridays; the women
wear headscarves and their role in the family is different from that of women
in Western secular societies. "Good" Muslims are the so-called secular
Muslims. They live like most Americans. "Many women believe that not
even three hairs should show beneath a headscarf," wrote the *Tribune*,
attempting to demonstrate the radical takeover of the mosque. "Men and
women are often separated at weddings." The *Tribune* failed to tell its
readers that a headscarf covering a woman's hair is the preferred form of
dress among many Muslims around the world, and at weddings from Cairo
to Amman and Karachi women and men are separated.

Unfamiliar with the workings of the media, the Muslim community in
Bridgeview and greater Chicago did not know how to respond. If they
wrote letters to the public editor, how could one letter of a few paragraphs
possibly counter the thousands of words that began on the front-page and
continued inside the paper? But they knew they had to do something.
They feared that the mosque community, like many in America, would
come under attack again. The day after September 11, a pro-American
demonstration in a neighboring district suddenly turned on the Bridgeview
mosque, and the police were called to keep protestors away. So, the mosque
leaders did what they had never done in the past. They demanded a meeting with the *Tribune*'s top editors, hoping a retraction would be published
once they made their case.

The editors agreed to the meeting and asked other reporters to attend. I never understood why I was invited to the meeting. Perhaps the editors wanted the Muslims to see the familiar face of at least one journalist with whom they had a positive relationship.

The day the meeting was held, the editors escorted the Muslim leaders into a conference room, where they sat on one side of the large circular wooden table. After pleasantries were exchanged, a young female teacher wearing a headscarf tried to explain that all practicing Muslim women, not only radicals, wear headscarves. While this might seem like an extreme practice in the United States, veiling is part of Islamic tradition and Muslim women all over the world cover their hair to maintain modest dress, she told them. "This doesn't mean a Muslim woman is radical," she said. She went on to explain that many Muslims across the world consider veiling a duty in Islam.

One editor, who had directed the series, was visibly hostile, as was the Muslim woman who helped report the story. At times they sneered at their critics. Another editor played the diplomat. He tried to make the Muslims feel their comments were being heard. But his disingenuous tone and the snickering faces of the other editors annoyed the head of the Bridgeview mosque.

"This story was biased and the idea was preconceived from the start," he blurted out, shattering the false harmony of the moment.

When the meeting ended, after about two hours, I wanted to assess the editors' reactions. I approached the editor who played the diplomat, not revealing my opinion about the discussion.

"So, what did you think?"

"These Muslims. They came to complain but they can't even agree among themselves what there is to complain about," he remarked, chuckling to himself before disappearing into his glass-walled office.

The editors seemed pleased with themselves. They had pacified the Muslims, who were fortunate to have been granted two hours with important editors from a large newspaper. What other newspaper would have given them such an audience, they thought? There would be no retractions, no corrections, and the Islam series would continue to run in occasional Sunday installments throughout the year. The paper continued to reject complaints sent in regarding the series, even after a group of renowned scholars of Islamic studies noted a number of historical misrepresentations.

Bridgeview's Islamic leaders asked the public editor, Don Wycliff, for permission to refute the story on the editorial pages reserved for readers' comments. Wycliff, an African American and former *New York Times* reporter, was the conscience of the *Tribune*. More sophisticated, educated, and open-minded than any other editor at the *Tribune*, he was displeased with the way the paper covered Islamic issues. On one occasion, when I had a particularly heated battle with my editors over a story about the Islamic community, I turned to Wycliff for advice. He spoke cautiously. As the public editor, the newspaper's liaison with its readers, he had no power to control directly the fate of each story. And, like most public editors, he had to phrase his comments carefully when he offered feedback to readers about the stories the newspaper published. Even if he did not agree with editorial decisions made near his office, Wycliff could not risk the wrath of the *Tribune's* management by raising formal objections about the Islam series or the paper's day-to-day coverage of Islamic issues.

Wycliff did publish one letter sent in for his consideration. Mohammed Sahloul a physician in the Bridgeview community and a member of the mosque governing board, had attended the meeting with the *Tribune* editors. Sahloul wrote:

> In the article titled "Hard-liners Won Battle for Bridgeview Mosque," the writers followed the same lines of misinformed accusations against the Mosque Foundation and the Muslim community in the southwest Chicago area. These accusations reinforce the stereotyping against Muslims, label any immigrant American-Muslim who sends donations to his or her family in the land of origin as "terrorist," or "aiding" the terrorists, and brand this community of American-Muslims as practicing a "strict version of Islam."
>
> Your article represents another media effort to link the Mosque Foundation, its leaders, its imam, its worshipers and the whole Muslim community in the U.S. to extremism and terrorism. . . . It strikes me as another step to discredit all Muslim institutions including houses of worship, schools, charitable organizations, financial institutions, political and social organizations, and to discredit prominent Muslim leaders and activists. It casts doubt on even the most basic activities of American Muslims, like holding prayer in proper Islamic way and abiding by the Islamic rules of modesty and Islamic attire. . . .
>
> We collect funds for worthy causes because this is an essential part of our religion and all religions. For example, we collected funds for Iranian earthquake victims, Turkish earthquake victims . . .
>
> My three children are scared to go to their schools and to the mosque because of your article. The sense of hopelessness and disappointment has intensified in this targeted community of peace-loving Muslims to a level I have never seen since the terrorist action of Sept. 11, 2001.

Sahloul had said it all. His sentiments echoed the feelings of many Muslims in Bridgeview, and those living across the United States. Shortly after the letter was published, I visited him in his office in Bridgeview, about a forty-five-minute drive from downtown Chicago. I did not go there to interview him; I simply wanted to understand what he and the others were experiencing. Sahloul, a Syrian from Damascus, is a soft-spoken, intelligent man. His weightless voice belies his determination to fight for his rights as an American. We talked about what could be done. I felt as hopeless as he did; individual reporters and editors at the *Tribune* were on a mission, and the only thing I could do as the religion writer was to publish stories to counter their distorted ones. Perhaps more thoughtful readers might come to realize there was a different vision of Islam than the one the newspaper was promoting in its series, "The Struggle for the Soul of Islam."

A few months later, Sahloul invited me to give a talk on a Saturday night before a packed audience at Bridgeview. I explained to the large Muslim crowd how the media operates in the United States and what steps they might take to get their point across. After the town meeting ended, near midnight, I realized that for the Bridgeview Muslims, mostly Arabs who have lived for many years in the United States, the media was as foreign as the streets of Damascus are to most Americans. They had few ideas about how to make their voices heard.

Long after I left the newspaper, I asked Wycliff what he thought in retrospect. He was more candid than I expected. "I think one of the things we write about worst in newspapers, and this newspaper is no different, is religion. We write about Islam worse than we write about other religions. The ignorance shows."

He also acknowledged that the *Tribune*'s coverage of the Palestinian-Israeli conflict is unfair, an obvious point to regular, objective readers. He recalled a trip he had taken to the Bridgeview mosque, where one Muslim worshipper talked about the paper's slanted coverage. "I think most American newspapers don't portray the situation fairly. Very seldom do you get the story in the Middle East from the Palestinian or Arab viewpoint," Wycliff said.

"I went with a group to the mosque in Bridgeview and one person said emotionally, 'You have been writing about the Israeli withdrawal from Gaza and it is always a painful step by Israeli government and you never talk about the pain for a Palestinian having his house destroyed.' He's right."

Two months after our conversation, Wycliff resigned from the *Tribune*. But before his resignation was made public, he wrote a column, which in my mind reflected the opinions he held all along. His column raised questions about the U.S. government's case against Muhammad Salah, the man who worshipped at the Bridgeview mosque. "What troubled me about the Salah case from the beginning was the secrecy of it all," Wycliff wrote in a column published on February 2, 2006.

> He and a couple of colleagues were arrested by Israeli military authorities during a trip to the occupied territories back in 1993. They were held incommunicado from the beginning, and the U.S. government seemed strangely lackadaisical about the whole business. In January 1995, after secret detention, secret interrogation (except, oddly, for a special command performance before the ubiquitous Judith Miller of the *New York Times*) and a non-public, military trial, Salah was found guilty of, as the *Tribune's* story at the time put it, "being a Hamas member and distributing hundreds of thousands of dollars within the organization."
>
> Only six years later, in August 2004, did the government get around to indicting Salah and two other men on the conspiracy charges for which they now await trial. So what does any of this have to do with journalism, and in particular, the *Tribune's* journalism?
>
> The premise of the court case against Salah is that aiding Hamas is illegal. The premise of the laws and decrees that make Hamas illegal is that it is bad. Sixty percent of the Palestinian voters in last week's election voted for Hamas. Is it possible that they see something in Hamas that American policymakers do not?
>
> Part of the reason we felt blindsided by Hamas' victory is that we don't see or hear things from the Palestinian perspective very often.
>
> On Sunday, for example, the *Tribune's* Commentary page carried two articles on Hamas' victory. One was by "an American-Israeli peace activist" from Oak Park, the other by the executive director of the publication of the Jewish United Fund/Jewish Federation of Metropolitan Chicago.

At the end of the column, Wycliff wrote: "I'm not sure what this has to do with Muhammad Salah and my conscience. Maybe what I feel is the anxiety that comes from knowing that, in this case anyway, ignorance isn't bliss."

There is a lesson, repeated over and over, that Muslims are learning from their interaction with mainstream America. As long as others interpret their lives and their faith, Islam will be judged strictly from a Western perspective. No matter how limited the audience and how meager the means, Muslims have come to know that their voices must be heard if there is any hope for them to be accepted into American society. Often, a single episode that is hard to ignore compels them to voice their views. Such was the case for Suleiman Khan, a young law student who, in 2004, launched the literary journal *Muslim Stories*.

For most of his childhood, Suleiman was glad his father's work had brought the family from Doncaster, England, to Boston. The move took place when Suleiman was almost seven years old and about to enter the first grade. It had meant leaving behind most of the relatives on his father's side of the family, all of whom had come to England from Pakistan. As soon as the family arrived in Boston, Suleiman felt America was more tolerant of Muslims than Britain had been. When he left class to pray, bringing his prayer rug, students looked at him with great interest, not bigoted anger.

His father was offered a new job, and in July 1998 the family moved to Chicago and then later to one of the city's most affluent suburbs, Lake Forest. When he started attending Lake Forest College in the fall of 2000, Suleiman came to believe that his identity as a Muslim was important to his success. As president of several campus organizations, ranging from the Muslim Students' Association to the prelaw society, he was widely respected by his peers. He took pride in coming to college dressed in his *kufi*, skullcap, and *shalwar kameez*, the leggings and long tunic that constitute Pakistani traditional dress.

Religion professors invited him to speak to their classes about Islam. And after September 11, Suleiman was often called upon to explain Islam not only to students in universities but at local high schools. As he spoke to large audiences after the attacks, he knew that life for Muslims in America was changing. The curiosity Americans once had about his faith had turned to suspicion. The change became clear when a teacher at one high school invited him to speak to four hundred students about Islam. After Suleiman's lecture, a question from an audience member deeply troubled him. An elderly woman, whom he learned was also a teacher at the school, raised her hand and asked the question, "Do Muslim women really pray?"

To the crowd, it seemed like an innocent question. But Suleiman was appalled. Did Americans think Muslim women are so oppressed that they don't leave the house, even to pray in the mosque? America, he thought, was far more ignorant of Islamic practice than he had ever imagined.

Suleiman decided he must do something to enlighten mainstream society. He wrote poetry as a hobby and he and a few friends thought that publishing a literary journal of poetry and essays expressing Muslim views about living in America would be one way to spread the word. The literary journal would not employ the blunt language of Islamic hip-hop. Its message would be subtle and evocative. The writings would be introspective and aimed at intellectual readers. Over the course of about a year, Suleiman created a Web site and posted a notice that he was accepting submissions. At first he received only a few essays and poems, many of them anonymous. Muslims weren't comfortable pouring their hearts out in public. But, by the end of 2005, he had a few hundred writing samples. One, called "Solace," was written by Abdur-Rahman Syed.

> When your scalding tears can't put out
> The ten thousand fires raging round,
> When your rubber thighs can't place
> Foot in front of foot on the ground,
> When you feel your insides fall away
> And just can't smile to play the part,
> When a warm shoulder turns cold
> And a horrid silence grips your heart,
> Look back to why you chose this path,
> Find those who see what you've seen—
> And while you wait with a wet gaze
> For the day we meet upon the green,
> Turn to the one behind the blink
> Of an eye, closer than you think.

I asked Suleiman in 2005 to send me a few writing samples to help me gain insight into the feelings of young, literary Muslims. Of all the pieces Suleiman sent me, I thought this one best expressed their frustrations. In the old world of just twenty years ago, Muslim immigrants from the Islamic world were able to remain unnoticed by playing the part of an assimilated American. But, now, their children would never be invisible in America. Now, they were forced to play *their* part. In creating a Muslim voice, whether through music, the media, or poetry, they are sorting out what they want to be, and hoping America will learn along with them.

SIX

Women in the Changing Mosque

જ

Ingrid Mattson sits gracefully on a hard white plastic chair, her hair covered in a flowing black scarf, her plaid skirt touching the tops of her ankles. Her large eyes, round face, and white skin give her features a classical appeal. Ingrid's modest demeanor belies her fierce intelligence; she has spent years in libraries, writing a dissertation, even a book. She will need all this brainpower not just to impress, but to galvanize her audience. She is lecturing a group of imams from different mosques across America. These men have volunteered to spend a day learning how to show respect for women in the mosque.

Ingrid scans the room. If she feels hesitant about what she is about to do, she doesn't show it.

"I want all the men to take their chairs and move down the hall. You won't be there for long," she says softly, and convincingly. An assistant appears in the doorway to help. The men have no idea what's in store, but they show no inkling of protest; they sheepishly move the portable chairs and disappear.

A few female imams remain in the room with Ingrid, as if nothing has happened. She asks them: "What kind of contribution do you make to the *masjid* [the mosque] in your community?"

The women reply with enthusiasm, relieved the men are no longer there. Then a faint male voice is heard from afar, "We can't hear you!"

Ingrid is silent and the chatting stops. A few minutes pass.

"Okay, you can come back into the room now," she says, ending their exile.

As they reenter the classroom, a bit confused, one imam blurts out, "What happened?"

It is a rhetorical question. Everyone understands the point of Ingrid's exercise. There's no need for an explanation, so she states the obvious: "Sometimes you can't understand someone's situation until you live it yourself."

The scene is all too familiar, only Ingrid has cleverly reversed the sex roles. For years, Muslim American women have complained about being secluded in a separate room, if not the basement, of a mosque during prayer time. Women in a mosque, at times, neither hear the imam's sermon directly nor see him. Often, they strain to make out his words coming through an old, scratchy speaker system. No matter where the mosque is located or whether it is old or new, it seems the quality of the speaker system is the same. It is as if someone planted old electronic equipment in all the mosques in America as part of a conspiracy to make it difficult for women to hear the imam. And even in those mosques where the speaker system works well, the children's chatter rises above all other voices. Children are usually the women's responsibility; an infant's cry is almost never heard in the men's prayer room.

Ingrid knows she is on slippery ground. Where a woman sits in a mosque is a sensitive subject. For some women, securing the seat of their choice is no small triumph; it defines their place in Islam. But, for many men, a woman in the same prayer hall is the end of society. This is why the whole issue has become so controversial, as Muslims sort out how to practice their faith in America. Women in American mosques are generally required to pray either at the back of the prayer hall behind men or on a second-floor balcony, where they can see and hear the imam. In conservative mosques, they pray in a separate room. In Islamic tradition, women are advised to pray in the back of the mosque so that when they prostrate themselves, their knees on the floor with their backs pointed upward, they will be out of the male line of vision. Islamic law says only men, not women, are obligated to pray in the mosque on Fridays, and nowhere in the holy texts does it say that women should pray in a separate room.

When I toured mosques across the country, some imams were eager to show me the space where women prayed, if it was in the main hall. They considered it a litmus test of the mosque's degree of modernity. They

Ingrid Mattson. (*Photograph by Dr. Abdalla M. Al. Courtesy of Islamic Horizons magazine*)

thought that, as a non-Muslim and a woman, I would surely conclude that if women prayed behind the men—not in a basement or a separate room—it must mean their worshippers were living a progressive life in America. When other, more conservative imams escorted me to separate prayer rooms for women, they made a point of noting the comforts there. Maybe the carpet was a bright color or there were large windows letting in the sunlight. With each visit, I tried to figure out how the separation got started. No one seemed to know for certain, but it appears there has never been a national consensus about where women should pray. Like most practices among Muslim Americans, it has evolved over time.

Many mosque leaders think the segregation of the sexes in American mosques dates back to the 1980s, when large numbers of immigrants began to arrive from Muslim countries. Before that time, most mosques enforced no such separation. But immigrants from South Asia brought their ideas and traditions with them. Some were influenced by the Islamic ideologue Mawlana Mawdudi, who established the Jamaat-i-Islami party, first in India and later in Pakistan. In his prolific writings, Mawdudi criticized the West, but his primary aim was to present an uncompromising worldview that would mobilize Muslims into forming a unified community. The strict separation of men and women in mosques was but a small detail in Mawdudi's vision for a worldwide *ummah*. When immigrants from the subcontinent arrived in the United States, they brought Mawdudi's views with them, including their experience of women either praying at home instead of the mosque, or being separated from men in prayer. At the same time, imams affiliated with American mosques were returning from religious studies in Saudi Arabia, and the conservative Saudi government was sending charismatic personalities to U.S. college campuses to organize Muslim Students' Associations. In Saudi Arabia in the 1980s as today, a rigid interpretation of Islam prevailed, particularly in religious schools; this interpretation included separating women from men in the mosque as well as in public. The Saudi students who became involved in the MSAs held strong views and were able to intimidate other Muslims, some of whom fled the MSAs, leaving the organizations vulnerable to Saudi influence.

In American mosques today, the form of separation depends upon the ethnic makeup of the worshippers and whether they have imported the traditions from their homeland to the United States. In many American mosques dominated by Muslims from India and Pakistan, women are either required to pray in a separate room or in a space in the main prayer room segregated by a curtain or other type of barrier. In India and Pakistan, it is rare for women to pray in a mosque. In some Turkish mosques, a barrier made of thick straw separates the men from the women. It allows the women to see out but prevents the men from seeing inside the women's section. By contrast, in most of the Arab world, for example in Egypt, women simply pray behind the men.

Some women, including Ingrid, believe in separation, as long as the conditions allow women to participate fully in the imam's sermons. Such women consider themselves Islamic feminists and view the place where women pray in the mosque as part of their struggle to gain more rights. They belong to a global movement of women in the West and East who believe the Koran and the Sunnah call for the equality of all human beings while recognizing the differences between men and women. These Islamic feminists are working to recapture the gender equality explicit in the Koran that has been lost over the ages as Islamic societies became increasingly patriarchal. This feminist movement emerged a decade and a half ago in parts of Africa and Asia, as well as in North America. In South

Africa, women who had participated in the postapartheid restructuring of their society fought for gender equality as part of their struggle for social justice, according to Margot Badran, a scholar specializing in Islamic feminism. South African Muslims were conscious of public space—having been denied access to such space in the apartheid era—and the women's struggle for rights inspired Muslim women to demand equal space in the mosque, according to Badran. This is where the mosque movement began.

The mosque struggle in America has intensified during the last few years for somewhat different reasons. For many decades, the mosque was considered simply as a place of worship. But as Muslim Americans became more interested in their Islamic identity, the mosque expanded literally and figuratively. Half of the several thousands of mosques now existing in the United States were founded after 1980, according to *The Mosque in America*, a 2001 study conducted by the Council on American-Islamic Relations. The increase after 1980 reflects the influx of immigrants and a renewed interest in practicing the faith. Rooms have been added for social activities. It is common in most mosques for worshippers to share meals together, especially during the holy month of Ramadan when the day-long fast is broken each evening at sunset. Young Muslims organize all sorts of activities on the mosque grounds, from basketball games to youth counseling.

The fight for women's rights is perhaps more fierce in America than in the Muslim world because when Muslim American women participate in activities at the mosque they expect to be treated in the same way they are at their jobs and schools. But, when they enter the mosque community, these rights are redefined by the Muslim men who generally control mosque life. This is not to say that all imams and mosque leaders are insensitive to women's concerns. But, in many mosques, women feel restrictions are placed upon them in the name of religion. There is little they can do to defend themselves because they lack the religious education that would make them authorities on Islamic law.

Later in the day, Ingrid Mattson tells the men a story that she hopes will inspire a change of heart. She was invited to speak at a conservative mosque in New Jersey, where the women are required to pray in a dark basement. "I assumed I would have to give the lecture in the women's section. But when I arrived, the imam announced on the loudspeaker, 'I'd like all the sisters to go upstairs and the men downstairs,'" Ingrid tells the imams.

"And the men said, 'It's so dark. We can't hear anything.'

"It was interesting. When you are in an environment and the light is coming in, it lifts your spirit. But that's not the feeling you get when you are in the basement."

The imams appear convinced. There will not be any more women praying in the basement, at least not in the basements of *their* mosques.

Ingrid is one of the few Muslim women with enough power to persuade a few imams that, no matter where women pray in the mosque, they should be able to hear and see the imam. As a professor of Islamic studies at Hartford Seminary in Connecticut and vice president of the largest Muslim American organization, the Islamic Society of North America, she navigates many worlds at once. Her blend of scholarly knowledge and real-life experience has made her an important voice for women as well as men.

She appeals to second-generation Muslim women with her idealized vision of Islam. As a young fine arts and philosophy student living in Paris in the summer of 1986, Ingrid met the first Muslims she ever knew; they were living in dilapidated apartments on the outskirts of the city. She calls this period "the summer I met Muslims." Their generosity toward one another as well as strangers made a big impression. Even now, she writes and talks about their well-mannered behavior, which reflects the Prophet's teachings.

She returned to Waterloo, Canada, where she was studying, and worked for about four months planting trees in northern Ontario and British Columbia, living in a tent and working from dawn to sunset. At the time, she knew she was drawing closer to Islam; when she went to bed each night under the northern lights, listening to the sounds of the wild, she played recitations of the Koran on a cassette player. Islam was slowly becoming the perfect answer to the soul searching that had begun for her as a young child growing up Catholic in Canada. The nuns in her school had taught her about social justice and women's rights to become leaders in their spiritual lives, but Catholicism never captured her heart. She left the church, and in college she became interested in art as a way to fulfill her spiritual needs. But the act of art appreciation felt like a solitary experience.

By the end of that year, Ingrid had converted to Islam. She applied to graduate school but felt she needed a break from her studies, and decided to find a way to do relief work. Her new religion, as well as her interest in the developing world, led her to a refugee camp in Peshawar, Pakistan, near the border with Afghanistan, during that country's occupation by the Soviet Union.

As the flood of Afghan refugees poured across the border, Ingrid experienced the dynamics of a patriarchal Muslim society, but also Muslim etiquette toward outsiders. She married a fellow refugee worker, Amer Aatek, an Egyptian engineer, and left the dusty camp for a few days. When she returned, the refugees wanted to know all the intimate details of her marriage ceremony. They were quickly disappointed. Ingrid showed them her modest gold ring and the simple dress she had borrowed for the wedding. The women refugees had been driven from their homes; they had sold their possessions to buy food; and they had lost their husbands in the Afghan war. But when they heard Ingrid's story, they were aghast. They brought her a wedding outfit—bright blue satin pants stitched with gold embroidery, a red velveteen dress decorated with colorful pompoms, and a matching blue scarf trimmed with shiny fabric.

Ingrid's compelling personal history and her conversion to Islam have given her an elevated status among Muslim Americans. Acceptance of converts within the Muslim community varies. Generally, the reaction is one of either skepticism of converts who know little about the faith or admiration of those who are well versed in Arabic and Islamic history. Ingrid earned her reputation through her work as a scholar and activist. When she tells imams that the Koran does not say women should pray in a dark basement, they listen. When she tells women not to listen to their husbands if they forbid them from going to the mosque for prayers, they follow her advice. And even in the non-Muslim world, which is often skeptical of a Muslim woman wearing *hijab*, Ingrid has influence. She gives the lie to the conventional wisdom that a woman wears a headscarf and loose-fitting skirt only if she suffers under the weight of male oppression.

Ingrid's best tool in her struggle to rebuild women's rights is her knowledge of Islamic history and her ability to cite early interpretations of Islamic law. The fight for women's rights from inside the Islamic tradition makes Ingrid and many other devout women part of a new movement. For them, women's rights were established in early Islam, but then taken away over the years. In the Prophet's mosque, women could see him and hear him speak. Aisha, the Prophet's wife, recorded many of her husband's sayings to create a vital historical and theological record. She also argued that women should be allowed to travel alone, as long as they avoid *fitna*, temptation that leads to chaos in society. These journeys should be allowed no matter the reason, not just to make the pilgrimage to Mecca, the only time traveling alone was allowed in her day. Many jurists disagreed with Aisha, and even now in some countries women are not allowed to travel without their husbands' permission. In Iran, men are the guardians of women's passports.

One Koranic verse Ingrid often cities is:

> For Muslim men and Muslim women, for believing men and believing women, for devout men and devout women, for true men and true women, for men and women who are patient and constant, for men and women who humble themselves, for men and women who give in charity, for men and women who fast (and deny themselves), for men and women who guard their chastity, and for men and women who engage much in Allah's praise, for them has Allah prepared forgiveness and great reward.

Other scholars point to another Koranic verse they believe shows that in Islam men and women are considered equal: "I shall never cause the deeds of any of you to be lost, male or female, you are of each other."

Ingrid and those who share her views, however, are at odds with a minority of Muslims who consider themselves "progressive." (It is virtually impossible to determine their numbers, but most Muslim leaders believe they are only a small minority.) While Ingrid refers to Islamic history and the holy texts to support her position, "progressive" Muslims say the holy texts should be adapted to modern times, and Muslims should not be wedded to literal interpretations of the Prophet's teachings. Not only should women pray in the same space as men, they argue, but women should lead the prayers just as men do.

A standoff between these two sides erupted in New York City in the spring of 2005 when Amina Wadud, a professor of Islamic studies, led Friday prayers before a mixed congregation. The incident provoked condemnation from Islamic jurists, scholars, and Muslim believers around the world. It was a rare moment when international Islamic scholars became directly involved with the Muslim American community. Sheikh Yussef al-Qaradawi, a respected scholar now living in Qatar, denounced Wadud's actions. He issued a fatwa, a religious decree, explaining his opinions. All four schools of Islamic jurisprudence, he said, are unanimous: Women do not lead men in performing religious duties. Women may lead prayers only before other women. "One wishes our sisters who are enthusiastic about women's rights would revive the practice of women leading women in prayers, instead of coming up with the heresy of women leading men in prayers," he wrote in his fatwa.

Many Muslims expressed outrage on Islamic Web sites. "We need not judge Amina Wadud only by what she is doing this Friday," wrote one writer on the site of Al-Jazeera, the Arabic-language cable television network.

We need to judge her by the pending issues on the agenda of her sponsors and supporters. To us, they have crossed all limits. To them, they have just taken the first step towards transforming Islam into a "progressive" and "moderate" form according to the wishes of the enemies of Islam. . . . Embracing Islam means Muslims have to submit themselves to the will of Allah, obey the Koran and follow the Sunnah. In this perspective, there is absolutely nothing in the Koran or the life of the Prophet Muhammad which can change the invalidity and impermissibility of women leading men in prayers, regardless of the wisdom behind it.

The progressive Muslims want their audience to believe that millions of Muslim women want to be emancipated and that believing in the totality of the Koran is something that makes Muslims "Islamists," "extremists," "radical," and ultimately terrorists.

The writer clearly identified one of the great challenges in creating a Muslim American identity: should Muslims interpret the holy texts in a non-Muslim society the way they would in the Islamic world? It was pretty clear Amina Wadud would never have tested the limits of Islamic tradition had she been living in Cairo or Lahore, Pakistan. Even in America, it is unlikely that an immigrant Muslim would have led the prayer. But Wadud is African American, and her ideas and approach as an Islamic feminist stem from her experience as an activist in the civil rights movement. Many within the broader Islamic community were unhappy with Wadud, in part, because of her approach. Louay Safi, a senior official at the Islamic Society of North America, summarized this sentiment in an article.

Several feminist Muslims, supported by a network of progressive activists, have been pushing the pendulum to the other extreme. . . . It is unfortunate that Muslim feminists are following in the footsteps of other secularist precursors, breaking all traditions, and engaging in experimentations that break with formative principles and values.

When I discussed the Wadud incident with several Muslim women, they were puzzled as to why she had created such a public spectacle. I realized there was a subtle reason they felt offended. Her brazen action was similar to the way a Western feminist might approach the problem. As an African American influenced by the civil rights movement, Wadud had used the tactics of an activist. The Muslim way of debating issues in public is far less confrontational. When Wadud led the prayer in New York, her action had the same spirit as the sit-ins for African American rights that took place in the 1960s. No matter how much disagreement there might be within the Muslim American community, it is considered taboo for Muslims to play out these differences in public.

Questions of concern to Muslim women such as Ingrid Mattson, as well as to the others, the self-declared progressives, come down to determining what it is to be a Muslim in the modern world: How should a Muslim interpret the Islamic sources in contemporary life? Should a Muslim distinguish the universal principles of Islam from cultural practices that are relevant only in a specific time and place? The progressives want to reinterpret Islamic texts based on the conditions of postmodern America. For them, the fact that women did not lead prayers in Islamic history does not mean women should not lead prayers in modern America; common sense should prevail. Women such as Ingrid Mattson, however, use the past rulings of scholars and theologians as their guide: women leading prayer is deemed forbidden in Islam. Ingrid believes that acts of worship are distinct from other areas of Islamic law, a differentiation also made in the *sharia*. She believes that the traditions established long ago regarding worship are sacred and should not be reformed; they have held Muslims together through all the centuries of change. But when it comes to other traditional legal interpretations of the holy texts, Ingrid believes distortions have occurred over time.

Amina Wadud believes that Islam in America should be an alternative to Islam as it has been understood in the past. She places interpretations of women in the Koran in three categories: traditional, reactive, and holistic. She believes her views fall in the last category, and she subscribes to the method of Koranic interpretation proposed by Fazlur Rahman, the twentieth-century reformer who taught at the University of Chicago. He says that all Koranic passages were revealed relative to the context of the time and can be reinterpreted to take into account changed circumstance. Wadud has written that to restrict Koranic interpretation to a single perspective that existed at the time of the Prophet limits its application and contradicts its stated universal purpose. For example, the United States offers Muslims civil liberties and freedoms that are not available in some Islamic countries, and these liberties should be adopted, even if they are alien to the Islamic tradition. Women may be segregated in mosques in the Islamic world, but this practice should not apply in the United States, where the role of women in society is different.

Ingrid Mattson and women like her do not view Islam through such a prism of relativism, and perhaps this is their fundamental difference with the "progressive" minority. Ingrid believes women should assert their rights for greater influence in mosque life and equal rights at home with their husbands. But she makes a distinction between this equality and the rights women were accorded in the Islamic texts.

The Muslim minority who describe themselves as "progressive," however, would ban all forms of separation. An Islamic Web site, Muslim Wakeup, which presents the views of progressive Muslims, condemned Mattson for public comments she made shortly after the Wadud incident. Mattson said simply that most Muslim American women prefer some degree of separation in the mosque. It was surely an accurate statement, one that I heard repeated in countless meetings and interviews I had with Muslim women. But, in a commentary, Muslim Wakeup dismissed her remarks as the "latest disappointing quote by Ingrid Mattson."

A fleeting organization called the Muslim Progressive Union (MPU) had endorsed the Wadud prayer in public and on Islamic Web sites. The leaders of the organization, which included Muslim American scholars and activists, said their purpose in helping to organize the prayer service was not to be provocative, but to initiate a serious discussion in the United States among Muslims wedded to the idea that prayers must be led exclusively by men. Some members of the Progressive Union attempted to refute the very basis of the ban on women leading men in prayer. In the past, jurists determined that a woman should not lead the prayer before a mixed congregation because she lacked the intellect to do so and she could spark sexual thoughts among men and create *fitna*. These conditions no longer apply in modern America, the progressives argued.

The MPU dissolved largely because their members failed to agree on a number of controversial issues. They enjoyed little popular support among Muslim Americans. Yet the group received a flurry of press attention out of all proportion to its numbers and influence within the Muslim community. Television networks and major U.S. newspapers reported on the Wadud prayer service. The progressives also managed to get coverage of some of their other events, including protests at mosques they felt restricted women's rights. They understood how to manipulate the mainstream media's interest in Islam: provide readers with a steady diet of stories that confirm their preconceived ideas of Muslims. The topic of women in Islam was the perfect choice.

The East-West Divide

In North America and Europe, politicians and the media today point to the lot of Muslim women to validate the Western consensus about Islam, namely that it is a backward, oppressive, and violent faith that must adapt itself to the values of the modern Western world. In the immediate aftermath of September 11, the White House successfully exploited Western anxieties and fears by casting its invasion of Afghanistan as a mission with an extra benefit—to free women from the depredations of the ultraconservative Taliban clerics, particularly their forced veiling of women in public. There were countless news reports about the U.S. liberation of Afghan women from their burkas, the traditional all-encompassing silk veil. On November 17, 2001, not long after U.S. and British bombs began falling on Afghan cities, towns, and villages, First Lady Laura Bush took to the airwaves to cast the war as a fight for women's rights. In a rare White House radio address made by a first lady, Laura Bush, not otherwise known for her feminist leanings, declared: "The fight against terrorism is also a fight for the rights and dignity of women." President Bush and other administration dignitaries posed for photo-ops with Afghanistan's new minister of women's affairs, Dr. Massouda Jalal, and the U.S. State Department promoted her as a "founding mother" of the new pro-American Afghan state.

For Afghan women in general, the burka was never their primary grievance against the Taliban; rather, this extremist movement had distorted Islamic doctrine to deprive them of their most basic civic rights. Yet, this was hardly the first time that the *hijab* was deployed to great effect in the West's running cultural war with Islam. George and Laura Bush and their White House handlers were merely following in the footsteps of Lord Cromer, Britain's one-time imperial proconsul in Egypt, who once approvingly quoted the following contemporary assessment of women and Islam: "The degradation of women in the East is a canker that begins its destructive work early in childhood, and has eaten into the whole system of Islam." Perhaps as might be expected, Lord Cromer was himself a vigorous campaigner against women's rights back home in England.

Leila Ahmad, a professor at Harvard and a leading scholar of women and veiling, points out that such Western attitudes toward Muslim women were used not only to justify the political domination of Muslims, but also to provide Christian missionaries with the basis for their general assault on Islamic culture itself. Muslim marriage, the missionaries declared, was "not founded on love but on sensuality." Women were "buried alive behind the veil," reduced to mere property in contrast to the Victorian ideal of wife as companion and partner, albeit of lesser status than her husband. Women, whose role in raising good Muslim children was central to the continuity of religious life, were explicitly targeted for conversion; missionaries encouraged many to throw off their veils in the name of modernity and civilization.

It is telling, Ahmad notes, that the alleged oppression of women under Islam only emerged as the central theme in Western thought in the nineteenth century when supposed concern for Muslim women became the ideological handmaiden to colonial occupation of Muslim lands. This "concern" paved the way for the West's armed civilizing mission to the East, a mission that justified, even demanded, the forced spread of the benefits of European culture. Before the nineteenth century, Western notions of Islam and Islamic life were often vague and based on imperfect understandings of Arabic texts and the often-exaggerated accounts of a few intrepid travelers and diarists. Many impressions still lingered from the West's initial, adversarial contact with Islam during the crusades, almost nine hundred years earlier.

Against this backdrop, it was almost inevitable that battle lines would be drawn over the practices of "modest dress" and women's seclusion. "Veiling—to *Western* eyes, the most visible marker of the differences and inferiority of Islamic societies—became the symbol now of both the oppression of women (or, in the language of the day, Islam's degradation of women) and the backwardness of Islam, and it became the open target of colonial attack and the spearhead of the assault on Muslim societies," wrote Leila Ahmad in her book *Women and Gender in Islam: Historical Roots of a Modern Debate.*

Although I had lived and worked for a number of years in Egypt, where an Islamic awakening, beginning in the 1970s, had inspired a renewed interest in veiling among younger Muslim women, nothing prepared me for the vehemence of the veiling wars I encountered upon moving to Iran in 1998. But I did have a brief foretaste. Before I moved there, I flew to Tehran to cover a meeting of the Organization of Islamic Conference; I slipped into the airplane's bathroom to pull on my new black chador, which I had had tailored for me in Cairo's central bazaar. The long black garment, stretching from head to toe, was cleverly fitted with clasps and hidden sleeves, providing the perfect "modest dress" while still allowing me the freedom to juggle notebooks, my tape recorder, and laptop. The style differed from the typical, sleeveless Iranian chador that keeps a woman's hands busy holding it together.

As I emerged from the lavatory, a pained howl went up from the assembled Western press corps flying in from Cairo. "Take that thing off," taunted one man, a correspondent from a major American newspaper. Journalists often dream of being a fly-on-the-wall at important news events, but apparently any real concession to Muslim sensibilities that would allow them to blend in with their surroundings and make their hosts feel comfortable enough to open their hearts to strangers was a step too far. Implicit in all the stories about women in Iran was this message: the United States should take punitive action against the Islamic Republic of Iran to save its female population.

Undeterred by my colleagues' consensus, I adopted my handmade chador after moving to Iran in the summer of 1998; it not only became a sort of trademark during my three years of reporting from the Islamic Republic, but it also helped open doors into the discreet, hidden world of Iran's most conservative clerics and politicians. To my interlocutors, many of whom had never spoken to a Western woman before, it was a reassuring sign that I was prepared to leave my own world behind and enter theirs.

Such was not the case for the small army of visiting foreign correspondents who regularly breezed into Tehran to observe the phenomenon of President Mohammad Khatami and his bid to introduce the notion of civil society into Iranian political life. No matter the publication and no matter the correspondent, I knew that soon enough the story would turn to the Iranian regime's treatment of women. The chador was always the central image used to illustrate this phenomenon. Few reporters ever stopped to consider that the majority of Iranian women feel comfortable wearing a headscarf; most Iranian women I knew believed they would retain the veil even if the authorities stopped mandating it.

Like much Western reporting of the Muslim world, and the developing world in general, such stories tell the readers far more about the correspondents and their own concerns and culture than they do about the society about which they are writing. This practice of reporting on the status of Iranian women became so common that I started calling it lipstick journalism. Reporters who came to Tehran to take the temperature of the Iranian reform movement would focus on the amount of makeup upper-middle-class women sported and how much hair might be showing beneath their veils. More lipstick, eyeliner, fingernail polish, or visible hair meant more personal liberty and ultimately better prospects for fundamental democratic change.

In earlier times since the 1979 Islamic revolution, such sartorial defiance was often met by arrest, fines, and even beatings at the hands of the so-called morality police, and only the brave or foolhardy would venture out without honoring the strict dress code. In a bit of slapstick comedy, an overzealous police officer once detained me on a reporting trip because the top of my foot was showing through my sandals. Officials of the press department and the foreign ministry soon sprung me, offering profuse apologies. By the late 1990s such incidents were more and more infrequent, at least in Tehran. In fact, the lipstick index was not only silly; it was often downright misleading. At least during my tenure in Iran, from 1998 until early 2001, the loosening of social rules generally accompanied periods when the conservative political and clerical establishment felt most confident. Periodic crackdowns came when the regime felt threatened. As a result, the prevalence of lipstick acted as a contrarian indicator, and it did not, as readers were told in often-breathless terms, indicate a coming Tehran Spring.

Media coverage mirrors the U.S. government's persistent misunderstanding of what Muslim women want. Even now, after the United States has maintained an armed presence in the heart of the Islamic world, old habits die hard. In September 2005, Karen P. Hughes, charged with spreading the American message in the Muslim world, was embarrassed on trips to Turkey and Saudi Arabia after Muslim women told her she didn't understand them. In Saudi Arabia, she expressed hope that women there would one day be allowed to drive cars—the cliché the West often points to when making the argument that Islam oppresses women. The women's response shattered the rhetoric of Hughes's scripted visit; they told her that just because they are not allowed to drive, it did not mean they were unhappy. They also told her that Muslim women do not aspire to live as women do in the United States.

The East-West divide over women's rights in Islam has obscured the fact that these same issues are being debated internally among Muslims across the world. Many Muslim are aware that women suffer discrimination at work and at home, and action is being taken in many countries where Islamic feminists are demanding their rights. In Iran, a reexamination of the *sharia* texts occurred in the 1990s, resulting in changes in the law. Bans on women studying topics such as mining and agriculture and on serving as judges were lifted. Even more important to women, divorce laws were also rewritten. A man's right to repudiate his wife (*talaq*) was curtailed, and a monetary value was placed on women's housework, entitling them to domestic wages.

Ingrid Mattson is the ideal for many Muslim women living in the East or the West. She is a complicated figure, too subtle to be widely understood. Even she struggles to find a category for her ideas. When I was at a loss for a description, fearing I would label her incorrectly, she told me she might call herself "a religious conservative" but a "legal modernist." Either way, she could never be a subject of "lipstick" journalism, nor could she be labeled an oppressed traditionalist. She appears to be a bundle of contradictions: She is a college professor who wears a headscarf. She was able to earn a Ph.D. because her husband, Amer, took responsibility for raising their two children during that time. She is an advocate for women's rights, yet she supports only those rights clearly permitted in the Islamic sources. But Ingrid's profile is becoming more common among Islamic feminists in the United States and Europe, particularly second-generation women. And like her, many Muslim American women are taking action to educate the next generation.

Portrait of a Devout Muslim Girl

Every Sunday, Rabab Gomaa visits a different mosque in a different Chicago suburb. She packs her books, her Koran, and sometimes her two teenage sons into the family's Suburban. Though she often arrives at the mosque late, there is always a crowd of boys and girls waiting for her. They look forward to their Sunday *halaqa* with the nurturing forty-seven-year-old from Egypt who could easily be their mother. With her bright headscarves, nicely tailored overcoats, and impassioned lectures about Islam, she transports the young Muslims to another life for an hour or two.

Rabab began her lectures in the mid-1990s after noticing that some Muslim women who were recent converts at the Bridgeview mosque were becoming disillusioned. They were trying to learn about Islam; many had married Muslims. But each time they came to the mosque, the sermons were in Arabic, the preferred language of the many worshippers at Bridgeview who are from Palestine or the Levant. Rabab began translating for them, and teaching them Koranic verse. The verse she chose was Surat Mariam, which teaches the distinctions between Islam and Christianity. Soon, the women invited her to their homes to give private lessons. So many women attended the lessons that Rabab began holding the sessions in the community rooms of mosques in the area. She felt she had taken on a large responsibility in trying to educate women about Islam.

She had no formal training in Islamic sciences or law; she had earned a degree in architecture from the University of Houston.

With no Islamic school in Chicago, she turned to the teachings of a sheikh she knew in Egypt, where she was born and raised. Sheikh Mohammad Mutawil-Sharawi was perhaps the most popular imam in the country at the time. In the 1990s, he gave religious lectures on Egyptian television on Fridays that were watched by millions because of the simple way he explained Islamic principles. He spoke colloquial Arabic, even though the language of the *ulama*, the religious authority, was classical Arabic. Although he had a large following among the masses, some feminists criticized him for his conservative views.

Rabab Gomaa also turned to the Islamic American University, one of the few Islamic colleges in the United States. The college is located in Southfield, Michigan, far from her home in South Barrington, Illinois. Rabab enrolled in an online program, and began studying for a degree in Islamic law.

When she told me how she prepared herself for the years of teaching that followed, I became curious about this university, one of the few in the United States that trains a Muslim to become an imam. I arranged a trip there to meet Sheikh Abdul Warith, Rabab's teacher and mentor.

As I arrive at the college, I notice immediately that it looks like a modern office building; the outside of the building offers no hint that it houses an Islamic college. As soon as I open the glass doors I meet Azeeza Mohamed, the patient and friendly voice I have come to know over the telephone as I made arrangements to meet Sheikh Warith. Azeeza, a Muslim convert, offers me an orange drink and some dates. At first I decline because it is Ramadan and I feel uncomfortable drinking or eating in the presence of Muslims who are fasting. But she insists, so I drink a bit once she leaves the room to let Sheikh Warith know I have arrived.

When the sheikh enters the room, he is accompanied by his wife, who with her stocky build covered with a long green *jilbab* resembles many women I used to know in Egypt. She and Sheikh Warith are from Cairo and she speaks only Arabic. She sits on a chair and Sheikh Warith joins me at a dining table nearby. He begins by explaining that the college wants to teach Muslims and non-Muslims how to understand the *real* Islam. He emphasizes "real"—not the uninformed Islam many Muslim Americans practice or the radical Islam of the extremists. He criticizes Muslim Americans for not knowing Arabic, the language of the Koran. The imams at the university, he says, were educated at al Azhar but are fluent in English, even though their first language is Arabic. "So why can't Americans learn Arabic?" he asks me. "People don't think of Islam in the right way. They don't think of it as a way of life, which it is. In order to do this, you must know Arabic to read the sources. Americans don't take Islam seriously. They might pay *zakat* [alms], but it is not just about paying *zakat*. It is a holistic way of life."

Then he tests my Arabic by asking me the meaning of a few phrases. My translation is imprecise, and he shows his disappointment, making me feel like an embarrassed schoolgirl.

He excuses himself for a few minutes and walks to an adjoining room to pray. When he returns, he explains the university curriculum. It is very structured, he tells me. There are two programs: one for Islamic studies and the other for Arabic. The courses are geared toward imams; teachers, like Rabab; and *khatibs*, those who give Islamic lectures before Friday prayer. "It is good for imams who will teach Americans to be educated in America," he says. "This way they understand the environment here."

This comment makes me realize that he has come to the United States from Cairo out of a sense of duty to help create a generation of American imams with a classical Islamic education. It is an admirable mission, particularly because it seems obvious he would rather be back home.

When I returned to Chicago, I wanted to attend one of Rabab Gomaa's lectures to see the fruits of Sheikh Warith's labor.

One Sunday during Ramadan, she is lecturing at *masjid* al-Hoda, a modern brick building in an affluent suburb. She leads the boys and girls into a social room inside the mosque. The walls are bright white and the only furniture is some beige folding chairs and tables. The room still smells of the food left over from the previous night's *iftar*, the daily meal at sunset ending the Ramadan fast. Rabab takes a folding chair and faces the young Muslims.

"Oh, Allah, we seek refuge from *fitna*," she says, beginning the lecture.

In many of Rabab's lectures, she cautions against *fitna* from too much interaction between the sexes, *fitna* from a lack of morals in American society, and *fitna* from too little dedication to Islam. She feels it is her duty to counsel adolescents so they will stay clear of drinking, drugs, and premarital sex.

This day, she decides to tailor her talk around Ramadan. She wants to take the youngsters back 1,400 years when the Angel Gabriel revealed the

Koran to the Prophet Muhammad. No one really knows exactly when that was, but Muslims mark this most important and sacred event as Laila al Qadr, "The Night of Power." It is a time spent reading the Koran and saying additional prayers. The Prophet said of this night: "Whoever establishes the prayers on this night of Qadr out of sincere faith and hoping to attain Allah's rewards, then all his past sins will be forgiven."

Like a professional storyteller with a vivid imagination, Rabab, or Mrs. Gomaa, as she is known to her students, relives that night for her students. "I hope you are with me and are ready for these nights, the Laila al Qadr. It's not just a night where you relax. You have to show Allah that you are working to reach that night. It is something we work for. Laila al Qadr was the night the Koran began.

"I'd like to give you a feel of the first night 1,400 years ago. The Prophet was in a cave, a deep dark cave. *Subhan Allah*. Praise be to God. The dark cave is embedded inside a mountain. This is where he meets the Angel Gabriel. *Subhan Allah*. The Prophet sees the Angel and he thinks, 'This is death.'

"The Angel says, 'Read!' But the Prophet says, 'I can't read.' The Angel hugs the Prophet and says, 'Read!'"

The young Muslims are captivated by the story; they seem transfixed. They vow they will go to the mosque on Laila al Qadr.

When the lecture ends, a few students who noticed I was taking notes ask me what I am doing. When I tell them I am writing a book, they are eager to tell stories about how Mrs. Gomaa educated them about Islam. One young woman says she started wearing a headscarf simply because Mrs. Gomaa advised her to be modest.

Of all the young lives Mrs. Gomaa touched, the one she influenced most profoundly was her daughter's. Yusra Gomaa's relationship with her mother is hard to fathom in the twenty-first-century West.

When I first met Yusra, she was one of many students sitting around a large wooden table in an aging but still grand dining hall at the University of Chicago. I had gone to the university to interview students who were members of the Muslim Students' Association. Yusra seemed to be the shyest in the group. At the time, I was looking for a researcher and a guide, someone who could be my mental shadow and give me insight into the Muslim community that could only come from an insider. When I left the meeting, I considered all the students there, but I thought Yusra might be too introverted; she was a freshman at the time. On a hunch, I called her a

Yusra Gomaa.

few weeks later. She was so eager to work on the project that I decided to give it a try.

I quickly learned that her relationship with her mother was perhaps the most important one in her life. She traced nearly every major decision she had ever made back to her mother's determination to raise a devout Muslim girl untainted by American values. The story of Yusra and Rabab is one Muslims can admire. They want their children to follow the faith strictly, no matter how difficult it might be to resist the temptations of growing up in America. Many Muslim parents I met struggled as they raised their daughters: Should they send them to an Islamic school to shield them from the decadence in public schools? Or are Islamic schools too sheltered, so much so that they will be unprepared for the real world once they graduate? Yusra was living proof that Rabab Gomaa seemed to have found all the answers.

When Yusra was in seventh grade at a public school in South Barrington, an upscale suburb outside Chicago where virtually no Muslims lived, Rabab noticed that she was becoming too interested in the adolescent adventures of her classmates. Rabab enrolled Yusra in the Islamic Foundation School in Villa Park, Illinois. The school was a new experience for Yusra; the majority of students were from the subcontinent. Before that, the only Muslims Yusra knew were her relatives from Egypt.

"I remember my first day. We had so many choices of Muslim friends. I had never seen Muslims from Pakistan before, but they quickly became my friends," Yusra told me one day. "The environment was Muslim friendly and I loved it because I was able to connect to Muslims on a spiritual level."

Although it is one of the oldest Islamic schools in the United States, Islamic Foundation was only a few years old when Yusra enrolled, and, as a pioneer, she helped start a basketball team and reading club. Everything seemed possible, especially because she had her mother's support. Mrs. Gomaa was very involved in making sure the curriculum at the school maintained high academic standards. She knew Yusra was a bright student and feared her daughter might suffer from being in an Islamic school.

Yusra entered Islamic Foundation when she was twelve years old, and she soon reached puberty, the time when practicing Muslim girls contemplate wearing a headscarf. When women wear headscarves they become ambassadors of the faith. But being an ambassador can be trying at times in a non-Muslim country. Some girls at Yusra's school dealt with this dilemma by wearing headscarves to school, required as part of the school uniform, and then taking them off once they boarded the bus to go home. But Yusra did not want to settle for half measures; she would either wear the *hijab* all the time or not at all. Rabab had started wearing the *hijab* seven years earlier, when she was in her early thirties. Yusra knew her mother wanted her oldest daughter to start veiling. Between her mother's example and her new Islamic school, she took the step she knew she must.

Exactly three weeks after she reached puberty, she dined with her family and a few friends at a chain restaurant. She wore her *hijab*, prompting one of her friends to ask accusingly, "Are you *muhajabat*?," Arabic for "one who wears the veil." Placed on the spot, Yusra said she was, even though her friend implied that cool girls do not wear veils. Making a public declaration was her vow to wear the headscarf whenever she was in public.

"My parents were so happy I said 'Yes,'" Yusra recalled one day, "even though my father quickly said, 'I had nothing to do with this.' Once I started wearing the headscarf it influenced me. It tells the world you are a Muslim."

Yusra remained at the Islamic Foundation until she began her freshman year at the University of Chicago. After six years in an Islamic school, she felt grounded. "That school really instilled my Islamic identity and made me content with it. When my class graduated, we were proud to be Muslims." But when she first entered the university, she realized life was not as black-and-white as it had been in an Islamic school. Being in an environment where Muslims were by far the minority drove her to do the obvious: she joined the Muslim Students' Association, an extension to what she had left behind.

Since the 1990s and particularly after September 11, the number of Muslim Students' Associations at universities across the country has grown. Many of the MSAs function more as social, than religious, organizations. The events that the MSAs organize, such as inviting speakers or hosting *iftars* during Ramadan, pertain to religion. But daily interaction among the Muslim students more commonly revolves around personal life. Like Yusra, many young Muslims at universities search for comfort from other Muslims, having left their families and close-knit mosque communities in their hometowns.

As I watched Yusra grow from a shy freshman into a self-assured junior—she completed college in three years—I realized that she had made a deliberate decision to be Muslim in America. She remained close to her family and to the Muslim students she met at the university. After a year of living in a dormitory, Yusra convinced her mother to allow her to live in an apartment near campus. It was a difficult decision for the Gomaa family; Rabab felt the dormitory would shield Yusra from the temptations of independent living. Then Yusra chose a Muslim who had attended an Islamic school as her roommate. That was enough to win the day.

Soon it was time to declare a major at the university. Yusra's parents wanted her to become a doctor, a common ambition among immigrant parents. Her father, a surgeon, wanted to guarantee his daughter's future financial security. And, like many Muslim parents, he believed that becoming a doctor signaled success in America. But Yusra wanted to devote herself to helping Muslims. She thought about psychiatry, social work, and then settled on law. She wanted to help Muslims juggle the laws pertaining to family proscribed in the *sharia*, Islamic law, with the laws in the American civil courts.

"I feel that I have a social responsibility to the Muslim community. A lot of Muslims get confused. They might ask the sheikh at the mosque for permission to get divorced or get custody of their children. But they don't understand that this is not legal in American law. Everyone wants to do things the Islamic way, but legally, we have to be protected by the courts. I see myself working closely with the mosques to help people when these issues arise."

When I talked with her about Muslim integration in America, she made a point of explaining that Muslims like herself have no grievance with non-Muslims nor do Muslims want to be isolated from mainstream society. But she felt it was important to stay close to Muslims.

We compared her feelings with those of my own family. The first generation of Lebanese immigrants who arrived in the United States chose not to integrate into American society. Like many immigrants, they were focused on making a living. Their children integrated a bit more, and by the time I came along, as a member of the third generation, I had few Lebanese friends. As I grew older, though, and my views diverged from the common American perception of the Middle East, I felt most comfortable with other Arabs. This is different, however, from the experiences of second-generation Muslims such as Yusra. They are building institutions, such as the Muslim Students' Associations, even at a young age, to enhance their Islamic identity. Yusra's feelings are perhaps more common among Muslim women than men because their *hijab* is a public symbol that sets them apart. In this way, they have already made a declaration of their difference.

Yusra was finishing her last year at the University of Chicago and preparing for law school just before I left the city for good. She had been accepted into many law schools and offered generous scholarships. Yet, her modesty, one hallmark of her personality, prevented any feelings of cockiness or arrogance. She talked about her new challenge ahead; she had heard so many stories about the difficulties of being a law student. But I was confident she would succeed in becoming a lawyer and giving back to the Islamic community what she had gained. By that time, she had taught me so much about Muslim life, without even trying. Her life reflected the dreams of many Muslim women in the new generation.

Recognizing women as equal partners has been a public issue over the last thirty years within Islamic communities in the East and West. Often specific events propel the issue to the forefront of public debate; reforms are then made or laws are adjusted, and the topic recedes again for some time. Such a scenario unfolded after the Amina Wadud prayer service in March 2005. While there was a backlash among conservatives who used the incident to reinforce their argument that the struggle for women's rights had gone too far, some Islamic organizations seized upon the moment. Muslim leaders who had tried before to draw attention to women's lack of inclusion in mosque life used the Wadud incident to take swift action.

A few women's groups and the Council on American-Islamic Relations distributed guidelines for treating women based on a study of 416 mosques in the United States. The pamphlet noted the difficulty of achieving equality, even in Western societies. "Living in a non-Muslim society and struggling to maintain our Muslim identity and values and to further instill them in our children requires spiritual and communal support. Muslim women are therefore seeking a dignified place in their *masjid*," [mosque] the pamphlet said. The survey showed that, on average, 75 percent of regular mosque participants are men. Although 54 percent of mosques reported regular activities for women, a sizeable portion—27 percent—reported only occasional activity, and 19 percent said they did not offer any programs for women. As many as 31 percent prevented women from serving on governing boards, and 19 percent said they allowed women to serve, but had not had women on the board for the past five years. The number of women praying behind a curtain or another form of partition had increased from 52 percent in 1994 to 66 percent in 2000.

The study, distributed among Muslim Americans, described current conditions in some mosques. Women are told to use fire exits rather than enter with men through the front doors. Sometimes, when imams deliver Friday sermons about women's issues, their comments are directed at older, more traditional women, not the younger generation. Younger women in particular are anxious to use their talents to improve mosque programs and activities, but are often discouraged from doing so. And the lack of participation from and visibility of women discourages women who might want to convert to Islam from going to the mosque, although the rate of conversion to Islam is higher among women than men.

It is not only the women who are exercising their rights; some Muslim men help along the way. Some imams, though they are still few in number, are teaching worshippers about women's rights through study sessions and other events in the mosques and by allowing women to participate in mosque governance.

Sheikh Ali Suleiman Ali, an affable man from Ghana who wears traditional African tunics and colorful caps, had been an imam at the Dix mosque in Dearborn's Southend from 1982 to 1987. He later served at a few other mosques before coming to lead a community in Canton, Michigan. Like other imams who had been at Dix, he left because he did not agree with the conservative ideas of the Yemeni worshippers. Sheikh Ali studied in Saudi Arabia and earned a Ph.D. from the University of Michigan in Ann Arbor, experiences that provided him a view of Islam from the East and the West.

The mosque in Canton, which is about one hour from Dearborn, is a relatively new mosque attended by Pakistani immigrants and is known officially as the Muslim Community of the Western Suburbs of Detroit. When he arrived there, Sheikh Ali wanted to foster a welcoming environment for women. The Pakistanis at the mosque had been living in Lavonia, a neighboring suburb, and they moved to Canton after raising six million dollars to build an Islamic school. There was no space for a school for their children at their Lavonia mosque.

At Canton, the women cooked to raise money for the mosque. But Sheikh Ali had more ambitious ideas. He asked the women to be members of the ruling mosque board. When I met him in the fall of 2005, there were two women on the eight-member board, rare for an American mosque. Sheikh Ali also started giving a *halaqa* to women every Wednesday to educate them about their rights in Islam, and on Friday evenings he invited well-known female speakers to talk about women's rights within the faith. His mission was not restricted to the mosque; by day, he worked as an adviser to Muslim Family Services, a nonprofit organization in Detroit that counsels Muslim women about whether their husbands are treating them well, their health concerns, and raising their children.

Of all Sheikh Ali's projects, one in particular shocked some of the worshippers. He removed the curtain separating men from women in the main prayer hall. "I've had to fight here for certain things," he told me. "I took down the barrier, but a majority overruled me and I had to put it back. A small number of women want the curtain, and about 20 percent of the men want it. There was little I could do."

Sheikh Ali certainly is the exception. But other imams have made similar efforts. Abdul Malik Mujahid, the executive producer of Radio Islam, is often invited to give the *khutba*, or Friday sermon, at various mosques in Chicago. He relayed this story to his friends and acquaintances: One day, he was set to give a sermon on a vague topic about Muslim life. When he had completed the notes he would use to deliver the sermon, he received an e-mail for an Islamic event for "brothers only." He had been annoyed about women's treatment in mosques long before he received this notice. The week before, when he had given a sermon in a new Chicago mosque, he overheard a few Muslim women speaking in the elevator. He asked them what was wrong. They explained that they could only see the imam through a television system in the women's section. One woman quipped, "If I wanted to watch television, I'd stay at home." At this same mosque, the leaders had assured Abdul Malik that they were encouraging women to become more involved in mosque life. This did not seem to be true.

Abdul Malik decided it was time to devote his *khutba* to women, whether the mosque leaders ever invited him again or not. He stood in the front section of the prayer hall that can accommodate about one thousand male worshipers. A few dozen women gathered in a small corner of the hall separated from the main space by a curtain. He preached that women in early Islamic history were not only mothers and wives, but participated in politics, the creation of Islamic law, and trade and commerce. When his sermon ended, a stream of worshippers thanked him, expressing far more praise than he normally receives. The feedback gave Abdul Malik hope that at least some Muslims are ready for change.

As I interviewed more imams, I learned the sheikhs at the Zaytuna Institute were hosting "An Evening of Gratitude, Honoring the Contributions of Muslim Women." I thought it would be interesting to compare the views of the Zaytuna sheikhs with the attitudes typical of the majority of imams. The idea of hosting an evening to honor women was in keeping with what the Zaytuna sheikhs had been teaching for years. Imam Zaid Shakir, the African American convert with Zaytuna, was known among Muslim Americans as a woman-friendly sheikh. In April 2004, he published a widely read essay offering evidence from the Koran about gender equality. Imam Zaid wanted to confront the perpetual line of attack against Islam—that women are treated as inferiors. Shakir wrote:

> The Koran emphasizes that men and women are equal in their essential physical and metaphysical nature. We read in this regard, "We have surely ennobled the descendants of Adam." This ennoblement of the human being precludes any claims to gender superiority, or any feelings of inferiority based on physical, or metaphysical composition. Such feelings underlie schemes of gender-based oppression, and have no place in Islam.

After a long day of travel, I enter the same Pakistani restaurant in San Jose where I had gone for my first Zaytuna event the year before. But this evening, there are fewer guests and less noise. The audience is mostly Muslim women, some of whom I have met at other places. I glance at the program and realize that Sheikh Hamza Yusuf is the last speaker, which means he may not emerge before 11 p.m. or midnight. Speaking at the end of the program is classic Sheikh Hamza; he would not want to steal anyone's thunder by appearing before them. And by being last on the agenda he will inspire the guests to stay through the entire program.

Wearing a long grey tunic with a white shirt and grey trousers, Sheikh Hamza rises from the head table to the podium. As I expected, it is near midnight.

"We fail in our homes to honor women," he says.

"It starts with assuming that the wife will take care of kids, clean, and do all the things women are expected to do. I was raised by a single mother. She divorced early and she had seven children . . . Much of how I view life is through my mother . . . The lives of women really infuse our religion with vitality . . . I think the women in houses are not getting the accolades they deserve. These women can do something higher."

He begins announcing the women being honored one by one. As he calls each name, his young son approaches the stage and takes a gold plaque inscribed with a Koranic verse, and then dashes across the banquet hall to deliver it to the designated woman. One goes to his mother, Yahya. She smiles, embarrassed by the public accolade. "My father was disappointed when I became a Muslim," says Sheikh Hamza over the microphone, as Yahya smiles from across the room. "I want to thank my wife for all she does."

Before he finishes calling out the names, he is interrupted. A shy African American woman approaches the stage with two other Muslim women. "We are breaking for an important announcement," he says, turning toward the women. "A sister wants to take the *shahada*. Welcome to Islam."

That night, the women leave the Pakistani restaurant satisfied that the men with authority have recognized their talents. For some, it is no great surprise. But for others, it is a miracle from God.

SEVEN

Heeding the Call

৵৹

Why, Chris Irwin wondered, would a Muslim volunteer to fight with American soldiers in Iraq? He had asked himself this question many times: at his military base in Fort Stewart, Georgia, when a few men in his unit asked him, "Are you with us or against us?"; in Kuwait, as he drank sugary tea and watched television news with local Arabs enraged over the impending war; and back home in San Antonio, Texas, when he first talked with his friends, just after September 11, about joining the military. At that time, Chris had just converted to Islam and was weighing his options. He could either work at a place like McDonald's or join the military to pay for his college tuition.

Now, he was compressed inside a Humvee, crossing the long stretch of no-man's-land between Kuwait and Iraq. With the sand from the desert peppering his dry skin and parched lips, he asked himself, "Could I, a Muslim, kill my brother?" He was too tired to find the answer. He and the ten men in his unit took turns dozing. If they were lucky, they got five hours of sleep a night, and those were interrupted by the powerful thrusts of gusty desert winds that shook the Humvee. They ate their MREs, ready-made military rations served in small plastic packages, to stay awake.

They approached Baghdad in March 2003. The war had been escalating for a few weeks, turning Chris's sleep deprivation into an adrenaline rush. The prospect of being in the middle of battle filled Chris with fear and excitement. On the outskirts of the city, their Humvee had narrowly escaped an artillery attack that struck across the street. Suddenly, Chris was face-to-face with the question that from afar he had managed to evade. He stared into the eyes of Iraqis, his Muslim brothers. He hoped no harm would come to them, even though such an idea seemed absurd during wartime. He wanted to go to a local mosque to ask God for guidance and to bury his head in the comforts of his faith. He wanted to cleanse himself of all the voices he had heard along the way. An officer in Kuwait made a joke in the briefing room about blowing up a mosque once the war began. His fellow soldiers raised doubts about his loyalty to America. A lieutenant in Kuwait scolded him for getting friendly with Kuwaitis by greeting them with "marhaba," a simple "hello" in Arabic.

Chris had gone to the war seeking truth about America's mission in Iraq. He wanted to know, was it a war against Islam? Was Saddam evil enough to justify the invasion? He looked everywhere to find answers, even in the most difficult places, including those hiding spots where Saddam Hussein might have kept all those weapons of mass destruction he supposedly had. Chris found a bit of truth, surprisingly, coming from a quiet voice in an unsuspected place. One day, when he was manning a U.S. Army military checkpoint in Baghdad, a crowd of children gathered around, as they often did when they saw American soldiers. They begged for money, food, even military memorabilia.

One precocious young boy stood back from the small hands reaching out toward Chris and asked innocently:

"Why are you invading Muslims if you are a Muslim?"

Chris smiled gently, "To help Iraqis."

It was the only answer he could give, whether he believed it or not. During his short time in Iraq, Chris watched as Americans rallied around their flag and the cultural bonds that united them against the country they had invaded. But Iraqis greeted Chris with "salaam aleikum," even as his glaring difference with them stared them in the face—in the guise of his camouflage military uniform.

By the time he left Iraq three months later, his answer to the question the Iraqi boy had asked him had become much more complicated. At first, Chris had been convinced that the American invasion and occupation, no matter how much violence it bred, must continue in order to prevent what he calls "an authoritarian Islamic republic." But as he watched it unfold, he was torn: Saddam was evil, he thought, but so many innocent Iraqis were being killed in the war. Surely, there could have been a better way. Chris had gone to Iraq as an idealist; he left as a cynic.

I met Chris one Sunday in December 2005 at an Islamic center used for prayer and social activities in San Antonio, where I was born and raised. I had gone there to get to know Muslim converts in an effort to learn why a dramatic number of Americans had been drawn to Islam since September 11. The trend was the opposite of what one might expect: in a country where public opinion is increasingly hostile toward Muslims and Islam, more and more Americans are becoming Muslims. Imam Ali, the head of the local Shiite mosque, knew many Muslims in San Antonio. He helped me arrange several interviews by phone before I traveled to Texas, and he gave me Chris's phone number.

Chris arrives at the Islamic center for our noon appointment while Sheikh Ali is giving a religious lesson. The sheikh urges us to talk privately in an enclosed room. Chris and I sit on a newly carpeted floor; as in many Islamic centers, there is no furniture. As soon as he begins telling me his story, I can tell that his mind is still in Iraq. He had gone to the Middle East believing that the war was justified. But after he returned home and the sectarian violence had spun out of control, his feelings became more complicated and he found it more difficult to defend his position around other Muslims. But even if he acknowledged the war was going badly, he still could not accept stinging condemnations of the United States. "In order to bring Islam to people, Muslims should stop insulting America. If you see the government doing something bad, don't focus on it," he tells me with great conviction. "You must embrace American culture. You are in a binding contract."

His ideas reflect a current of thought among some contemporary Muslim theologians, who say Islam does not permit believers in a non-Muslim country to rebel against the values of their host nation. At times, Chris tries to convince other Muslims that Saddam Hussein was training Muslim extremists in Iraq, and that this alone was justification for war. But he found this argument hard to make once it became well established that, in fact, Saddam Hussein had no weapons of mass destruction.

His views are unlike those of the majority of Muslims I have met; most openly criticize the U.S. invasion and the rise of Islamic militancy it has caused across the Muslim world. They did not support Saddam Hussein's tyranny, but do not find American colonialism to be much of an improvement. Many Muslims think the occupation could have been avoided if the United States had allowed sanctions to continue pressuring Hussein's government. They wonder if Muslims have become the target of the occupation, as the war has dragged on. But, as a convert, Chris views the United States and many things about Islam differently than those born into the faith. In Chris's case, going to Iraq was a true test of where his loyalties stood. He is torn between his American identity and his new one as a Muslim.

Chris's choice of Islam as his new religion was a great leap of faith. As a child, he had no religion; his parents discouraged him from going to church. This was especially unusual because half of his family is from Guatemala, a part of the world where Catholicism is strong. "I knew almost instinctively that there was one God, but I felt that He never helped me in anything. Rather, he kept me humble by causing me to fail at everything," Chris explained. He did not know what religion was right for him, or what he wanted to become. In elementary school, he thought he was an atheist. He had no god to pray to so he used good luck charms to try to influence his fate.

As a high school student, Chris met a young girl who, in his eyes, was a good Christian, which led him to try her faith. He began to study Christian and Jewish teachings. He read the Old Testament, but he was confused and frustrated. He prayed to God for guidance, but he just became more depressed.

One day he picked up a few books off his grandfather's shelf. One was about the early Islamic period. It explained in detail how the Angel Gabriel revealed the Koran to the Prophet Muhammad. At first Chris was skeptical; he had thought Islam was a religion of the Devil. Still, he kept reading. He learned that the Prophet had received the revelation with great humility. He read more from his grandfather's books, and then delved into material he found on the Internet about anything Islamic. He found information about Saudi Arabia's royal family and a book about Islamic history, a work he later realized distorted history. He had so many questions, so he used the Internet as his guide. Every day he found new literature; he discovered that Islam is compatible with science and modern knowledge. For Chris, it was no longer a religion for devils or mystics.

At the time, he was a freshman at San Antonio College and, while he still did not know even one Muslim, he started to feel like a Muslim. He called God "Allah," and fasted secretly during Ramadan. He was afraid his family and friends would frown upon his interest in Islam. "At this time in my life it was revolutionary to do this. I had been conditioned by society and the television to hate Muslims . . . to believe Muslims are evil. Later, I realized society had deceived me."

Chris Irwin. (*Courtesy of Chris Irwin*)

The next logical step for Chris was to recite the *shahada*, the proclamation of the faith. Chris called a number he found on an Islamic Web site. A woman answered and arranged to drive him across town to one of the few mosques in San Antonio. "I was scared," Chris recalled. "Satan tried his best to prevent me from becoming a Muslim, but I was brave and resisted."

As he took his vows, he was confused about Muslims. It seemed all the Web sites were about Islamic extremism. He loved his country and he came to love the true Islam. "What could he do?" he wondered. Chris promised himself he would try to change Muslim relations with America.

"There are a lot of people in the country who try to root out Muslims because they think they are evil people. Likewise, conservatives in Islam complain about the media being biased against them. Islam is a religion to show people how to be really good human beings. This is why I converted."

Memories of al-Andalus

Latinos like Chris are converting to Islam in growing numbers. National Islamic organizations estimate there are tens of thousands—perhaps as many as seventy-five thousand—Latino converts in America, many of whom only discovered Islam recently. This is out of an estimated 33 million Americans who identity themselves as Latino, according to the 2000 Census. Not surprisingly, the largest Latino Muslim communities are in those cities with large Hispanic populations: San Antonio, Chicago, New York, and Miami.

Few studies have been published about Latino Muslims because their conversion is such a new phenomenon. In one study conducted by Samantha Sanchez, a scholar at the New School for Social Research, 25 percent of those surveyed said they had actively sought a new faith and had considered other religions before choosing Islam. Unlike Chris, many Latinos took three to twelve years to convert. Her survey found that 73 percent were former Catholics.

When I asked Latinos why they chose Islam over other religions, many described the Muslim experience as an intellectual one. They felt that other religions demanded blind faith, but Islam required analyzing the holy texts. Former Catholics, in particular, said they left the church for the mosque because they were frustrated with the Vatican's demand for unquestioning acceptance of religious doctrine and church teachings in the absence of educating the faithful. This might be an oversimplification of the Catholic Church, but many Latinos clearly were negatively affected by the scandal in the church involving homosexual priests who sexually abused young boys. This scandal appeared to color their views of the church in general. They expressed skepticism, for example, of Christian doctrine that Jesus Christ is the Son of God. Islam's belief that Jesus is one in a string of revered prophets, but not the Son of God, seemed more believable to them. Islam's concept of *tawhid*, the oneness of God, seemed more intuitive, especially when set against the complexity of the Holy Trinity.

Latino converts also told me they didn't believe in the infallibility of the pope and appreciated Islam's tradition of individual interpretation of the holy texts. Most mainstream Muslims believe Islam calls for them to interpret the Koran and the Sunnah for themselves, with the help of learned scholars. And because Islam does not have a hierarchy like the Catholic Church, the faith may appear less absolutist to them than Catholicism.

Islam's glorious history in medieval Spain, known to Muslims as al-Andalus, where Muslims built a world-class civilization—the accomplishments of which in science, mathematics, philosophy, and the arts dwarfed those of neighboring Christendom—also influences Latinos to convert. Some assume their own ancestors were born Muslim and they are merely "reverting" back to Islam, rather than converting. Some Muslims born into the faith would also describe the transformation of those who are new to the faith as "reversion," rather than "conversion," because they believe everyone is born a Muslim.

When Islam first began to spread during the time of the Prophet Muhammad, there was certainly reason to believe this was true. Conversions were numerous, so much so that a *surah*, one chapter in the Koran, states: "And you saw people entering Allah's religion in throngs."

At first, Latinos' regular references to the past riches of al-Andalus—its great city Córdoba was once known as the Ornament of the World for the countless cultural wonders that later helped fuel the Renaissance—came as something of a surprise to the non-Muslims they encountered. In the Western imagination, the wildfire spread of Islam from its birthplace in the Arabian Peninsula in the early seventh century to Iberia, Sicily, North Africa, the Indian subcontinent, and beyond was a matter of forced conversion by marauding Arab armies. In practice, "conversion by the sword," when applied at all, was reserved for idol worshippers, not the fellow People of the Book. The victorious Muslims generally permitted their fellow monotheists—Jews, Christians, and often Zoroastrians and Mandaeans—to live pretty much as they had before, as "protected peoples." Like the Muslims, the other People of the Book believed in one god, they followed revealed texts, shared some fundamental beliefs, and recognized many of the same prophets. However, these so-called *dhimmis*, non-Muslims living in a state governed by Islamic law, were required to pay a special tax and were relegated to second-class status in the new social and political order under Muslim rule.

The Muslims first came to the Iberian Peninsula in 711, when Arab and Berber forces crossed over from North Africa under the command of General Tariq ibn Zayid. His landing spot, known as Mount Tariq, or Jabal Tariq in Arabic, gives us its present-day name, Gibraltar. Soon, the Visigoth Christian masters of Spain were overthrown, and the oppression of the local Jews gave way to a more tolerant approach under the Muslims. Native Christians and Jews could, and often did, thrive in al-Andalus, and some obtained positions of considerable power and influence. However, social advancement could only be ensured by conversion to Islam, a process that also freed the new believer from the burdens of poll tax and from a series of legal and social restrictions placed on the recognized non-Muslim communities. By the mid-tenth century, according to some scholars, as much as 80 percent of the indigenous population had converted to Islam, although it took at least another two centuries for these new Muslims to be accepted by the ethnic Arab elite.

Over the next 750 years, the Christians gradually pushed their Muslim rivals from the Iberian Peninsula, essentially completing the Reconquista in 1492 with the fall of the last Islamic stronghold, Grenada, to Ferdinand and Isabella. The so-called Catholic Kings, best known in America for their patronage of Christopher Columbus in that same year, soon issued their infamous expulsion order directing all Jews to convert or leave the kingdom within four months. The Catholics ordered the forced conversion of the Muslims, in violation of the terms of Grenada's surrender in 1502, and a period of often-violent ethnic cleansing and suppression began. A little more than one hundred years later, those Iberians of Muslim origin were expelled under a decree that enjoyed wide public support among the dominant Christians but was also economically disastrous. An estimated three hundred thousand "Moriscos" headed for North Africa, the New World, and points beyond.

Once American Latinos discover this historic connection to Islam, for many becoming Muslim has an even greater appeal. The Latino experience thus bears some similarities to Islam's attraction among African Americans, who also feel connected to the faith's long history in Africa. Latinos and English speakers also have a linguistic affiliation with Arabic; Islam's long stay in Spain has bequeathed the West countless Arabic words and concepts, familiar to speakers of both Spanish and English—from "adobe" to "zenith." Finally, many Latinos feel Islam is compatible with their cultural practices, particularly their emphasis on family life.

The Draw of Modern Life

Several contemporary conditions lead Latinos to convert. Those who settle in large American cities become exposed to Islam in one of two ways: they live near mosques, or they have African American neighbors who are familiar with the Nation of Islam. The two populations find common ground, for both often feel disenfranchised in America and seek comfort in the personal relationships they form in mosque communities. It is clear that many African Americans have converted because they believe Islam will correct the social injustice in America. Whether they joined the Nation of Islam or mainstream Sunni mosques, as the scholar Sulayman Nyang writes, "Islam was used as an ideological weapon against racial discrimination."

Intermarriage is another important impetus for Latino conversions, particularly when Hispanic women marry Muslim men. It is perfectly acceptable for Muslim men to marry women from outside the faith; verses in the Koran give men permission to marry women among the People of the Book. Typically, these women convert when they marry a Muslim.

After September 11, Latinos, like many other Americans, began searching for more information about Islam. Some found it in mosques in their communities, where organizations were distributing pamphlets, books, and tapes to dispel misconceptions about Islam and educate Americans about the true face of their religion. The Council on American-Islamic Relations (CAIR) sponsored eight thousand reading corners in mosques and Islamic centers, which are filled with books and other religious literature. The vast education campaign led Latinos, as well as others, to convert. Nihad Awad, the chairman of CAIR, told a Saudi newspaper three months after September 11 that thirty-four thousand Americans had converted to Islam after the attacks. Generally, the converts were students, single mothers, or women who married Muslim men. According to a November 2001 study conducted at Georgetown University's Center for Muslim-Christian Understanding, a majority of converts—38 percent—were moved toward their decision by literature about Islam. Fellow Muslims influenced 22 percent to convert, 13 percent married a Muslim, and a variety of other reasons accounted for the remaining 24 percent.

Similar trends can be seen in Europe. The French newspaper *Le Figaro*, citing French intelligence sources, reported that between thirty thousand and fifty thousand conversions to Islam took place in France in 2004. Many were French women who married Muslim men. In France, at least in the eyes of state security sources, male converts were generally disaffected young men from unstable backgrounds. In the United States, however, this profile does not apply to male converts.

The rise in conversions has caught American mosques and Islamic centers by surprise. Some mosques, including the Dix mosque in Dearborn, began hosting open houses or organizing study sessions for outsiders interested in converting. Some of the new classes I attended for converts were very basic. In some cases, the sessions amounted to little more than people narrating their life histories.

Most of the time, however, while mosque leaders might boast of the large numbers taking the *shahada* in their mosques, converts are often left out in the cold from that day on. Some turn to the numerous sites on the Internet listing testimonials from fellow converts. Others find sympathetic worshippers willing to teach them about the faith. Even after September 11, when tens of thousands were said to have converted, most mosque leaders failed to create ways to educate their new fellow Muslims.

In Dearborn and Detroit, where there is a high concentration of mosques and Muslims, the problem of educating new converts became so troubling that Cherine Abdulah created the Ummah Project in 2004. Her own experiences had inspired her to help converts. She was born into a secular, nonpracticing Muslim family, but when she reached her twenties she wanted to learn about the faith. She called a few imams in Dearborn, but no one was willing to help her. The organization Cherine now runs provides a series of classes to teach converts everything from the basics, such as how to pray, to the theological tenets of the faith. Cherine says many mosque communities do little to show acceptance toward new converts and, as a result, she estimates that 50 percent of those who adopt Islam eventually leave it. The greatest problem new Muslims face today is emotional and psychological isolation. Once they give up certain activities that draw people together, such as attending events at which alcohol is served or that pose obstacles to practicing their new faith, they need a new social life. For Muslim immigrants, that social life revolves around the mosque. But, if converts are not made to feel welcome there, they have no support group to replace the one they left behind.

The counseling they receive from imams or mosque leaders, Cherine told me, often creates more frustration. If a new convert is having trouble with her non-Muslim husband, for example, an imam might advise her to get a divorce, rather than lead her toward a solution. In some mosques, female converts are pressured to immediately start wearing the *hijab* or *jilbab*, and for many women this requires a complete change in lifestyle. Cherine believes all these pressures lead to what she calls "new Muslim burnout," causing immigrant Muslim communities to lose an opportunity to tap into the growing interest in Islam among non-Muslims.

Such disinterest toward converts is surprising considering that some of the most influential Muslim leaders in America were not born into the faith: Sheikh Hamza Yusuf and Imam Zaid Shakir, the influential sheikhs at the Zaytuna Institute; Dr. Umar Faruq Abd-Allah, one of Sheikh Hamza's mentors; and the prominent Muslim activist Ingrid Mattson. Their popularity among immigrant Muslims might seem to contradict the usual reaction to converts. However, during my travels it became clear that immigrant Muslims born into Islam make a distinction between converts who are well educated about the faith and those who are not.

The lack of acceptance of converts among imams in mosques goes against one of the fundamental principles in Islam, called *dawah*, literally to invite one to Islam. Since the time of the Prophet Muhammad, *dawah* has been the avenue through which Islam has expanded to now include 1.5 billion Muslims worldwide. In the Koran, *dawah* generally refers to God's invitation to live according to his will. In contemporary times, *dawah* is used to encourage Muslims to be pious in all aspects of their lives.

In the United States, the obstacles to accepting converts generally reflects the historical ethnic segregation in most mosques—the same segregation Rami Nashashibi and other young Muslim activists are now working to eradicate. The converts represent to some degree the "other"; they do not fit neatly into particular mosque communities, many of which are divided along ethnic lines. In a study conducted by Ihsan Bagby, *The Mosque in America: A National Portrait*, the congregations of 64 percent of mosques were composed of one dominant ethnic group, generally either African American or South Asian.

The size of the Latino Muslim population remains small and the conversion rate in no way compares to that of African Americans over recent decades. According to a CAIR study published in April 2001, 64 percent of Muslim converts were African American, 27 percent were white, 6 percent were Hispanic, and 3 percent fell into the "other" category. According to the same study, 44 percent of mosques reported one to five conversions per year, while 23 percent reported eleven to forty-nine conversions per year. There has been no definitive study since then on the numbers of conversions, but imams say they have seen a dramatic rise at their mosques since September 11.

African Americans make up the overwhelming majority of all converts, and their numbers have increased significantly over the last century. The rise in their numbers can be traced in part to Sheikh Daud Faisal, an African American musician. Faisal and his wife, who is an African American with a Pakistani father, played a key role in spreading the faith among blacks in the New York and New Jersey area. According to Sulayman Nyang, the Nation of Islam also circulated their ideas of Islamic doctrine in the same region of the northeast in the 1930s. Nyang goes as far as to say that Elijah Muhammad did more to multiply the numbers of Muslims in America than any other leader or group in the country.

Despite the far greater number of African American converts, I have chosen to write about the conversions of Latinos. I think the reasons they are converting—their attraction to the intellectual nature of Islam and

their disillusionment with religions they feel are guided by blind faith—
reflect powerful global trends that will continue, and even accelerate, in
the foreseeable future. African Americans, on the other hand, have converted for reasons that are particular to their history in America, often as
recourse against their discrimination at the hands of white society. For
decades, African American conversions have been most prevalent among
prisoners. A 2004 U.S. Department of Justice study found that 6 percent
of the country's 150,000 federal inmates are Muslims, and 85 percent of
these Muslims converted in prison. Islamic organizations of many stripes
have worked for decades to spread the *dawah* to the black prison population, which is ripe for conversion to Islam. Yet, there are still few Muslim
chaplains; of more than two hundred chaplains in the U.S. Federal Bureau
of Prisons, less than a dozen are Muslim.

A 1972 publication called *Ijtahad* described how Muslim Students' Associations were soliciting support in the 1960s and 1970s to convert inmates.

> An increasing number of inmates in various correctional facilities are now
> accepting Islam as their only salvation in this life and thereafter. Most of them
> have accepted Islam after they have been in contact with sincere Muslims at
> the prison. The unity of God, justice, brotherhood, equality of mankind, at-
> tracted most of them to become Muslims. With all the rigid regulations of the
> prison facilities, the new Muslims are still able to study and practice Islam . . .
> The MSA committee for Correctional Facilities, therefore, solicits the sup-
> port and cooperation of all the MSA local chapters and Muslim communities
> to provide them with dedicated Muslim teachers knowledgeable in Islam for
> the effective rehabilitation of the sincere inmates.

After Malcolm X found Islam in prison through the Nation of Islam,
he expressed thoughts similar to those of many black converts over the
decades:

> America needs to understand Islam, because this is the one religion that erases
> from its society the race problem. Throughout my travels in the Muslim world,
> I have met, talked to, and even eaten with people who in America would have
> been considered white, but the white attitude was removed from their minds
> by the religion of Islam.

The tradition of spreading Islam in prisons continues to this day as
Muslim chaplains deliver Friday sermons, distribute Korans and other literature, and give religious study lessons. Inmates are particularly attracted
to Islam because of its lack of hierarchy. A prisoner does not need a cleric,
priest, or even a mosque to practice the faith. Islam places great importance on self-reformation without the intervention of a third party. Often

denied regular contact with a religious authority, inmates can teach themselves about Islam and still feel they are diligently practicing the faith.

For decades, the conversions have happened with ease. But only about 25 percent of prison converts pursue their new faith once they are freed. Faced with the demands of finding a job and making the effort required to find a local mosque or Islamic community center, a great majority never makes it to a mosque. There is no longer a national organization equivalent to the Nation leading converts to the faith, or charismatic leaders like Malcolm X who can stand as reminders of how their prison conversions transformed their lives.

"So Many Muslim Sisters"

After talking with Chris at the Islamic Center, I met Amira, a twenty-six-year-old Latina convert who grew up along the Mexican border in Amarillo, a Texas town more often associated with the old southwest than with the rise of a new religious trend. Amira immediately stood out in the crowd when she entered the main room where Sheikh Ali was giving his religious lesson. Some of the women in the class did not wear headscarves, and others from South Asia or Southeast Asia placed them delicately on the crowns of the heads, exposing some of their hair. But Amira, a tall, slender woman with a soft face, was wearing a long black chador similar to the floor-length veil I had worn during my years in Iran. Her dark eyes, accented with black mascara and liner, made her look nearly entirely black. I had never seen a convert in America dressed so conservatively, although this type of veil is common in many countries, particularly in the Persian Gulf. Some Muslims had told me that converts sometimes try to compensate for not being born into the faith by taking extreme measures, such as wearing conservative veils, in order to prove their commitment.

Amira guides me outside the center, into the bright sunlight. She says she prefers to talk at her apartment nearby, where her small son and daughter can play. I hop into the front seat of her Chevy Suburban, where they are waiting in the back seat. As Amira drives, we pass all the shopping malls and streets I remember from my own childhood in San Antonio. Back then, it seemed there were no Muslims living in the city and certainly no recognizable mosques. San Antonians generally had very little knowledge about the Middle East or the Muslim world. When I was a student in an all-girls Catholic school, most of my classmates thought I was Mexican because of my dark features. When I told them my family was Lebanese, they had no idea that there was a country called Lebanon. As I think about how Islam has spread, even in this unexpected corner of the country, Mariah, Amira's six-year-old daughter, proudly recites the opening verses of the Koran, something I never heard in this city twenty-five years ago. "Show this lady what you learned in your Islamic school," Amira tells Mariah. Soon, she is proudly reciting the letters of the Arabic alphabet.

As Mariah sings in the back seat, Amira tells me her story. A tragedy and a Muslim husband led her to Islam. She was raising her two children in San Antonio alone, having divorced her first husband, a Catholic from Mexico. She could not afford a babysitter so she left the children alone during the day while she attended a vocational school near their apartment. A neighbor reported her to Child Protective Services. Amira knew it was wrong to leave her two small children alone in the apartment, but she felt she had no choice if she wanted to get an education and a good-paying job. Officials from the agency were unsympathetic; they took her children away and placed them in a foster home for a year and three months. Amira was heartbroken. At first, she was allowed to visit them only two hours a month.

Two months after her children were taken away, she converted to Islam at one of the city's central mosques. She had come to know several Muslims in town and was briefly married to a Palestinian man. She started reading literature about the faith, including books and tapes from Sheikh Hamza Yusuf. Through all this, she felt convinced she had made the right decision, even when her marriage ended after only two months.

"There is acceptance in the Islamic community that you don't find anywhere else," she tells me. "I have so many Muslim sisters and I never had so many friends." By this point in our conversation we had arrived at her somewhat Spartan apartment. I sat on her living room sofa as she fetched some peanut butter and jelly from the cupboard for her children.

Knowing Muslims brings stability to her life. The Islamic community has started giving her support. It helps her to pay the rent for her apartment, which has allowed her to quit her part-time job at a dry cleaners so she can continue studying at a local college to become an X-ray technician. "I am organized and I function much better now," Amira explains, slapping the gooey peanut butter on slices of white bread. "When you become a Muslim, you have much more control over your life. On Saturdays, I go to a study session for converts at the mosque, and they teach us how to pray correctly, they teach us about the Prophet, and how to raise your kids to be good Muslims."

The Saturday study sessions are typical of the ways many converts across the country become educated about Islam. About six years ago, when more and more Muslims started attending the Islamic Center of San Antonio, a couple from Jordan began giving *halaqas*, or study sessions. After about a year, they returned to the Middle East, and the community asked one of their students, Jameelah Ohl, to become the new teacher. Jameelah, born into a Christian family, converted to Islam in 1996 in what she calls a "stop 'n' go" mosque in the city. She had tried several religions, but chose Islam after meeting Palestinians and Lebanese who told her a bit about the Koran. Aside from the Islamic conferences she has attended in nearby Houston, Dallas, and Austin, Jameelah has no formal Islamic education. What she knows about the Koran and the *hadiths* she mostly taught herself and picked up from her husband, a Muslim from Uganda. Yet, each Saturday the number of students in her "Classes for Sisters" grew, and, about forty Muslims, mostly converts like Amira, diligently attended each week. Many of the women had converted because they had married Muslim men. Finding a Muslim husband was important to the women who were unmarried, a common desire among female converts. In Dearborn, some converts scan matchmaking sites on the Internet for available Muslim men from the Middle East, and then travel to countries such as Yemen to marry.

Amira longed to find a Muslim husband. "Marriage is so important. I want to marry a very religious man because it is good for raising children."

I ask her about her life back in Amarillo, but she is not interested in talking about her distant past. She was born Catholic, but became disillusioned with the church and became a Jehovah's Witness. That is about all she says. Although she gives no details, I get the impression that she does not communicate much with her family.

What did they think about her marriage to a Muslim?

"When I married the Palestinian man, they told me, 'He is going to take you to his country and kill you.' They don't understand much about the world."

Straight to God

On a hot September Sunday morning in 1999, Marta Felicitas Ramirez de Galedary and four other Muslim women gathered in a room at the Islamic

Center of Southern California. They first met out of frustration; they could never fully understand the imam's sermons or much else at their local mosque, located in the heart of a predominately Hispanic Los Angeles neighborhood. Some did not know English well and none knew Arabic, the language used on occasion at the mosque. They felt the language barrier prevented the mosque leadership, who was generally open-minded, from reaching the few Latino Muslims who worshipped there. So, they decided to help one another.

First, they had to map out their strategy: They needed books about Islam written in Spanish, but how could they find them? There certainly was no demand for Spanish books about Islam in the United States, and, in Mexico, there were too few Muslims for the publishing industry to translate English books into Spanish. But Marta was familiar with one book, *Reading the Muslim Mind*, written by Hassan Hathout, a scholar living in California. Somehow, Marta had discovered a Spanish translation. This book and a Spanish biography of the Prophet Muhammad that Marta found on the Internet were the extent of their library. They chose various themes relevant to Latinos, and each person volunteered to give a presentation each week summarizing the topic. Eventually, Hassan Hathout agreed to lecture to the group on the last Sunday of each month. So began their study sessions. Each Sunday, the women met for lessons and eventually expanded their circle.

Marta was used to routine and discipline. She was born into a traditional Catholic family in Mexico in the state of Guerrero. Her father was a rancher and was as demanding of his eleven daughters—Marta was the youngest—as he was with his cattle. His daughters attended a strict Catholic school to get a good education and develop moral values. During Holy Week, a sacred time for Catholics before Easter Sunday, when Jesus Christ is believed to have risen from the dead, Marta was not permitted to go to the movies or eat meat. She was expected only to pray. When Marta completed secondary school, she convinced her father to let her attend a good college in Mexico City. He agreed and she and two of her sisters rented an apartment so Marta could attend el Colegio Hispano Americano, where she studied Western literature, psychology, art, and existentialism. From her studies in Marxism and philosophy, Marta seriously began to question Catholicism for the first time in her life. "I was lost, confused and living an extremely conflicted and painful life," Marta wrote in an essay, describing her feelings at the time.

In the midst of her soul searching she married and had a son. But she continued studying and enrolled in English classes at an institute created by the British Embassy in Mexico City. She was so inspired by her lessons that she arranged to enroll in an English-language exchange program in Bath, a small city west of London, which in the late Middle Ages was a center for the study of Arabic texts. Her stay there changed her life. She met three classmates: Hassan, Ismael, and Kitar, all Muslims from Brunei. Marta did not know what a Muslim was. Still her friends almost never talked to her about Islam, aside from assuring her that she was born a Muslim.

She returned to Mexico City after her summer studies had ended, and felt like a different woman. She had just divorced her husband, and she missed her Muslim friends. Something about their personalities and what little they told her about Islam stayed with her. She wanted to be part of it. She wrote to them diligently, but she needed human contact with other Muslims. At the same time, she wanted to keep improving her English, so she moved to the United States as part of an exchange program. Once there, she met more Muslims, including her English teacher—a Jew who had converted to Islam. Her renewed contacts with Muslims inspired her to say the *shahada*.

Marta Felicitas Ramirez de Galedary. (*Photograph by Chris Martinez. Courtesy of* La Opinion *newspaper*)

"I was in tears during my first prayers. Finally, I had found peace in my heart. I knew that Allah was with me, and I knew what was my role in the world and the reason for my existence. I have returned to the one God and I will never be lost again." These were the words Marta wrote in her essay to document her life at that time.

While she felt satisfied that her long search had ended, her family was displeased with her decision. Islam was little known in her native Mexico. One of her sisters, a nun, blamed herself for not teaching Marta enough about Catholicism when she was a young girl. Her grieving mother called the local priest for comfort. She wanted to know how to convince her daughter to return to the Catholic Church. Much to her surprise the priest told her Islam was not a new religion and that Marta was on the right path.

I met Marta many years after her conversion, in December 2005, at a café in Santa Monica. I had tried desperately to get the phone numbers of Latino Muslims in Los Angeles by calling Latinos I knew in San Antonio and Chicago. But I quickly discovered that there is no national organization or network connecting Latino believers. When I finally got Marta's e-mail address, she responded quickly, with the same efficiency with which she had started her study circle in Los Angeles back in 1999.

I asked her if her feelings have changed since those passionate days in Mexico when she left her country and her family to pursue her faith. She told me her commitment to Islam had become even stronger, but that she had tried over the years to practice Islam in ways that suit her personality. For instance, she wore a headscarf for only a few weeks before realizing that she felt more comfortable without it. As she told me this story, it was clear that Marta's youthful independent streak had stayed with her. This became even clearer when she compared Islam to Catholicism.

"Latinos are attracted to Islam because they like the fact that you pray straight to God and you don't have to tell anyone your sins, especially to a person who is probably more sinful than you are. And no one is trying to intimidate you or manipulate your brain. In Islam, you are forced to use your intellect. For many of us, Islam has given us the meaning of life, why we are in this world."

Marta did her best to create a national Latino Muslim organization that would cooperate with well-established mosques and Islamic groups. She was in touch with Latinos in Chicago, San Antonio, and New York, but they had reservations about forming an organization identified strictly as Hispanic. They want to be considered part of the broader Muslim

American community, without an ethnic marker. But Marta suggested that, as more Latinos convert to Islam, some of their differences with other Muslims are becoming more apparent. In deciding not to wear the *hijab*, for example, Marta's views are at odds with many other practicing Muslim women.

There are also cultural traditions among Latinos that set them apart from other Muslims. Latino Muslims believe it is important for people, men and women alike, to shake hands when they first meet. But many traditional Muslim men, the vast majority in the Islamic world, feel uncomfortable shaking a woman's hand. "Being Latino means expressing yourself. We kiss one another and shake hands and I don't understand how this can be considered un-Islamic," Marta said. "We give seminars every year because we have some Latinos who say you can't celebrate Thanksgiving or birthdays anymore. We tell them they can keep their culture. You just have to change certain habits. Don't go to bars and drink alcohol."

"Ricardo, the Muslim"

Ricardo Pena was once a full-fledged Catholic in Chicago, a Catholic town. He went to catechism class and he made his first communion. His Puerto Rican mother and Mexican father were not particularly religious but they encouraged Ricardo to fulfill his spiritual obligations.

By the time he was a young teenager his interest in the church had waned. He asked himself why he should go through the trouble of praying when he didn't have the energy to do his homework. He tried not to think about God and ignored anyone who wanted to talk to him about organized religion. His visceral rejection of religion made him realize one thing: his anger was based on fear of the afterlife. From this realization came a new way of thinking about religion. Ricardo considered other faiths; he shopped around for the perfect fit that paired his spiritual needs with the fundamentals of a faith.

Years passed, and when Ricardo was twenty years old he developed a close friendship with Danny, whose family had moved next door to Ricardo Pena's family in Roger's Park, a working-class Chicago neighborhood. Danny had converted to Islam in high school, about four years before he moved to Roger's Park, after his Muslim classmates convinced him to embrace the faith. It was not an easy transformation; Danny had resisted, but his Muslim friends with whom he had formed a close bond by playing sports together and going to Cubs games at the stadium near their homes, persuaded him over a few years.

Danny then turned to Ricardo, his lost neighbor, to try to teach him about Islam. He told Ricardo that God sent Muhammad, the last prophet, to Earth. This was news to Ricardo who had no idea about Islam.

"What Danny told me broke my heart," Ricardo explained, when I met him at a Chicago coffee shop.

"I started intensively studying and comparing Christianity with Islam. I did this for seven months and every night I asked God to show me the way.

"I realized over time that if I stuck with Catholicism it would be because of an attachment, not because I had a rational argument. When I was a Catholic everything was based on emotion. But in Islam, they ask you to use your brain."

During the months he studied Islam, Ricardo turned to his brother for support.

"I told Danny and my brother that I wanted to convert and they implied that I was too emotional, that people were not supposed to become Muslims out of emotion. I realized later that they wanted me to be sure I really wanted to embrace Islam. They knew how serious it would be for me to become a Muslim and then decide to leave the faith."

Shortly thereafter, in September 1995, Ricardo and his brother took the *shahada* together at the Muslim Community Center, one of Chicago's most established mosques. He was twenty-one years old. "Once it became public, I didn't know what to do. The sheikh came in and said a few words and there were witnesses."

So Ricardo began to change his lifestyle. First, he stopped his occasional drinking. "It took awhile for me to begin to drift away from my friends and drift more towards Muslims. I didn't know many Muslims and it wasn't until later that I became connected to them that I knew I needed a support structure."

Of all the negative reactions Ricardo and his brother experienced after publicly declaring their new faith, the worst came from their parents. "We broke the news to our parents and it was a fight that started at eight in the evening and we didn't get to bed until four in the morning. My parents were so upset. It turned into a big drama. It was a shock. It is the fear of the unknown. And when they asked why, we got into things they didn't want to hear. They didn't know what we were getting into.

"But after my parents realized there was nothing they could do, they let it be. They thought at least our new religion had some moral standard. They knew we were adults, not kids and could make our own decisions.

"But my sister remained hostile to the idea of Islam and was very hostile toward the fact that Islam was in her life. She would say, 'I don't want to hear about it.' I would say, 'Okay, it is fine.' Then she had a daughter out of wedlock when she was seventeen and that changed everything."

She got married and started thinking more about religion. She started going to mass on Sundays at the local Catholic Church. When things bothered her, she turned to the Bible, but she was sinking deeper into depression. "Then one day she was sitting in a library studying and she started crying," Ricardo explained. "At that moment, she put her head in her hand and when she turned she saw writing on the wall written in orange marker and it said, 'Jesus is not God and is not the son of God. Jesus is the messenger of God.'"

That day she decided to become a Muslim. "She was finally able to overcome all the things she thought were barriers to becoming a Muslim, like wearing *hijab*. She was ready, no matter the difficulties."

When I met Ricardo, he had been a Muslim for ten years and had a network of Muslim friends. His wife, Diana, was a Latina convert from Puerto Rico, and they had settled in Chicago with their two children. Yet, while he seemed to have all the support he had hoped for, he still felt disconnected to the broader Islamic community. Part of the problem was the amount of time he devoted to his career. As a computer software developer at the Chicago operations of the Chicago Federal Home Loan Bank, he spent much of his free time outside work reading literature to try and keep up with rapidly changing technological trends. When he wasn't working on computers, he attended night school to become a certified public accountant. With little time left for attending prayers at the mosque or starting a group for Latino Muslims, one of his dreams, he felt a bit lost. He wanted desperately to create a national Latino Muslim organization, but he needed funding, and raising money was time consuming.

Most people at work and other places thought of him as "Ricardo, the Hispanic," not "Ricardo, the Muslim." On Fridays, he did not ask permission from his boss to leave for prayers in the mosque, as some Muslims do. Instead, Ricardo asked a Shi'ite Muslim who owned a photo shop downstairs from his office if he could pray there. Even the mere idea of working at a federal bank troubled him. He feared that working for the

U.S. government was a betrayal to Islam considering the U.S. invasion of two Islamic countries—Iraq and Afghanistan.

"I have a hard time," Ricardo told me. "I feel like a Muslim in the closet the way gays used to be in the closet. I don't wear a *kufi*. I don't look the part. If I went for a job interview, no one would be biased because they wouldn't know I am a Muslim. They would just see Ricardo, the Latino."

Like many converts I met, Ricardo faced different obstacles and dilemmas than those Muslims born into the faith. Whether thousands of new converts will remain Muslim could depend upon to what degree the broader Islamic community steps in to help them deal with their new lives in America.

EIGHT

The Future of the Faith

⟨⟩

Farhan Latif always knew it was only a matter of time before the slow-burning anger would erupt. His conservative Muslim enemies had made their intentions clear to him. They had sent threatening e-mails and left menacing messages on his cell phone. In their eyes, Farhan's ideas were criminal. The Western world might call him a moderate Muslim, but his foes thought he was an apostate, luring young Muslims away from the faith.

The day Farhan feared came in September 2004. As he was about to enter his modern apartment in Dearborn, about one mile from his university, three young men jumped him and pushed him to the ground. They beat and kicked him without saying a word. Farhan recognized one of his attackers; the guy did not bother to hide his face under a mask.

"Why are you doing this?" Farhan cried, trying to shield his face from their blows.

The attackers did not reply. Within minutes, they got back into their car and tried to run Farhan over before they sped away. He managed to avoid the oncoming wheels by rolling away just in time.

As he rested in the hospital, nursing a swollen head, several cracked ribs, and a broken arm, Farhan was depressed more than shocked over the beating. It was one thing to endure the daily blows from the non-Muslims who criticized Islam. But now he was in a battle with his fellow believers. "I fight against everything people say against my religion every day, on television, on the radio, everywhere," Farhan remarked, reflecting on the incident later. "I was not so much scared when this happened but sad that fellow Muslims would do this."

Months before the attack, in the spring of 2004, Farhan was elected president of the Muslim Students' Association at the University of Michigan's Dearborn campus. In a short time, he revolutionized the association, making it more attractive to a majority of Muslim students on campus, many of whom had refused to join when the conservatives were in charge. Farhan and the new leaders decided there would no longer be radical imams unleashing hate speech at Friday prayers. All lecturers would be required to follow certain rules. They lifted the ban that prevented women without headscarves from joining the association. All Muslims would be welcome, no matter their political ideas or their sect; minority Shi'ites, often scorned for their separate ways and different approach to the faith, were just as acceptable as the Sunni student majority. Farhan organized events to show how the three monotheistic faiths have much in common. A drama called "Children of Abraham" made its debut before the Muslim association.

None of this sat well with members of Dearborn's Muslim Students' Association who were either radical Salafis or affiliated with the Hizb ut-Tahrir al-Islami, the Islamic Party of Liberation. The movement, a clandestine, radical Sunni Islamic group that is banned in several countries around the world, advocates the replacement of individual Muslim governments with a single caliphate governed under a strict reading of the *sharia*. The students who are members of Hizb ut-Tahrir al-Islami share a common creed that calls for strict adherence to the Koran and the rejection of applying human reason and logic when interpreting the Islamic holy texts.

The movement traces back to the early 1950s, when a Muslim judge in Jerusalem founded it in order to campaign for a return of the community of believers to an Islamic lifestyle within a single, shared religious space, the *dar al-Islam*. After its initial success in recruiting members in Saudi Arabia and Jordan, Hizb ut-Tahrir al-Islami soon established a foothold throughout the Muslim world, where it has often been violently suppressed and its members have been jailed and even killed. Based these days primarily in Western Europe, it has recently concentrated on establishing a presence in the repressive Central Asian states of the former Soviet Union, particularly Uzbekistan. Regional leaders, alarmed by the threat the groups pose to their own unpopular rule, regularly denounce Hizb ut-Tahrir al-Islami members as violent terrorists, as does the Russian security service, which fears the group's influence in the state's restive Muslim regions, including Chechnya. Neither the U.S. government nor independent experts have linked the group to armed extremist activities.

Before Farhan had arrived on the campus, radical students had turned the Muslim Students' Association into a virtual training camp for conservative ideologues. Under the influence and guidance of an imam at a Dearborn mosque, the students believed their fellow Muslims were straying dangerously from the faith. In their eyes, being a dedicated Muslim meant that men should work to pressure the U.S. government to change its policies in the Islamic world, Muslim women should wear headscarves, and Muslims should have little to do with Jews and Christians. This was the crux of the ideological battle the Salafi students and those belonging to the Hizb ut-Tahrir al-Islami were determined to win against Farhan and his friends and allies.

Farhan's parents pleaded with him to stop his activism on campus. Farhan usually listened to them. He had come to the United States alone in 2000 hoping to attend medical school. A cousin in Dearborn offered to help him, so Farhan left his parents at their current home in Qatar. For years, his family had traveled from country to country, as his father pursued a career as a Pakistani diplomat and later a lawyer. They were often strangers in a new land, and the bond among them remained strong even as Farhan became more independent. Farhan's father's expertise in *sharia* law offered Farhan a scholarly and enlightened view of the Islamic tradition, putting him at odds with the students from the Hizb ut-Tahrir, who blindly followed the ideas of a radical imam.

Other students, if beaten for their beliefs, might have given up. But Farhan and his close group of friends inside the student association wanted to press on with their ideas, no matter the cost. Together, they had been the leaders of the MSA at a nearby college for two years before enrolling at the University of Michigan in Dearborn. During that time, they watched literally from across the street, the distance from their university to the University of Michigan, as the radical students drove more measured Muslims away from the MSA there. Farhan and his friends worked on a strategy for transforming the organization from a distance, even before

they were elected to lead it. They believed they had the support of a majority of Muslim students and others on campus, and they were not going
to surrender to violence or intimidation.

They were strong willed. Patrick Cates was a Muslim convert and activist who spent years studying the intricacies of Islam until he knew far
more than many born into the faith. These young students were dedicated
Muslims, but had different beliefs from those in Hizb ut-Tahrir al-Islami.
During one of my first trips to Dearborn in the summer of 2003, I met
Patrick and Farhan through a friend, Saeed Khan. Saeed asked Farhan
and Patrick to give me a tour of the mosques in the area.

For hours that Saturday, they drove me around town, from one mosque
to another, trying to make introductions so that I could later return to the
mosques on my own to begin my research. Sometimes, we were turned
away, if the worshippers or leaders were fearful of outsiders. I was surprised that anyone in America would spend an entire day helping a complete stranger. As I came to know Farhan and Patrick, I quickly realized
they were committed to educating people about Islam and Muslims in
America, no matter the amount of time or effort it might take.

The vehemence of the debate among young Muslims in America, as
captured in Farhan's own violent experience, highlights the central role
Muslim Students' Associations are playing in charting a new Muslim American identity after September 11. Though association members rarely re-
sort to violence, many young Muslims are tangled in debate and
disagreement, particularly as the associations' membership grows. As the
Muslim community of believers becomes more established and more visible across America, the stakes in this debate have increased exponentially.
No longer content—or even able—to exist in their own segregated universe, out of sight and out of mind of mainstream society, today's young
Muslims are coming together in student associations, mosques, and Islamic
centers to work out for themselves just what it means to be a Muslim in
contemporary America. Adherents of what the sheikhs at the Zaytuna Institute in California call a new rejectionist tendency, many are seeking neither
to assimilate into the national melting pot nor to live "separate but equal,"
like their parents. Rather, they are determined to put their Islamic identity
first, but within an American context; it is, they say, their country, too.

For many educated, upwardly mobile young Muslims, the student associations are defining how to live as a devout Muslim in a secular and often
hostile society. The racial politics at the core of black Islam and the isolation-
ism of the early-twentieth-century prairie Muslims both ended in failure—

a fate today's believers are determined to avoid. As this second generation of Muslims becomes more attached to their distinct religious identity, the student associations are rapidly becoming the main platform for debating religious and social issues, ranging from whether women should be veiled to how much contact Muslim Americans should have with non-Muslims. The battle is being waged not only by schools of thought at either extreme of the ideological spectrum, but also among students who would not define themselves as either progressive or conservative Muslims.

Since September 11, Muslim Students' Associations have become more visible and more active across the United States. Their ranks are increasing from all directions: young Muslims who grew up in secular families are becoming members in order to learn about their faith and to surround themselves with other Muslims; conservative students join because they want their ideas to dominate the organizations; and non-Muslims are entering those MSAs that will make room for them because they are curious about a religion and way of life that is capturing the daily headlines.

In the two and a half years since Farhan graduated, the Dearborn chapter has grown significantly, from around two hundred students to six hundred. This includes about one hundred non-Muslims, an unusually large number for a Muslim Students' Association on any American campus. Farhan's commitment to making the organization more inclusive and to eliminate the rules and practices that alienated not only non-Muslims but also many Muslims has clearly paid off.

Part of the allure of the associations is simply that they are no longer invisible. At one time they were relegated to the basements of student union halls and forced to compete with more glamorous, mainstream student activities for scarce resources. Now, however, universities have begun to realize that the MSAs have a powerful role to play, not just in campus life but in broader society. Some MSAs seek funding from their universities, just like any other campus group. But, in most cases, the associations are defined as religious organizations, and are thus barred from receiving such money by state and federal laws protecting the separation of church and state.

Since September 11, Muslim student leaders have found themselves in great demand; they are often called upon to explain the basics of Islam to campus audiences of hundreds of students. With the spotlight unexpectedly focused on what was a closed, sectarian world, when asked to explain publicly what it is to be Muslim in the modern world, many young student leaders have risen to the occasion.

"Magic Muslim"

One star of the September 11 generation is Hadia Mubarak, a petite woman with a girlish smile and fresh complexion, who does nearly everything faster than most people; she talks fast, and she finished college in three years. She was the first woman president of the MSA national organization, the umbrella group for all such associations in the United States and Canada. She was also one of the first girls daring enough to play high school sports wearing a *hijab.* The sight of her headscarf blowing in the wind as she dribbled a soccer ball down the field brought Hadia a bit of fame among the two thousand students at her public high school in Florida. Her teammates called her Magic Muslim, a reference to the retired basketball star, Erwin "Magic" Johnson.

This reputation as a groundbreaker followed her years later. She truly seemed to have a magical appeal, speaking to Muslim youth across the country, lecturing to the U.S. Congress, and writing opinion pieces and columns in newspapers. Hadia is best known for helping defeat a discriminatory bill in the Florida House of Representatives that would have used national origin as a criteria to eliminate state funding to students. Hadia led a statewide campaign, debating a sitting congressman on television.

When she was the president of her MSA at Florida State University, she articulated what second-generation Muslims were feeling but were

Hadia Mubarak. *(Photograph by Dr. Abdalla M. Ali. Courtesy of* Islamic Horizons *magazine)*

generally too timid to say out loud. "Walking into an airport at Mobile, Alabama, I am watched as if I were the object of examination," Hadia wrote in the *Tallahassee Democrat*, a local newspaper.

> Accustomed to the curious stares, I disregard them and walk up to the ticket counter, speaking to the agent in perfect English. Perhaps the surprised eyes that glance up are asking the same question that a lady asked on Oprah's "Islam 101" talk show. "Why have you failed to assimilate," she asked the Muslim girls sitting in the audience, their hair covered beneath a scarf, their bodies hidden beneath long-sleeved shirts, long dresses, shirts or pants. "Everyone in this country has assimilated," she continued, "except for Muslims."

The column raises the central idea Hadia Mubarak is spreading across America, one that has made her a heroine among many young Muslims. If they choose, devout Muslims can have it all. They can display the symbols of their faith, such as the headscarf. Like Hadia, they can enjoy sports, achieve academic success, and pursue a professional career. One of Hadia's role models is Ingrid Mattson, the vice president of the Islamic Society of North America who taught imams about women's rights in Islam. While Ingrid's success and assertiveness are unusual for her generation—she is about twenty years older than Hadia—young Muslim women are learning to express their views and pursue demanding careers, while also embracing Islam publicly and privately in ways their parents never did when they first arrived in the United States. Hadia's generation is breaking many taboos that were once alive and well among Muslims everywhere, not just in the United States. And those who are taking the lead are also serving as a bridge between Muslims and non-Muslims. Hadia and a handful of other young Muslims are often invited to speak when non-Muslim scholars, experts, and policymakers are examining contemporary Islamic issues. In the past, when these issues were discussed and analyzed, no Muslims were ever offered a seat at the table. Although this is still often the case, times are changing in part because of articulate young Muslims who are not afraid to speak out.

As Hadia wrote later in the same newspaper column, many women from the Middle East who had not worn headscarves in their home countries started wearing them after visiting America. The attraction of displaying the faith publicly for all to see, a mission among many second-generation Muslim Americans, was catching on even among Muslims from the Islamic world. But, as Hadia often explained, being a proud Muslim is never easy.

> As my *hijab* is mistakenly viewed as a failure to assimilate, I am reminded of the obstacles that lie ahead as I struggle to validate my roots as a Muslim Arab

American. . . . I began to realize that people didn't see me when they looked at me, but rather saw an image they had formulated in their minds from Hollywood movies showing Arab fanatics hijacking a plane. . . . Before they've even learned my name, heard my laughter or witnessed my tears, before they've seen me kick a soccer ball or debate an argument, they have judged me and think they know who I am.

The umbrella campus organization, the Muslim Students' Association of the United States and Canada, tapped Hadia to be its first female president in 2004, prompting fierce debate among young Muslims. Some young women feared a backlash; Hadia did not just have to be competent, she had to be an extraordinary president. Otherwise, the male skeptics who openly questioned whether a woman should ever hold such a post would win the day. By the end of her year as the organization's president, Hadia had more than fulfilled everyone's expectations. She had spread her convictions and ideas, honed over her years as a young student activist, to Muslim Students' Associations across the country, strengthening the individual chapters and championing women's roles within the organizations.

Each campus's MSA generally aims to provide basic religious services to students at the university. A space for Muslims to pray now exists on most campuses, ranging from full-fledged mosques to small rooms in basements or student centers. The MSA also organizes lectures each week, followed by discussions. On weekend evenings, the associations generally host social events. While non-Muslim students might be living it up at fraternity parties, the Muslims students are getting to know one another at alcohol-free concerts or dinners. At least once a year, the MSAs sponsor "Islamic Awareness Week," an event that is giving Muslim students visibility on campuses across the country. Events held during this week educate non-Muslims about Islam. On some campuses, the Muslim students consider this a form of *dawah*, drawing non-Muslims into the faith.

Another big draw at MSAs is Islamic hip-hop music. Muslim associations often invite bands with a national following, such as Native Deen, to attract non-Muslims and Muslims alike. The concerts are great icebreakers; they unify Muslims from all political and religious persuasions and show non-Muslim crowds that being a Muslim is not only about praying and fasting.

In the post–September 11 world, Muslims hold a range of events for Muslim students, and they bring more Muslim speakers to campuses. They are also placing greater demands on university administrators on behalf of the Muslim student body. These demands typically include larger prayer spaces, the availability of religiously permitted *zabiha* foods in campus caf-eterias, time off to attend Friday communal prayers, and recognition of the two religious Eid holidays—the Feast of the Sacrifice and the end of Ramadan. The MSAs encourage young Muslims to make Islam public, so that the faith will not be privatized at home but active at all times in the hearts and minds of every Muslim. These organizations fulfill the need of many young Muslims to stand up and defend their faith.

The aim of the national MSA organization is reflected in a statement on its Web site: "to serve the best interest of Islam and Muslims in the United States and Canada so as to enable them to practice Islam as *a com-plete way of life*" on campuses. Making Islam inseparable from normal life has had several effects. At some Muslim Student Associations I visited, young women told me they started wearing the *hijab* after they joined and began to pray regularly on Fridays. They found the courage to be pious once they were surrounded by like minds.

It is a fundamental aspect of Islam that it is a prescription for all facets of life not simply a matter of visiting the mosque once a week the way many Americans go to church on Sunday. This is what most sets it apart from contemporary mainstream Western faiths. This difference is also the source of the deeper conflict today between the Muslim world and the West, where critics of contemporary Islam can often be heard demanding a so-called reformation to dilute the influence of religious doctrine and to allow greater space for secular life and activities. With the exception of a few high-profile "progressive" Muslims who have attracted considerable U.S. media attention, there is no evidence that such a reformation is any more welcome in America's mosques, Islamic centers, and student asso-ciations than it would be in Cairo, Karachi, or Kuala Lumpur.

These developments within the Muslim Students' Associations are shap-ing the future direction of Islam in America. By creating a unified, close-knit social and religious group on campus, Muslim students are forming bonds that did not exist among Muslim Americans of earlier generations. The associations instill confidence in the students as practicing Muslims. These young Muslims then tend to become more assertive when they re-turn to the mosques in their communities. Their influence can be seen in the effort today among young Muslims to make the mosque more diverse and dynamic. For example, activists are encouraging religious leaders at mosques to talk about social ills such as drug and alcohol abuse among young Muslims—behavior many imams pretend does not exist because it

suggests that Muslims have not been successful in warding off the negative influences of Western society.

At times, when enthusiastic Muslim students try to recreate campus life
back in their home mosques the result is a clash between the old and young
generation. This was certainly true when Nedaa, an active member of the
Muslim Students' Association at DePaul University in Chicago, organized
youth counseling sessions at her mosque in one of the city's suburbs. After
a series of discussions on drug and alcohol abuse, the mosque board decided to close the youth center. Nedaa, an articulate, charismatic young
woman was enraged.

"The older generation lives in denial," Nedaa told me one day, as we
sat together at an Arab youth center in South Chicago.

"There is a drug problem, people are getting pregnant before they marry.
The fact that we want to talk about this and confront it is causing huge
difficulty. The older generation has a different mentality. When I was
growing up, I was told 'There is us and there is them,' them meaning the
Americans. We Muslims don't drink alcohol. We don't have premarital
sex. Why? Because we are better. But now for some young Muslims, there
is little difference between Muhammad and Mike and we have to face this
new reality.

"The purpose of the youth center at our mosque was to deal with these
issues. We are now in a situation in America where the entire country is
against us, the world is against us. We only have each other and if we don't
face our problems, our community might break up."

America's Muslim student movement has done more than simply shake
up the way the community looks at the challenges of modern life. It has
also gone a long way toward creating a multicultural Islam among second-
generation Muslims. Students from diverse ethnic backgrounds join the
Muslim Students' Associations and encounter, often for the first time,
Muslims outside their own ethnic groups. Just as Rami Nashashibi has
worked for a decade to bring multicultural Islam to an impoverished corner of Chicago, the student associations are creating a color-blind faith
among educated, socially mobile young Muslims by drawing them to events
such as hip-hop concerts. Muslims sometimes meet their future spouses in
the student associations, in which a variety of ethnic groups are represented. This growing multiculturalism has in turn added considerable
momentum to the drive for a unique Muslim identity that can face the
challenges of post–September 11 America.

In many ways, the goals and aspirations of the young people in today's Muslim Students' Associations have come full circle since the first North American MSA was founded in the early 1960s. Surely, the times were different compared with the post–September 11 world, but the members' ideas were similar to those of students now leading the associations. It took almost forty years, however, for the Muslim students' earlier vision to be realized.

In the 1960s, Muslim students had a yearning to be Muslim "out loud" and the first Muslim Students' Association of the United States and Canada was established in 1963 at the University of Illinois at Urbana-Champaign. In contrast with today, the original MSA members were mostly foreign students who planned to return home once they graduated. There were few, if any, Muslims born in America on college campuses at this time. Although these visiting students created the association primarily as a comfort zone during their years in the United States, they had a lofty goal, which is only now being realized; they wanted to institutionalize Islam in America by creating a powerful movement of young Muslims.

In one of its earliest publications, the new national organization proclaimed that among its chief goals was the promotion among young Muslims of a "self definition [that] involves, initially, and fundamentally [an] Islamic identity." At the time, the founders and activists in this budding student movement were driven by a desire to create conditions for pursuing a proper Islamic lifestyle during their time in America. Unlike students today, they were not responding to widespread persecution nor did they feel the need to carve out a permanent place in mainstream society. These sentiments were spelled out in *Al Ittihad*, a publication the MSA of the United States and Canada started in its earliest days. An editorial in the March 1968 issue entitled, "The Message of the MSA," stated: "The idea for working among Muslim students of different countries living in this part of the world was that we are Muslims first, Muslims last, and Muslims forever. We should live as Muslims, we should die as Muslims."

Over time, the Muslim student movement began a series of steps to help institutionalize elements of Islam and the Islamic lifestyle in America, primarily through education. Soon the MSA began to distribute books about Islam and Islamic practice to Muslims and non-Muslims on college and university campuses. The group's journal *Al Ittihad*, which members refer to as its "mouthpiece," was filled with articles about contemporary Islamic issues. For the first time, Muslims in America began to discuss leading problems in the Islamic world, including the role of women in

Islam and the population explosions in some of the students' home countries. The journal also began to call for the creation of Islamic schools in the United States, with one article on a proposed Islamic boarding school published in 1973. At the time, virtually no such schools existed.

As part of its educational campaign, the Muslim Students' Association began to publish brochures and books and to translate the works of prominent Islamic thinkers into English. By 1966, the MSA of the United States and Canada launched the Islamic Book Service, a clearinghouse for books and periodicals. The list of titles was often featured in *Al Ittihad* so students could place their orders. The association's work continued throughout the 1970s, with the establishment of a *fiqh* (legal) council for North America. The council issued legal opinions on issues facing Muslims living in a secular society. At first, the council offered opinions on relatively limited concerns, such as the proper starting point of Ramadan, based on the first sighting of the crescent moon. But by 1988, its role had broadened to issuing decrees on a wide range of social and religious topics.

Emblematic of the student movement's increasingly influential role among Muslims across America was the creation in 1982 of the Islamic Society of North America (ISNA), an offshoot of the student associations led by former members now pursuing professional careers. Founded in part with funding from Saudi Arabia, which went toward building its headquarters in the middle of farmland in Plainfield, Indiana, ISNA has since become a prominent advocate for Muslim Americans. Although former students in the MSA created the organization, its purpose was to be a voice for all Muslims. In recent years, its annual conventions held in Chicago draw an estimated thirty thousand Muslims from across North America to discuss their religious and political concerns.

With the rise of the Islamic Society of North America, the MSA of the United States and Canada narrowed its focus to Muslim students. The organization promoted unity among students by integrating those from different ethnic groups at religious events, created prayer rooms on campus, and published articles in various magazines about recent conversions to Islam, and created sexually segregated summer youth camps that continue today.

The Way Ahead

As young Muslims lead the way toward creating a well-defined Muslim American identity, non-Muslim America often asks: "Will the outcome be a segregated community? Will the young Muslim Americans embracing their faith also become radicalized like their peers in Europe?" Each time I lecture at conferences hosted by think tanks in Washington and attended by policy makers, these are the issues of greatest concern.

On the surface, there are many outward signs that might suggest young Muslim Americans have much in common with Muslims in Europe. More women in America are wearing headscarves, just as in Europe. Islam is more institutionalized in American and European societies than ever before, as social and political organizations and Islamic schools develop. And perhaps more significant, young Muslims are proving that they are not choosing to integrate into Western societies in the ways typical of other religious and ethnic minorities in the past. While it is common for the second generations of religious and ethnic groups to distance themselves from the culture, religion, and language of their ancestors, young Muslims are taking the opposite approach. They are learning Arabic, attending Islamic schools, adopting Islamic symbolism, and joining organizations, such as the MSAs, to form a more unified Muslim community.

Today, there is a new Europe. Countries that were once largely homogeneous now have significant Muslim populations who have introduced new languages, cultures, and beliefs, and who consider Islam central to their lives. This poses a great challenge to secular countries, such as Germany, France, and Denmark, where there is little place for religion in the national identity. Although Muslims are still very much in the minority in the European Union—they comprise only 5 percent or between 15 and 20 million of the total population of 425 million people—Muslims living in Europe have three times as many children as their non-Muslim neighbors. As early as 2020, Muslims could comprise 10 percent of the population in the EU, according to some surveys. Unlike the United States, a country built of immigrants, in Western Europe, immigrants, for the most part, are a post–World War II phenomenon. And, unlike in the United States, Muslims in countries such as France, the Netherlands, Germany, and Belgium, comprise the largest of the immigrant populations.

Second-generation Muslims in some European countries are vulnerable to the recruitment campaigns of extremist Islamic organizations, which have stepped up their efforts since September 11 and the invasion of Iraq. The numbers of young Muslim recruits vary greatly, but they are estimated to be in the hundreds, according to European intelligence reports, and increasingly include women and Muslim converts. After September 11, al-Qaeda and other groups searched for recruits with clean records and who could travel within Europe and abroad without scrutiny. Women and converts, some of whom do not have dark features, are proving suitable for this purpose.

So far, there are no real signs that Europe's non-Muslim majority is prepared to make any concessions to this increasingly large and visible segment in their societies. In France, lawmakers fearful of what they saw as rising sectarian tensions in public schools have banned students from wearing or displaying what they called "religious symbols." These include Christian crosses, the Jewish skullcap or *kippah*, and veils for Muslim women and girls. Needless to say, the intent of the law backfired. While there is no doctrinal requirement that Christians wear the cross, many devout Muslims believe that God has commanded the veil. In other words, the state was openly interfering with their ability to practice their faith, exacerbating suspicions among many pious Muslims that Western society is out to destroy them and their beliefs.

This same approach could be seen in 2006, when newspaper editors in Europe, Canada, and New Zealand—all majority Christian countries— insisted on republishing a series of inflammatory Danish editorial cartoons that insulted the Prophet Muhammad, including one that portrayed him as a terrorist. The newspaper editors and their allies asserted their actions were not only within their rights but also necessary to defend the principle of free speech. Setting aside the fact that free speech was never seriously under attack in Jutland, Denmark, where the cartoons originated in 2005, the entire affair still smacked of a gratuitous assault on the beliefs and values of the world's Muslims. Besides, argued the Islamic world, the same Danish newspaper had earlier rejected a cartoon that poked fun at Jesus, while laws in France, Germany, and Austria specifically limit free speech by making it illegal to deny the Holocaust.

The bond of the *ummah*, the collective Islamic community, draws together second-generation Muslims in America and those in Europe. Each landmark event—September 11, the invasion of Afghanistan, the occupation of Iraq, the French government's ban on headscarves, and even the decision of some European news organizations to publish the insulting cartoons of the Prophet Muhammad—gives this collective community a reason to unite to protect Islam from attack by the Western world. Faith has now become the bond among young Muslims that transcends ethnicity and tribes, if not yet the historical Sunni-Shi'ite divide.

Will this growing religiosity radicalize young Muslims in America? So far, there is little evidence to suggest that second-generation Muslims are answering the call of extremist groups. One of the most intriguing characteristics of America's young Muslims is their ability to pick and choose those aspects of American values and culture they want to adopt and those they wish to reject. Hadia Mubarak, the Magic Muslim of the soccer field, has every intention of becoming a successful lawyer or an academic, but this does not mean she will stop wearing the *hijab*, or end her regular prayers at the mosque, or halt her activism to create a strong, close-knit Muslim community.

The young Muslims I have profiled might consider their Islamic identity more important than their American one, but that does not mean they reject what America has to offer. Rather, young Muslim Americans could be the first Islamic community in the world to reconcile what has become a perceived conflict between the Muslim world and the West. They could be the first to take advantage of the historical commonalities of two civilizations that were intimately intertwined for centuries until the modern age. They could be the first to disprove the misguided notion advanced by many scholars and pundits that Islam must undergo a reformation in order to become "modern."

When there are bombings in London or Madrid or when the conservative establishment in the United States makes unsubstantiated declarations about al-Qaeda cells on American soil, I am reminded that the goal of the young generation of Muslim Americans sets them apart from some of their more radical European peers. I am reminded each time Yusra Gomaa, the devout Muslim and future lawyer, sends me an e-mail, always ending with this saying from the Prophet Muhammad: "None of you truly believes until he likes for his brother what he likes for himself."

Bibliography

Abraham, Nabeel, and Andrew Shryock, eds. *Arab Detroit: From Margin to Mainstream*. Detroit: Wayne State University Press, 2000.

Ahmed, Leila. *Women and Gender in Islam: Historical Roots of a Modern Debate*. Cairo: The American University in Cairo Press, 1993.

Aidi, Hisham. "Jihadis in the Hood: Race, Urban Islam, and the War on Terror." *Middle East Report* 224 (Fall 2002). www.merip.org/mer/mer224/224_aidi.html.

———. "Let Us Be Moors: Islam, Race, and Connected Histories." *Middle East Report* 229 (Winter 2003). www.merip.org/mer/mer229/229_aidi.html.

Al-Hibri, Azizah. "Islamic Law and Muslim Women in America." In *One Nation under God? Religion and American Culture*, edited by Marjorie Garber and Rebecca Walkowitz. New York: Routledge, 1999, 128–144.

Anjum, Umaymir. "Women's Role in Muslim Communities: The Ideal and the Challenge." *Al Jumah* 16, no. 6 (July/August 2004).

Anway, Carole L. *Daughters of Another Path: Experiences of American Women Choosing Islam.* Lee's Summit, Mo.: Yawna, 1996.

Athar, Shahid. *Reflections of an American Muslim.* Chicago: KAZI, 1994.

Austin, Allan D. *African Muslims in Antebellum America: Transatlantic Stories and Spiritual Struggles.* New York: Routledge, 1997.

Ayalon, Ami. "The Arab Discovery of America in the Nineteenth Century." *Middle Eastern Studies* 20, no. 4 (1984): 5–17.

Bagby, Ihsan. "A Profile of African-American Masjids: A Report from the National Masjid Study 2000." *Journal of the Interdenominational Theological Center* 29, no. 1–2 (1998): 205–241.

Bagby, Ihsan, Paul M. Perl, and Byran T. Froehle. *The Mosque in America: A National Portrait: A Report from the Mosque Study Project.* Washington, D.C.: Council on American-Islamic Relations, 2001.

Bayyah, Shaykh Abdullah bin. "Muslims Living in Non-Muslim Lands." Introduced by Shaykh Hamza Yusuf, 2001. Available at www.zaytuna.org/sh_bin_bayyah.html.

Ben, Kimberly. "Women's Issues: Maintaining Marital Happiness: The Wife's Role." *Islamic Horizons* 17, no. 5 (June/July 2005).

Berg, Robert. "Camels West." *Saudi Aramco World* (May/June 2002): 2–7.

Bukhari, Muhammad Ibn Ismail, and Yusuf Talal Delorenzo. *Imam Bukhari's Book of Muslim Morals and Manners.* Al-Saadawi Publications, 1997.

Diouf, Sylviane A. *Servants of Allah: African Muslims Enslaved in the Americas.* New York: New York University Press, 1998.

Ebaugh, Helen, and J. S. Chafetz, eds. *Religion and the New Immigrant.* New York: Altamira, 2000.

Eck, Diana. *A New Religious America.* San Francisco: Harper San Francisco, 2001.

Floyd, Jennifer. "Why I Chose Islam." *Al-Ittihad.* 2, no. 2 (March 1966).

Galvan, Juan. "Latino Muslims: Leading Others to Enlightenment." *Islamic Horizons* 31, no. 4. (July/August 2002).

Gardell, Mattias. *In the Name of Elijah Muhammad: Louis Farrakhan and the Nation of Islam.* Durham, N.C.: Duke University Press, 1996.

Gomez, Michael A. "Muslims in Early America." *The Journal of Southern History* 40, no. 4 (1994): 671–710.

Haddad, Yvonne Y., and Adair T. Lummis. *Islamic Values in the United States: A Comparative Study.* New York: Oxford University Press, 1987.

Haddad, Yvonne Y., and John Esposito, eds. *Muslims on the Americanization Path?* Atlanta: Scholars Press, 1998.

Hasan, Asma Gull. *American Muslims: The New Generation.* New York: Continuum, 2000.

Jackson, Sherman A. *Islam and the Blackamerican: Looking toward the Third Resurrection.* New York: Oxford University Press, 2005.

Koszegi, Michael A., and J. Gordon Melton, eds. *Islam in North America: A Sourcebook.* New York: Garland, 1992.

Lawrence, Bruce. *New Faiths, Old Fears: Muslims and Other Asian Immigrants in American Religious Life.* New York: Columbia University Press, 2002.

Leonard, Karen Isaken. *Muslims in the United States.* New York: Russell Sage, 2003.

Mamdani, Mahmood. *Good Muslim, Bad Muslim: America, the Cold War, and the Roots of Terror.* New York: Pantheon, 2004.

McCloud, Aminah Beverly. *African American Islam.* New York: Routledge, 1995.

North Dakota Public Radio. "First Mosque," hosted by Merrill Piepkorn, written by Merry Helm, and produced by Bill Thomas. Dakota Datebook (project): Prairie Public Broadcasting (June 2, 2005). www.prairiepublic.org/programs/datebook/bydate/05/0605/060205.jsp

Nuruddin, Yusuf. "The Five Percenters: A Teenage Nation of Gods and Earths." In *Muslim Communities in North America*, edited by Yvonne Haddad and Jane Smith. Albany: State University of New York Press, 1994.

Nyang, Sulayman. *Islam in the United States of America*. Chicago: ABC International, 1999.

Osman, Ghada, and Camille F. Forbes. "Representing the West in the Arabic Language: The Slave Narrative of Omar ibn Said." *Journal of Islamic Studies* 15, no. 3 (2004): 331–343.

Ramadan, Tariq. *To Be a European Muslim*. Leicester, England: Islamic Foundation, 1998.

———. *Western Muslims and the Future of Islam*. New York: Oxford University Press, 2004.

Rauf, Feisal Abdul. *What's Right with Islam: A New Vision for Muslims and the West*. San Francisco: Harper San Francisco, 2004.

Roy, Olivier. *Globalized Islam: The Search for a New Ummah*. New York: Columbia University Press, 2004.

Safi, Omid, ed. *Progressive Muslims: On Justice, Gender, and Pluralism*. Oxford, England: Oneworld Publications, 2003.

Schmidt, Garbi. *American Medina: A Study of the Sunni Muslim Immigrant Communities in Chicago*. Lund, Sweden: University of Lund, 1998.

Shakir, Evelyn. *Bint Arab: Arab and Arab American Women in the United States*. Westport, Conn.: Praeger, 1997.

Smith, Jane. *Islam in America*. New York: Columbia University Press, 1999.

———. *"Women's Issues in American Islam."* Hartford, Conn.: Duncan Black Macdonald Center for the Study of Islam and Christian-Muslim Relations. Available at www.macdonald.hartsem.edu/smithart1.htm

Smith, Wilfred Cantwell. *Islam in Modern History.* Princeton, N.J.: Princeton University Press, 1957.

Taylor, Charles. "Two Theories of Modernity." *Public Culture* 11, no. 1 (1999): 153–174.

Waugh, Earle H., Baba Abu-Laban, and Regula B. Qureshi, eds. *The Muslim Community in North America.* Edmunton: The University of Alberta Press, 1983.

Yusuf, Hamza. *Purification of the Heart.* Chicago: Starlatch, 2004.

Index

꿍